NINJA FUTURE

NINJA FUTURE

SECRETS TO SUCCESS
IN THE NEW WORLD
OF INNOVATION

GARY SHAPIRO

WM
WILLIAM MORROW
An Imprint of HarperCollins*Publishers*

HarperCollins books may be purchased for educational, business, or sales promotional use. For information, please email the Special Markets Department at SPsales@harpercollins.com.

FIRST EDITION

Library of Congress Cataloging-in-Publication Data has been applied for.

ISBN 978-0-06-289051-1

19 20 21 22 23   DIX/LSC   10 9 8 7 6 5 4 3 2 1

THIS BOOK IS DEDICATED TO THE INNOVATORS: THOSE
WHO TAKE RISKS, SOLVE PROBLEMS, AND MAKE LIFE
BETTER, HEALTHIER, AND SAFER FOR ALL OF US

CONTENTS

PREFACE

"The world that we live in today is unrecognizable to that of just twenty years ago . . . nothing is ever static . . . we can never tell where we'll be in five years." I wrote these words in my 2013 book, *Ninja Innovation: The Ten Killer Strategies of the World's Most Successful Businesses.* Since then, the world has changed all over again, in some ways I predicted back then and in other ways few of us could have imagined. Much of the credit for this goes to ninja innovators.

I coined the phrase *ninja innovation* to describe the people and organizations that demonstrated the attributes of ancient ninjas—Japanese warriors who survived battles against extraordinary odds. Using stealth and surprise, they triumphed over adversaries, despite often being outgunned and outmanned by fierce competition or hostile conditions.

I have used the idea of the ninja as a standard for my children and employees since the television series *Teenage Mutant Ninja Turtles* came on the scene in the mid-1980s. My sons watched the show religiously and begged my first wife and me to enroll them in karate classes. Eventually we relented and signed up for tae kwon do as a family.

The experience was humbling. Sometimes work required me to miss classes, so my kids often became my instructors. Over time, we developed the discipline, self-confidence, and respect required to earn our black belts. We also learned a way of thinking that relies on surprise, strategy, and adaptability. We learned to adjust our tactics, change course, ignore conventional wisdom, and find creative ways to solve intractable problems.

As I trained, it occurred to me that there were parallels to my professional life. As the head of Consumer Technology Association (CTA), I have the opportunity and privilege to see ninja innovators in action every day. For our member companies, success doesn't mean preserving the status quo, no matter how great that might be. It means reaching previously insurmountable heights. It means achieving seemingly impossible goals.

Part of my personal and business lexicon is challenging myself and others to "think like a ninja." Ninjas innovate. Ninjas do the unexpected—and in so doing, produce value. That value can be survival, a successful product launch, or agreement on a deal. It can mean greater revenue, lower costs, increased efficiency, better results, or happier customers. Often it means connecting the dots among different areas of knowledge. It can mean almost anything—but it always requires creative thinking.

At our Innovation House, CTA's home base on Capitol Hill in Washington, D.C., we display a phrase I often use: "Innovate or Die." These words are a mandate not just for businesses, but also for humanity. I passionately believe our survival—past, present, and future—is due to our unique ability to innovate. We are different from other species in our ability to cause our own destruction, but also in our ability to change course and ensure that we continue to thrive.

In some ways, the future looks a bit grim: We face major threats, now and in the not-too-distant future. Disease, nuclear weapons, climate change, debt, social upheaval, war, and natural disasters loom large. Successfully navigating these complexities will require all citizens and companies to become ninja innovators. Ninja innovators aren't limited to the tech industry, though of course my focus will be there. Ninja innovators can be found in schools, hospitals, stores, restaurants, theaters, private companies, and government agencies.

Amazon is a clear example. It is not so much inventing products but constantly reinventing itself. Led by CEO Jeff Bezos, the company morphed from an online bookstore to a multibillion-dollar global behemoth that sells, well, everything. Once the company dominated bookselling, its leadership shifted its focus to becoming the go-to online retailer for customers seeking convenience and speed of ordering and delivery. They developed their own e-readers and tablets to capitalize on the changing reading, watching, and listening preferences of consumers. They offered digital file storage, including photos, on their cloud service Amazon Drive.

The company launched Amazon Prime, a subscription service that gives members free shipping and access to digital content (music, videos, original programming). They established a publishing imprint and bought Audible—the largest audio book company. They introduced Amazon Echo, launched Amazon Fresh for grocery delivery. They bought a robotics company to automate and hone their fulfillment distribution processes to such an extent that customers can order and receive a product on the same day. And Amazon has now come full circle, in a way, by purchasing Whole Foods and building brick-and-mortar Amazon bookstores.

In 2017, *Fast Company* named Amazon "the world's most innovative company."[1] And it's no wonder; Amazon "has continued to be nimble even as it has achieved enviable scale." Not only does Amazon anticipate changes in the marketplace and in consumer habits, it also drives them—which makes it a classic example of a ninja innovator.

Ninja innovators possess the strength, cunning, intensity, and adaptability needed to outwit or outrun the competition and achieve victory. They assemble a strike force of colleagues committed to creating a better future. They take risks and absorb and learn from setbacks. They lay out a strategy for overcoming obstacles, both known and unknown, but are flexible enough to adjust to changing circumstances. They constantly evaluate the opportunities and threats around them and are poised to take advantage of their surroundings. Ninja innovators never settle, and they are never satisfied. They appreciate what is, but focus on what can be.

This future will be marked by disruption. But the people and organizations who possess these qualities also view the challenges ahead as opportunities to generate a better future—a ninja future. In the midst of social, political, and physical upheaval, they will create progress. Growth. Integration. Diversity. Resilience. But that only scratches the surface. What does the landscape of the ninja future look like, and how do we prepare for it?

It's a daunting challenge—so complex and so fast-moving that it would take a ninja to navigate it. *Ninja Future* is designed to do just that.

NINJA FUTURE

INTRODUCTION

We are entering a new era of innovation. The pace of change is accelerating. More fundamental human problems will be solved in the next two decades than we have solved in the last two centuries. Self-driving vehicles will dramatically reduce the more than one million driving-related fatalities we have each year. Diseases will be cured through focused ultrasound and gene-specific treatments. Production of food and availability of clean water to sustain the world's growing population will increase. We will reduce our reliance on coal and oil. We will outsource dangerous work to robots. Further in the future, artificial intelligence (AI) will match the capacity of a human brain, and robotics will mimic the human body. We may not only avoid extinction—some argue we'll eliminate aging and even death by downloading our minds and relying on indestructible bodies.

Such ideas may terrify some and energize others. Whatever your view, technology already powers nearly everything we do. Just think about how much of your average day is fueled by tech: Your phone tells you how to avoid traffic, helps you buy merchandise, and lets you share your life via social networks. Your watch tells you how far to jog, how many steps you've taken, and when it's time to get up and move—you can even use it to make phone calls. Your home appliances may be powered by a smart speaker, letting you turn up the heat or set your alarm simply by making a verbal request into the air.

This ubiquity means that we can no longer think of innovation in terms of discrete, vertical technology silos like TV, audio, automotive, and smartphones. Think back to Amazon, which now does all this and much more, with monstrous success. The silo approach limits productivity and stymies creativity. All these things are now interconnected, so we need to think horizontally: How can technology power an entire ecosystem, from a home, to a city, to an entire country?

This shift has become increasingly apparent over the years at CES®, the world's largest and most important tech show, which is owned and produced by CTA. While we organize the show around some distinct silos, new themes emerge that drive myriad innovations. A few years ago, we saw how the Internet of Things (IoT) could connect us in ways we never imagined. Then self-driving cars, robotics, and consumer drones shifted from ideas to reality. Soon voice burst onto the scene as a new way to interface with devices. Most recently, we have seen how AI and 5G open the door to a world of convenience, precision, and high-speed broadband.

Ninja Future reflects that shift from tech silos to tech landscapes. In my first book, *The Comeback: How Innovation Will Restore the American Dream*, I discussed independent, straightforward topics such as tax reform, energy reform, and trade reform. I took a similar vertical approach in *Ninja Innovation*, structuring my argument around ten discrete, clear-cut strategies by which an organization can reach ninja status.

But when it came to writing *Ninja Future*, I had to, well, innovate. This time I took a "horizontal" approach. All the systems and structures I'll discuss cross multiple industries and categories. You'll see AI crop up in multiple chapters; you'll see blockchain discussed in wildly different contexts; you'll see self-driving vehicles invoked throughout. The next twelve chapters are meant to be a primer on the technologies and innovation that people, businesses, and governments should consider, prepare for, adapt to—otherwise they will be left in the dust of today's technological revolution.

It's no longer feasible to innovate just enough to turn a profit. In the ninja future, everything is interconnected: things, people, governments, financial networks, cultures. A breakthrough technology or a piece of legislation that impacts one nation or industry will inevitably impact them all. So future ninja innovators cannot work in silos. Future ninjas must reach across industries, international borders, and the political aisle to create the innovation-friendly work and regulatory environments needed for society to flourish.

The structure of the book reflects the interconnected and ubiquitous nature of tomorrow's innovation. It's a fluid, adaptive setup that mirrors the fluid, adaptive nature of the ninja future.

In Part I, we'll explore how innovation has shaped the modern world, and speculate on what life will be like in the ninja future. In Chapter 1, we'll zoom through the history of technology, with a particular emphasis on the explosion of innovation in the past fifty years. We'll discuss the challenge we face in anticipating the unknown, and the importance and ease of access to information. In Chapter 2, we'll survey the major cultural and commercial shifts in modern life. Chapter 3 will explore the implications of these shifts on the future economy. In Chapter 4, we'll examine the innovations that have brought us to the edge of the ninja future—such as sensors, algorithms, and broadband. And Chapter 5 will outline the ways we will combine these building blocks of innovation to drive progress—think virtual reality, drones, and artificial intelligence.

In Part II, we'll explore how we can create the proper macro conditions for innovation to flourish. Chapter 6 will evaluate some of the risks and rewards of innovative technologies, particularly their impact on our privacy, security, health, and environmental sustainability. Chapter 7 dives deep into regulation and its effects on innovation; we'll study various nations' regulatory approaches to try to find the sweet spot that rewards innovation instead of squelching it. In Chapter 8, we'll take a world tour, visiting the best and worst countries for innovation. And in Chapter 9, we'll take a road trip through the United States, highlighting hotbeds of innovation and extracting their best practices to build thriving businesses and communities in what might seem like unlikely places.

In Part III, we'll zoom back in and consider how to create the proper micro conditions for innovation to flourish. Chapter 10 offers strategies for individuals and businesses to go from merely surviving in the fast-paced future, to thriving. Chapter 11 examines two areas—diversity and resilience—that set savvy companies and governments up for success, no matter what unknowns the future holds. Finally, in Chapter 12, I'll distill all these best practices into a set of guiding principles and advice for leading the way in the ninja future.

I hope you enjoy the ride.

PART I

PAST, PRESENT, AND FUTURE NINJA INNOVATION

CHAPTER 1

THE EDGE OF TOMORROW

TECHNOLOGY IS INESCAPABLE. THROUGHOUT HUMAN history, ninja innovators—people, companies, and institutions that live by the mantra "Innovate or Die!"—have changed the way we live, work, communicate, and travel. They've revolutionized our health, education, military, politics, economy, and art. Looking at the history of technology stretching back across centuries and countries, we see long fallow periods of cultivation interspersed with brief seasons of spectacular growth.

The harnessing of fire (one million years ago). The advent of farming (12,000[1] years ago). The invention of the wheel (5,500[2] years ago). The written word (5,000[3] years ago). The invention of the printing press (550 years[4] ago). The control of electricity and invention of the phonograph and the camera in the 1800s. The Wright brothers' first flight in 1903 and the development of the Model T[5] in 1908. The discovery of antibiotics and proliferation of vaccines. The conception, blossoming, and widespread adoption of the radio, television, telephone, and computer.

We are living in such a moment right now. Milestone after technological milestone races by us so fast that it's hard to keep track of their exponential growth and impact. No sooner do ninja innovations enter the market than they change the market. Sometimes they merge with other ninja innovations, creating something entirely new. Wireless broadband connects us anywhere, anytime, untethering us from our desks. Today's smartphones are more powerful than the computers that took the Apollo spacecraft to the moon. More than one billion hours[6] of content are streamed on YouTube every day, and you don't have to live in Hollywood to be a producer. Using our own DNA, gene therapies can cure some cancers, regrow skin, and restore sight. And the Mars Rover is taking us beyond the confines of planet Earth to chart what's possible for the future.

This trend won't slow down anytime soon. Ninja innovators will continue to race toward the next century, thanks to advancements in physics, mathematics, and engineering.

These innovations will bring with them tremendous changes—and tremendous challenges. Some are predictable, so we can prepare ourselves, our businesses, and even our governments for the opportunities and obstacles that rapid change will bring. Automation and artificial intelligence (AI) will make some jobs obsolete—but they will also create new categories of jobs that don't exist today. Self-driving cars will eliminate car crashes caused by human error, saving hundreds of thousands of lives every year. Faster broadband connections and 5G will open up new job and tourism opportunities for people living in remote places.

Other changes are still up in the air: Will bitcoin upend traditional banking? Will we still have malls? Which companies will lead in social media, search, and online shopping? Will drones replace trucks for daily deliveries? Will governments give the tech industry breathing room to innovate? Or will new technologies be squashed in their infancy? We can guess, but we won't know for a while. Fifty years ago, we could not have foreseen how the internet would transform the global economy. Fifty years hence, we will again be adjusting to things we don't yet know—changes that will eventually seem inevitable, but right now are unimaginable.

Stability seems sensible in the midst of so many unknowns—but sameness is not a winning strategy. In our fast-moving economy, businesses that stick with what's worked in the past will eventually be left in the past. And consumers who consciously avoid the opportunities available via connected devices risk missing out on the wealth of jobs, products, and experiences we can now create and share with each other.

Change has always cast doubt on forward progress. And some among us work overtime to preserve the status quo. It's an age-old tension. The Luddites in England destroyed weaving machines in the early 1800s, as they feared losing work as hand weavers. Bank tellers in the 1970s dreaded the introduction of the automatic teller machine (ATM)—yet their ranks have nearly doubled[7] between 1970 and 2010, since banks could afford to open more branches. And now the number of branches is falling again, thanks to new technological innovations such as mobile banking and artificial intelligence.

It is human nature to fear and even resist the uncertainty of the future. Yet our very humanness is defined by the certainty that we have a limited amount of time. Winning in the digital world means making the most of that time. Winning in the digital world means making a conscious effort to embrace innovation.

Tomorrow's Luddites will struggle to preserve driving, brick-and-mortar retail, and even certain white-collar jobs: travel agents, postal clerks, insurance underwriters.[8] Tomorrow's ninjas will strive to leverage the building blocks we have to construct a strong and secure future.

The question is: How do we prepare for the technological progress of the next century, when so much is uncertain and unpredictable?

Known and Unknown

A few years ago, I found myself sitting across from former secretary of defense Donald Rumsfeld on a flight to Washington, D.C. Rumsfeld had recently published *Known and Unknown*, in which he reflected on his life and the challenges he navigated as secretary of defense under Presidents Gerald Ford and George W. Bush. The book's title was taken from his comments at a 2002 news briefing,[9] when he said: "There are known knowns. These are things we know that we know. There are known unknowns. That is to say, there are things that we know we don't know. But there are also unknown unknowns. There are things we don't know we don't know."

This concept captivated me. I don't follow defense issues closely, and am not making a case for or against Rumsfeld as secretary of defense. But his analysis, using this two-by-two matrix, struck me as precisely the kind of thinking I encouraged in *Ninja Innovation*. Ninjas must anticipate myriad situations. They can plan, prepare, and practice. But Secretary Rumsfeld knew from history and experience that the plan rarely survives the first encounter on the battlefield.

In the tech industry, the marketplace is the battlefield. Businesses fight for survival, and it's not necessarily the strongest that survive. It's those that break the mold entirely and those that can adapt the quickest.

Ninja business leaders must be flexible in response to changing market conditions. You can anticipate trends. You can assemble a great team with complementary strengths. You can do everything right ahead of time. But whether or not you actually survive in the long run depends entirely on how cunning and nimble you are when the unexpected occurs—and it *will* occur. Can you shift your strategy? Can you redirect your resources? Can you ask the right questions—and really listen to the answers? Can you rely on your judgment and the people on your team?

Surprise Hits

As I sketched out *Ninja Future*, I thought back to an introduction I made in Las Vegas in the mid-1990s between Bill Gates, who was then the CEO of Microsoft, and Norio Ohga, who was then the CEO of Sony. I had the privilege of introducing these two behemoths of global technology companies and listening in as they discussed with concern an upstart company from Korea—Samsung, an anticipated competitor. What they did not discuss (at least not that morning) was a little company called Apple.

Neither anticipated the major impact Apple would soon have in key hardware and software markets they were used to dominating. Nor did Gates foresee the shift from desktops to mobile devices. Apple soon replaced Sony in the Walkman-handheld device market. Apple's operating system never replaced Microsoft's for business, but it certainly became a persistent competitor. And while both Sony and Microsoft recovered from Apple's market entry and are still thriving today, they missed a massive opportunity. Apple sits in an enviable position as the first publicly traded U.S. company ever to reach a market value of $1 trillion.

For Sony and Microsoft, Samsung was an up-and-coming, known competitor. Apple was not a total "unknown unknown," but it was close. Hindsight is twenty-twenty; it's easy to look back and determine what Microsoft and Sony could have done differently. They have wised up and adapted some key strategies from Apple's playbook: an emphasis on aesthetics and a willingness to defy established industry wisdom to put consumer needs first. Ninjas learn from mistakes and quickly adapt, which is why Microsoft and Sony are prospering today.

Sometimes it just takes one product—one new idea—to upend an entire industry. Sony shocked the world with the Betamax and the Walkman, but it was Apple—a noncompetitor—that seemingly came out of nowhere to redefine the way we experience music with the iPod.

IBM used to own the personal computer market and then shared it with RadioShack. But it was two 1980s startups, Dell and Gateway, that lured customers away with their lower-cost alternatives. In 2010, the iPad arrived on the market, putting a noticeable dent in the PC and notebook markets. If you took a road trip twenty years ago, you probably used an atlas, local road map, or a customized TripTik travel planner from AAA. Fast-forward to the twenty-first century and handheld GPS units made those bulky paper maps a thing of the past. Everyone wanted a Garmin—until one day, Google enabled millions of phones to use a digital mapping app that was higher quality and completely free. Apple soon followed. Virtually overnight, hand-held GPS units for cars were no longer in demand. Garmin's business model was gravely threatened—but they adapted and thrived by shifting to aviation, wearable tech, and other special-ized products.

Rumsfeld's two-by-two matrix applies to businesses, govern-ments, and even people when analyzing a given situation. For businesses, "known known" is the easy box to complete: It's pure metrics. Your present competitors, your market position, the size of the market, your revenue, product mix or profitability—all of that is measurable.

The "known unknowns" are trickier: variables like the future health of the economy, interest rates, employment, adop-tion curves, and pricing of competitive technology.

Then come the "unknown knowns," which are the compet-itors, technologies, services, and trends that are out there today, but not yet on your radar (or not high enough on your radar). Careful market research and analysis can mitigate the dangers that might spring any moment from this Pandora's box.

The "unknown unknowns" vexed Rumsfeld most. These are the events and risks that are nearly impossible to imagine, but which end up disrupting everything—the "black swans" described by Nassim Nicholas Taleb. These are outliers with an extreme impact that we struggle to rationalize. Terrorist attacks. The unexpected or irrational behavior of a market, leader, or government. A nuclear reactor explosion. A tsunami. An unexpected market entrant.

A few decades ago, few could have predicted the massive growth of the internet, let alone a wireless environment and an explosion of apps. The death of classified advertising, the shuttering of newspapers, the demise of video rental stores, the reduced demand for travel agents, and the decline of malls at the expense of online shopping were "unknown unknowns."

Knowing there are unknowns often sparks anxiety. That's natural, but it's much more productive to view rapid change due to innovation as a series of opportunities. It allows us to grow, develop our potential, and try new things. It allows for the creation of new businesses and services. It stretches us, tries us, and improves us. We can't know the future—but we can still shape it. If we understand and embrace the change we are already witnessing, we can harness the excitement, potential, and beauty of a world where everyone has access to more opportunities and better experiences.

Ninja innovators possess the qualities and strategies that set them up for success today. Future ninjas are already planning for those "unknown unknowns" right now. If they don't, not only will their businesses not thrive—they won't survive.

The key to the ninja future? Access to information. Thanks to innovation, that's never been easier.

Spend Less, Know More

When I was growing up, access to knowledge meant a straight, shining row of encyclopedias. If you had told me my own kids would be able to "look up" vitally important childhood questions such as "How do dolphins breathe?" "What is a black hole?" and "How were pyramids built?" by addressing the question aloud to a small black cylinder on the kitchen counter, I'd have assumed you were a serious sci-fi fan, or you'd lost your mind. Yet many of us now consider Amazon's Alexa or Google Home part of the family.

This is a far cry from my childhood. My mother, Milly, was a part-time Hebrew teacher, a part-time market researcher, and a part-time door-to-door salesperson for *World Book Encyclopedia*. My father, Jerry, was a sixth-grade teacher who tutored to make extra money. My Jewish family grew up in a Levitt house, in a lower-middle-class neighborhood of mostly Italians and Irish Catholics. (It took me years to understand that pedestrians and Protestants were different—I used to think the "No Pedestrian" signs signaled religious segregation.)

Built on top of the rural potato fields of Long Island, Levittown was a large community of mass-produced single-family homes designed for servicemen—like my dad—returning from World War II. The houses were nearly identical. They had no basement, no air-conditioning, and no garage. They had a carport, one bathroom, three bedrooms, and a cesspool instead of sewage pipes. The Levitt & Sons sales brochure boasted, "Regardless of the Levittown house which you choose, you will be acquiring the latest in modern design with the most up-to-date appliances and features."

Levittown became the prototype for suburban living in the United States. We could bike to community pools and play in open fields. My brothers and friends and I played football outside every day; we used the "no ball playing" signs as our goalposts. Little League was big, and only later did it embarrass me that our team sponsor, "Emergency Cesspool," was also our team name, splashed boldly across our team shirts.

My parents paid $9,000 for our Levitt house in 1952. Like other families in the neighborhood, we added rooms over the years, including an extra bathroom and a one-car garage. By the time I left in 1977, one room had air-conditioning, and I would occasionally sneak in there to sleep on hot summer nights.

My mother believed in the power of education and was passionate that every family should have an encyclopedia. Back then, the twenty-two-volume encyclopedia set sold for several hundred dollars. Most of my mom's customers would buy one volume at a time, at about twenty dollars per book. My mother always told me you should believe in what you sell, and she felt *World Book* was a special learning tool for families. One perk of her job was that we got a complete encyclopedia set, plus *Childcraft* (an encyclopedia-like series aimed at younger children), yearbooks, and a mechanically interactive circular teaching and testing device called "Cyclopedia." I spent hundreds of hours using these resources, occasionally without being required to! In retrospect, I realize that they inspired in me curiosity and a love of learning new things.

My mother advocated lifelong learning. She would listen to

radio talk show programs whenever she had the chance. I recall often asking her why she was wasting her time, and her response was always the same: "If I learn one thing for each hour of listening, it is worth it."

I try to apply that philosophy to everything I do. When I sit next to a stranger at a dinner or hop in a Lyft or Uber, I ask questions. Everyone is great at something or has some life experience that they may be willing to share. I find joy in discovering these unexpected gems and obscure pockets of expertise in my daily interactions.

Learning from others is also fun. As my wife and I go on our weekly five-mile run together, we never lack things to discuss and insights to share. Her biggest concern about marriage was being bored, but several times a year now, we turn to one another amid the chaos of kids, school, and work, and remind each other that, busy as we are, at least we are not bored. We cringe when we notice many older couples—we call them the "dining dead"—sitting across from each other at restaurants, eating but never speaking. So we both take ownership of the relationship and work to ensure that in the course of our hectic lives we continue to challenge and entertain each other. (Although sometimes we lament that it would be nice to be bored.)

My six-year-old son is always asking "How?" and "Why?" He's fixated on convincing me to invent a time machine, both so he can avoid repeating the mistakes of the past and so he can travel back to a different time period or relive a great day like his birthday. He's not the only one who's interested in the idea. I also love time-travel stories and discussions of alternate realities—my all-time favorite movie is *Groundhog Day*. But I'm also a realist and recognize that we can't go back, only forward—and that our best bet is to try to learn from the past instead of wishing we could return to it.

So, this thirst for knowledge is not just learning for learning's sake. It's more than honoring my mother's memory or bonding with my family. It's also practical. The more I know—and the more creatively I can think—the better decisions I make and the more I can help others.

With every failure at work or at home, I ask, "What did we learn from this?" Success teaches you certain things—but failure is also an opportunity to grow and learn. I try to push through the natural emotions of denial, excuses, shame, and anger to see the upside of every failure. What did we miss? What did we learn? How can we be better? And I hear my mom's voice: "If I learn one thing for each hour of listening, it is worth it."

My mom listened to consumers and clients every day. She often went to malls to do market research for big companies. Today, this sort of face-to-face investigation has given way to robocalls, internet research, user data harvesting, and instant polling at everything from sporting events to political debates. In my mother's time, the cost of knowledge was extremely high. Ad-supported radio and television programs were free, but they had limited content and variety. Market research was expensive and scarce. Encyclopedias seemed exorbitant. Libraries were available, but generally had limited offerings; research using microfiche was difficult and tedious.

The same held true for the telephone. I grew up with a black rotary phone. It cost about twenty dollars a month and was cheap for local calls, but calling out of state cost a dollar a minute. My mom called her family in Canada about once a month, and the call was limited to three minutes. Today, not only is calling anywhere in the world almost free, but for about the same inflation-adjusted price of monthly service for that rotary phone, you can get video chat, music, texting, dozens of apps, from banking to photography, and many other services. Plus, you can take the phone with you, get navigational information, and read customer reviews before walking into a restaurant or buying a product. Today everyone with a device and a broadband connection literally carries a row of encyclopedias in their pocket.

Information and entertainment have also become more affordable. In 1954, a new fifteen-inch color TV set cost $1,000,[10] or around $10,000 in 2018 dollars. It displayed a slightly grainy picture with terrible coloring and received only a handful of channels. Today, for a fraction of that inflation-adjusted price, you can get a flat-screen 4K Ultra-High Definition TV with around 4,000 horizontal pixels.[11] Plus, you can pay a hundred dollars a month to have thousands of choices of channels and programming.

These technological innovations were unforeseeable, if not unimaginable, for my parents—and they've changed the way we measure wealth. A generation ago, nobody had access to a smartphone. Two generations ago, no one had a computer at home. In 2018, the computing power of the smartphone in your pocket rivaled that of most desktop computers.

We see this trend across all different kinds of technologies. Just take a look at books. My two younger sons use their Kindles and Fires to blaze through hundreds of books each year. If we were to purchase those same books on dead trees (paper), we would have four-figure reading bills.

Transportation is another example. A base-model Toyota Corolla comes with standard driver-assist features that ten years ago were not even available in high-end luxury models. Soon every new car will have a backup camera. Many have passive collision-avoidance systems that can alert the driver of a possible crash in the making. Increasingly, cars have active collision-avoidance systems that can activate brakes or take other action to prevent the accident at all. An array of technologies is saving lives by addressing distracted driving. The difference between standard cars and luxury vehicles isn't really about transportation—all brands can get you from point A to point B. But tech innovation is closing the consumer-affinity gap between mainstream and luxury cars. Almost all cars can hit 65 mph fairly quickly, but cars that are decked with technology from heated seats to video monitors and internet access command a luxury premium. It's less about status and more about style and experience, which are boosted by innovative technology.

Accessing the internet is also getting easier, cheaper, and faster. When I began working in the tech industry in 1982, pre-internet, a 300-baud modem was the standard, so I would work in my office several hours each Saturday to download information from around the country. Today I can click on hyperlinks while I'm drinking coffee in my kitchen and information is instantaneous. Innovation changes things—often for better, occasionally for worse in the short term, but ultimately for good. Change, like risk, is unavoidable. But it doesn't have to be unexpected.

If we pay close attention, we can see how tiny forces beneath the surface—no matter how insignificant or disconnected they may seem—can irrevocably impact modern life. Looking carefully, we can start to see the small shifts that, taken together, give rise to big trends. Innovators must anticipate and understand these global trends in order to excel in the ninja future. So let's examine them together.

CHAPTER 2

CHANGES IN CULTURE AND COMMERCE

EVERY DAY BRINGS EVIDENCE THAT small undercurrents of human evolution and innovation are coming together to produce tidal waves of cultural, social, and economic change. Some are already well under way, and others can't be far behind. In this chapter I break them out into two categories: culture and commerce. The reality, of course, is that all these changes—whether natural or technological—are inextricable. Like waves breaking on the shore, each trend derives in part from another, and in turn will spur change in another direction. It is in this complex interplay of human and technological forces that we find the promise—and peril—of innovation.

A Connected Generation

My teen self would have been stunned to discover that in 2018, 95 percent[1] of U.S. teens had a smartphone or have access to one, according to Pew research. Remember, I grew up with a shared, black rotary phone!

The cell phone was invented in the 1970s, but the classic movie *Lethal Weapon*, which came out in 1987, was the first to show a "modern" mobile phone. IMDb's trivia page identifies it as a portable RadioShack Model 17-1003: Sergeant Murtaugh held the handset (complete with a cord) in one hand and the immense electronics and heavy battery in the other, making fleet-footed police work rather challenging.[2] And one of the tensest moments in the 1992 movie adaptation of Tom Clancy's *Patriot Games* featured slightly less old-school tech: After surviving an attack outside the U.S. Naval Academy, Jack Ryan (played by Harrison Ford) tries desperately to call his wife (a retina surgeon like my wife!) but gets a busy signal. He finally gets through in time to warn her that she's in imminent danger, but is too late to prevent a terrible car crash.[3] Both are using what we used to call "car phones."

Teens today would probably see these first car phones, the size of bricks and hardwired into the vehicle, as just as old-fashioned as rotary phones. Still, those steady, iterative technological advancements were a harbinger of the explosion of smart, mobile technology we now take for granted. The appearance of those unwieldy devices in blockbuster movies is the first sign of a seismic shift not just in technology, but also in our relationship to it.

Born between 1995 and 2012, Generation "I," or "GenIs," grew up entirely in the age of the internet. They can't remember a world without smartphones—or at least cell phones—and can't imagine not having one at their fingertips 24/7.

These GenIs spend hours a day searching, chatting, texting, posting, and swiping. Many are coding. Others are gamers or they watch e-gamers. Some take unhealthy risks and may be sexting, cyberbullying, trolling, and engaging in other bad online behavior ending in -ing. Others have complete conversations using only emojis. GenIs rely on social media platforms such as Instagram, Snap, WhatsApp, and Twitter to search for and share information. In just a few years, we have created a whole new lexicon simply to define how people interact with technology. We've also created new categories to diagnose over-indulgence in tech. In 2018, the World Health Organization added[4] gaming disorder (as in video games) to its comprehensive list of disease classifications.

The ubiquity of mobile devices has obvious benefits for GenIs: they can easily call for help in case of an emergency. They can connect with people across the world they might never get to meet "IRL," as the kids say. Parents can monitor online activity and keep track of their kids' location. On the flip side, having unlimited access to information means young people will likely be exposed to content that parents would rather they avoid. Having instantaneous access to other people makes it tempting to waste time texting or checking social media instead of using time mindfully. With so much of life happening virtually, teens are likely to spend a great deal of time with their eyes on a screen instead of the real, five-sense world around them.

If you're a parent, you've probably had the frustrating experience of competing with your child's phone for attention—and losing. Intermittent silences, grunts or one-word responses, and fast-typing fingers are all telltale signs that he or she has—believe it or not—found something more interesting and amusing than you. It's often not even a close contest.

Psychologist Jean Twenge, who analyzed generational data in America going back to the 1930s, concludes that while most recorded generational changes "appear gradually, and along a continuum," recent change has been seismic. As she observed in *The Atlantic*,[5] "the changes weren't just in degree, but in kind. . . . The experiences they have every day are radically different from those of the generation that came of age just a few years before them."

Around 2012, Twenge saw something surprising in her study of teen behavior and emotions: Today's teens are dating less. They're less likely to play outdoor sports, and, sadly, more likely to commit suicide. They are spending less time having face-to-face conversations with their families and friends and more time alone, interacting with only their screens. According to Twenge, this trend coincided with the moment that more than 50 percent of Americans owned a smartphone.

Are these dramatic shifts in behavior due solely to technology? It's hard to prove in this traumatic era of school shootings, terrorism, and political divisiveness. Technology is certainly a factor, but the trend is undeniable in teens across the spectrum, from different geographic, socioeconomic, and ethnic backgrounds. "Where there are cell towers," says Twenge, "there are teens living their lives on their smartphone."[6]

Before we start wringing our hands over technology's influence on the next generation, we need to take an honest look at the example we're setting with our own tech habits. One teen in Twenge's *Atlantic* piece said of her own generation, "I think we like our phones more than we like actual people."[7] What about the rest of us? Are we using technology creatively and actively, or are we passively and idly letting our technology use us? Are we spending our time wisely, or letting life pass us by as technology sucks us in?

Most adults are not digital natives. We're relatively new to anytime/anywhere connectivity, and the benefits and challenges it brings. The truth is, many of us have failed to set effective boundaries and are just as distracted as our children. To be the role models our children deserve, we must create a healthy household culture, including how and when we use technology.

This means insisting that conversations and relationships are a top priority. Practically, this will look different for each family. Some might find it useful to create a tech-free zone in their house or car, where no phones, tablets, or laptops are allowed. Instead, families can play card games or listen to audiobooks. Others might use parental control apps to set limits on screen time. Whatever rules or boundaries you create, the goal is the same: reconnecting with the people you care about by disconnecting from your devices.

But we, as adults, also face increasing isolation and decreasing empathy. America's political leaders are locked in battle, prioritizing party over country. Their divisions are so extreme that they can't even agree on facts. And each side believes the media is distorting the truth to advance a political agenda.

Our confidence in the American Dream, our common commitment to fundamental values, and our belief that our nation can and should be a moral leader for the world are threatened from both inside and outside the United States. For many of us who came of age in the last century, life seems like a step-by-step erosion of things we assumed and took for granted. It's no wonder our kids act differently than we did at their age.

I don't blame technology for these changes. Correlation is not causation, after all. The fact that kids are turning away from my generation's symbol of freedom—the car and the driver's license—is easily explainable by technology. The smartphone now provides autonomy and peer connection. And car services like Lyft and Uber provide the means to be physically free and independent.

But we have to be clear-eyed about how technology detracts from the human experience as much as it enhances it. For better or worse, technology has enabled like-minded people to find each other and shift to electronic tribalism. And in this way, technology divides us at least as much as it unites us. We must honestly acknowledge these real differences to plan for the future.

An Aging Population

Let's take a break from psychoanalyzing our teens and turn to some startling trends in another demographic: our adult population. The percentage of older adults is growing. There were 48 million seniors in the United States in 2017, and that figure will balloon to 98 million by 2060—about one-quarter[8] of the U.S. population. Today, as many as 6.4 million[9] seniors live at or below the poverty line, and four million[10] seniors are homebound. Nine in ten[11] seniors would like to stay in their homes as they age, according to AARP research. And in 2014, more than one-quarter (12.1 million[12]) of older adults lived alone.

Technology presents an opportunity to dramatically improve the quality of life for older people. Active-aging tech amplifies our lives across multiple dimensions: physical, social, emotional, and cognitive. Advances in health care and nutrition let us live longer. We are connected to our friends and family like never before. And thanks to human-centered voice interfaces, like Amazon's Alexa and Apple's Siri, you don't have to be a digital native to understand how to use technology—you just have to talk to your smart speaker.

But perhaps one of the greatest gifts that technology can offer older adults is peace of mind. My mother suffered from Alzheimer's for more than a dozen years before she passed away in 2005. In the early stages, she started to forget the names of loved ones. For several years, my father would use pictures of family and friends and talk about them to help her remember. Often he was rewarded with her smile or knowing comment. He discovered that she was particularly responsive when he'd play the music of her youth, such as Frank Sinatra and the big bands. Since then, researchers have confirmed his experience: studies have shown that familiar or significant music has remarkable benefits to Alzheimer's sufferers. Several states and Canadian provinces use music therapy as an alternative to the marginally effective and expensive drugs now available. (As a side note, the documentary *Alive Inside* takes a heartrending but hopeful look at the promise of music therapy—made more readily accessible than ever through increasing connectivity—for Alzheimer's patients.)

For the moment, Alzheimer's remains a cruelly progressive disease. By the time my mother died, she seemed to have no mental or physical capability. I live with the understanding that I may carry the Alzheimer's gene and suffer that same fate. I think of it every time I forget where I parked the car or struggle to come up with a word. Most of all, I think of it when I see a person I know and blank on his or her name.

Granted, I've always been forgetful, especially with names. And so I have been following with great interest the rapid developments in facial recognition technology and artificial intelligence. When memory fails, technology can help. I was thrilled in 2012 when it leaked that early versions of Google Glass included facial recognition capability. I imagined my personal ninja future: never forgetting another name. I figured it would be only a matter of time before this technology could be incorporated into my daily routine. My excitement was short-lived, however, as before the official launch Google withdrew the facial recognition feature due to privacy fears. In my view, facial recognition technology is an innovation we should embrace. The benefits far outweigh the risks, from helping us remember names in social situations to promoting public safety. We can mitigate risk and protect against abuse with codes of ethics and, if necessary, carefully drawn legal restrictions. We'll talk more about this in Chapter 7.

Now, I'm excited about how people living with Alzheimer's and dementia can harness the power of AI to regain their sense of self. Rick Phelps, who was diagnosed with early-onset Alzheimer's in 2010 and founded Memory People, an Alzheimer's and dementia support group on Facebook, wrote[13] this about Amazon's Alexa: "It has afforded me something that I have lost. Memory. I can ask Alexa anything and I get the answer instantly."

These technologies do more than just make life easier for seniors living with disease or disabilities—they also benefit caregivers and open up new business opportunities to a large and growing sector of Americans. The market for active-aging technology includes 962 million [14] adults over the age of sixty—about 13 percent of the global population as of 2017. And this total multiplies when you take into account family caregivers—so the innovation and independence that consumer technology can offer can improve lives across age demographics. CarePredict helps caregivers better tend to seniors: From sleep behavior to eating habits, the wearable tracks activity and machine learning uses the data collected to discover patterns and flag for abnormalities in seniors' daily routines. Best Buy recognizes the value inherent in this market and the unique role technology can play: In 2018, it announced plans to acquire health company Great Call, which offers senior-friendly tech products and medical alert devices, for $800 million.

According to CTA research, seniors living in the United States will represent a $42.7 billion [15] market opportunity by 2020, including tech products that help people balance aging with a proactive, healthy, independent lifestyle. As a welcome bonus, these consumer benefits can translate into billions of dollars in savings for the health-care industry. The United States is facing a retirement wave—the baby boomer generation is turning sixty-five, and at the same time, the "Silent Generation" (those born roughly between 1925 and 1945) is living longer than past generations.

Most long-term-care providers are already contending with

When the generations will end

Analysis by The Post.

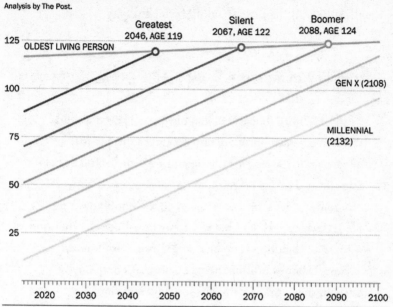

Figure 1: "When the generations will end," Courtesy of *The Washington Post*.

rising demand amid a capacity shortage and limited funding. Wider adoption of consumer technology can go a long way toward promoting preventive care and easing the burden on our health-care system.

As the market for active aging technology expands and the Internet of Things (IoT) evolves, there are endless opportunities for assistive tech. Future ninjas will seize the opportunity to develop technical solutions for safety monitoring, remote care, even wellness and fitness. The biggest challenge lies not in developing technology, but in designing it with the correct audience in mind so they will try it, trust it, use it, and stick with it.

This brings us to another trend: In the ninja future, how will we use all the time freed up by technology?

IoT for You and Me

By 2020, more than 30 billion devices will be digitized, sensorized, Web-enabled, and connected to the IoT, according to Cisco. Just as the internet connected people to news and other information, IoT is creating a network of people, places, and devices. In an IoT-enabled world, objects we use all the time will connect with each other and with us, automating tasks and information exchanges.

Smartphones are the driver behind IoT connectivity, pushing down the price of sensors and spurring improvements in battery life. The less expensive it becomes to connect "things," the faster and more broadly the market will grow. Our smartphones will continue to play an important role in the proliferation of IoT, serving as a hub for our connected devices. And smart speakers have accelerated growth of IoT in the home by giving us the most natural interface of all, our own voices, and finally shattering the ease-of-use barrier.

This technology will touch every aspect of our lives, from chores like watering plants, grocery shopping, and commuting to monitoring our health and home security. We will be safer. We will be more efficient as our tech can anticipate and meet many of our needs. We will even have more control over our time—for example, traffic lights will respond more effectively to traffic dynamics and cars will drive themselves. These innovations and countless others will enable us to worry less about our inanimate things and more about the living creatures around us.

Time Will Tell

Time is our most valuable resource, and we'll have more of it as more tasks are automated.

Ninja innovators have already dramatically cut the time required to accomplish everyday tasks. Look around your home: you no longer need to grow your own food, clean your own dishes, or wash your clothes by hand. When we leave our homes, we have much better ways to travel: we've gone from our feet to horses to trains to cars to jets with electronic ticketing.

But even with online check-in, many of us hate waiting—so ninja innovators developed "skip the line" technologies such as ATMs, Lyft and Uber, StubHub, and drive-through pharmacies. We can place a Starbucks order from our phones and have a latte ready and waiting within minutes. We can order from hardware stores and restaurants alike with apps like Postmates and have it delivered to us immediately. We click through online aisles of groceries on apps like FreshDirect and have our weekly food stock delivered the next morning. We can buy tickets and reserve our seats at movie theaters, allowing us to settle in just in time for the opening credits.

And communication? We began with cave etchings, hieroglyphics, and smoke signals. Yesterday's ninja innovators brought us the printing press, telegraph, radio, television, copy machines, cameras, and computers. Then came smartphones, texts, audiobooks, video calls, social media, and apps including Instagram, Facebook, and Twitter that let us document our every move in real time. If today's communication is easy and instantaneous, imagine what future ninjas will do.

It's undeniable that time-saving innovations have impacted our personal lives, and unimaginable that the same won't be true for our professional lives. In 1930, economist John Maynard Keynes predicted we'd eventually enjoy a fifteen-hour workweek[16] thanks to tech advancements. In some ways, Keynes wasn't far off. Many people work fewer hours now than their predecessors did in the 1950s. As Derek Thompson wrote[17] in a 2014 *Atlantic* essay, "Between 1965 and 2011, time spent on housework and childcare for women declined by 35 percent (or 15 hours each week), thanks to dishwashers, TVs, and other appliances that assist the work of stay-at-home parents." Of course, Thompson argued, this downward trend isn't benefiting every worker equally: Single parents and higher-educated workers tend to work much more than the national average. Those of you running businesses probably don't feel this lighter load. But technology certainly helps you work more efficiently than a decade ago, and there's every reason to believe this trend will continue—especially if you use ninja strategies (assemble a strike force, prepare strategically, take risks, innovate or die) to prepare your business for tomorrow's challenges.

Newer, Smarter Cities

Ninja innovators are already preparing by making our cities smarter—and not a moment too soon. In 1960, one-third of the world's citizens lived in cities. Today roughly half do. By 2050, the United Nations projects that two-thirds of people will live in cities. The world population was three billion in 1960 and is expected to be 9.8 billion[18] by 2050; much of that population growth is happening in urban centers. How will cities be able to handle this growth? How can urban citizens get provisions, water, electricity, broadband, and reliable transportation?

Carnival Corporation offers a sneak peek at what smart cities will look like. Cruise ships are self-contained floating cities, so an envelope-pushing company such as Carnival is instructive for urban planners. Through its world-famous brands—Princess Cruises, Holland America, and Carnival Cruise Line, to name a few—Carnival controls roughly half the berths in the cruise industry. On the CES keynote stage in Las Vegas in 2017, Carnival CEO Arnold Donald revealed an ambitious plan to transition many of the ships within the corporate fleet into smart cities. His vision was that each passenger's needs could be anticipated. As guests swim, stroll, relax, or even visit port destinations, they are known by the crew and their needs are met—all through internet-connected technology.

Arnold hired the team from Disney that had created the MagicBand, a connected wristband for park guests. The brains behind the MagicBand promised to change not only the cruise and hospitality industry but several other customer-oriented, high-experience industries as well.

On the CES stage, Arnold introduced the device that would make this happen: a tiny, beautiful, connected medallion passengers can wear like a watch or a necklace. The OceanMedallion™ conveys the passenger's identity and interests. Passengers receive their medallions prior to leaving home, so they don't have to fish out paper, tickets, or itineraries when they arrive at the ship. Each passenger is recognized by sensors, greeted by name by the crew, and made to feel like royalty upon embarking on the cruise experience.

I visited the first cruise ship outfitted with this technology in 2018, and it blew me away! The medallion serves many functions. It replaces keys—each berth has a sensor outside the door matched with the passenger's medallion. Visit any bar on board and the bartender knows who you are and what you drink. Sit in a lounge and your favorite refreshments magically appear. It transforms a passenger's cruise ship experience to one of anticipated service and customized delight.

I met the team crunching customer data to track correlations in activity and food consumption. Seamlessly, they analyzed how guests spend their time on board; the data allowed them to adapt cruise entertainment and activity offerings to returning passengers' specific preferences or needs. They talked about fundamentally redesigning future cruise ships based on data demonstrating how customers actually move around a ship and spend their time.

Think of the energy that will save: energy is roughly half the cost of running a cruise ship. If the OceanMedallion can tell that no one is in or near a room, the air-conditioning intensity can be reduced. Hallway lights can be dimmed. Food and beverages actually needed on board can be ordered based on consumption patterns from returning guests.

So what will this look like on land in the ninja future? Well, many cities are already becoming smart: Smart streetlamps light up only when people are around. Smart traffic lights respond not only to old traffic patterns but to actual cars—and even pedestrians.

Future ninjas will adapt this same technology to other environments. Imagine simply using the hotel app on your smartphone to check in to and unlock a room customized with the pillows and hangers you prefer, the humidifier you need, and personalized deals from nearby businesses appearing on your phone. The same goes for health clubs, stadiums, and cultural centers of the future. Companies offering these special services will be rewarded with engaged and enthusiastic customers.

And the benefits aren't for ninja businesses alone.

Imagine a local government using this connected technology. Town leaders would get real-time information on how people live and move, allowing them to schedule staff and design services responsive to people's real needs. Understanding the ebb and flow of people means that shifts for police, fire crews, park and parking attendants, information providers, and even office workers could be scheduled with greater predictability.

This technology is also valuable for parents and caregivers—and even pet owners. They could monitor and quickly locate their charges, receive alerts if any set geofence is violated, and avoid the paralyzing anxiety of losing track of those you love, even for a few seconds.

Rana Sen, managing director, Deloitte Consulting LLP, and its government and public services practice's Smart City leader, says we're in the midst of the next generation of urban evolution: He calls it Smart City 2.0. "More cities have begun to move beyond infrastructure, and are now tapping into data and the wisdom of their residents and visitors," he said. "Ultimately, the success of smart cities of tomorrow will depend on how well they engage the citizens, visitors, and businesses in a meaningful way through an intelligent, integrated ecosystem built on a sensor-based physical infrastructure."[19]

Technology that learns about and communicates human needs is just one possible aspect of a smart city. As technology continues to enhance urban living and recreation, smart cities will be a staple of the ninja future.

Retail Apocalypse

What types of stores will we see in smart cities? No industry has been more disrupted by the internet than brick-and-mortar retail. Mainstays such as Sears, JCPenney, and Kmart are shuttering stores across the country as they struggle to compete against online retailers. Many of these stores are "anchor tenants" for malls, leaving giant gaps that can't be filled by, well, Gap. And because many smaller retailers sign cotenancy agreements, pegging their leases to bigger stores next door, smaller stores are shuttering, too.

In 2017, roughly 2,500 stores[20] closed in malls nationwide. Credit Suisse estimates that of the 1,100 malls still open today, one-quarter[21] of them are at risk of closing in the next five years.

Others are less optimistic. Former JCPenney CEO Mike Ullman told an audience in 2018 that only about three hundred malls[22] across America will make it through the next five years. Analysts call this shift "the retail apocalypse"[23] and warn that local jobs will be hit hard when malls close.

But some ninja businesses are reinventing themselves and finding innovative ways to compete with online giants. Macy's surprised everyone—including itself[24]—by posting higher-than-expected profits in the first quarter of 2018. It got a lift from a strong U.S. economy, an increase in spending from international tourists, and the 2018 tax cuts (which left more money in consumers' wallets). But the company is also making physical changes to its stores to compete, launching pop-up marketplaces called "The Market @ Macy's." These pop-ups dedicate space to specific brands for limited periods of time. Marc Mastronardi, Macy's executive vice president of new business development and innovation, said pop-ups such as these give shoppers "a constant break of discovery."[25]

Best Buy is another ninja success story. Facing stiff competition from online retailers, which toppled some of its brick-and-mortar competitors, Best Buy embarked on a turnaround plan that included price-matching, upgrading its website, enhancing the customer service experience, and faster delivery to boost sales both in stores and online. Moving past its turnaround phase, Best Buy is now investing in new services such as In-Home Advisor (a free, in-home consultant for technology) and Total Tech Support (a service plan for all your technology, no matter where or when you bought it), offering customers a more customized experience, and helping to develop a deeper relationship with the company. As my friend the CEO Hubert

Joly told Reuters in 2018, "We have not only survived but thrived and I don't believe this is a winner-takes-all market."[26] This ninja strategy is working: the company's share price has been multiplied by more than five in six years, since the fall of 2012.

In the 1950s, Sears had more than 700[27] U.S. stores. By 2011, that figure had jumped to 3,500 stores.[28] The Great Recession caused its stock to plummet and forced a string of store closings, and today, Sears is back down to about 550 stores.[29] Yet Sears *started* as a mail-order business—they were among the original ninja innovators in retail. "A hundred years ago, Sears was thriving by offering customers the products they needed without the inconvenience (and cost) of a physical store," wrote *Tire Review*'s Michael Ingram. "Sears did this with their iconic catalogue instead of a webpage, but the basic model would be the same as Amazon: Keep overhead costs low, simplify distribution, and let the customer shop from home."[30] Since then, the company has endured the ups and downs of the marketplace, suffering the most during the Great Recession. Stock plummeted and stores closed across the nation. But recently, Sears has made some strategic moves toward attempting to reclaim its ninja identity, though as of this writing, it still faces challenges in today's changing market. It is creatively capitalizing on its large physical spaces by a recent partnership with Amazon: customers can order tires online, then have them delivered to and installed at Sears Auto Centers. The Sears-Amazon partnership is one example of a behemoth retailer recapturing a sense of ninja innovation.

Physical retail remains powerful. True, the e-commerce sector is growing—but it still represents a fraction of what's spent each year at brick-and-mortar stores. In 2017, 59 percent of U.S. holiday shoppers shopped for tech online and 79 percent shopped in physical stores.[31] Amazon, the leader in online shopping, has opened brick-and-mortar bookstores and grocery stores, and ultimately purchased Whole Foods. Niche high-end, online outlets including Warby Parker, Bonobos (owned by Walmart), and Rent the Runway have opened physical stores, too. At the same time, budget-friendly Dollar General announced it would open 1,800 stores between 2016 and 2018.[32] Their goal is that more than 75 percent of Americans will live within a five-mile radius of one of their stores by the end of 2018. (At its heyday in 2004,[33] 95 percent[34] of Americans lived within three miles of a RadioShack, but it filed for bankruptcy in 2015.)

Robin Rivaton, a young French economist, cowrote *Make Real Estate Great Again* with Vincent Pavanello to describe how real estate is in the midst of a major disruption. As malls decline, we have opportunities to repurpose that land and those buildings. Big companies are seeking interesting office space to attract employees. Buildings can become event, concert, and wedding venues. Some have already become classrooms and shared workspaces for startups.

Commercial real estate companies are rethinking how to transform urban, downtown spaces into "un-malls"—areas where you want to spend the day shopping and exploring outside the confines of a shopping mall or plaza. Brookfield Properties is reviving Bleecker Street in New York, which ballooned with high-end stores in the early 2000s that were forced to close when rents skyrocketed. Describing the renewal of Bleecker Street and the new face of retail in *New York* magazine in 2018, Carl Swanson wrote, "The new retail beginning to rise is, like the rest of our lives, mediated by the digital: Shops without shopping bags that act as showrooms for products you have to order later online; stores as places to hang out and drink coffee, maybe pick up a set of millennial-pink dinner plates or sniff a candle, and then Instagram that you were there. . . . [W]ith the old models for retail broken, or at least a good deal less sturdy, and rents finally in decline, risks are being taken. That willingness to experiment means that certain seemingly threatened—but perhaps more resilient than imagined—retailers . . . are returning in new forms." [35]

What Will Become of Retail Jobs?

As online sales flatten or shrink retail space, the surviving brick-and-mortar retailers are using technology to enhance the customer experience and save on labor costs. Thanks to increasingly humanlike robots, service kiosks, and automated helpdesks, customers can complete a transaction without interacting with another person.

Long-term, this means fewer jobs for salespeople, cashiers, and clerks. We need to think about other avenues for these workers. Some of them can be retrained to help people in their homes. La Poste—the French national postal service—relies on public trust of its mail carriers to sell in-home installation of everything from alarm systems to entertainment. In the United States, retailers like Best Buy and Amazon have focused on new delivery techniques, installation, and other managed services in the connected home. These services help consumers ensure that their devices are working properly, and have the added benefit of driving increased engagement with the retailer.

Ultimately, retail is about helping other people—so it makes sense that some displaced retail workers could reskill for other "helping professions" where we have severe shortages, including elder care, security, and child care.

A Digital Economy

Internet platforms help build businesses, too. In 2017, Google's search and advertising tools generated $283 billion in economic activity for more than 1.5 million U.S. businesses and nonprofits.[36] Google's primary business revenue stream is advertisements tied to search, connecting local businesses with people searching the Web for exactly what those small businesses offer. These ads give small business big reach—helping them connect with customers around the world. In fact, more than 30 percent of clicks for American businesses advertising on Google came from outside the United States in 2017.

Even social media platforms create jobs. Facebook Marketplace, for example, is a localized internet forum to buy and sell unwanted items. More than 700 million people use it every month to exchange goods through safe, verified transactions.[37] Rather than going unused or to the dump, your neighbor can list that patio furniture or kitchen appliance online and sell it to nearby Facebook users in one convenient mobile app.

Facebook Groups have emerged as more than a place to discuss shared causes or activities—they're also a virtual forum to build communities and companies. Businesses on Facebook have formed 20,000 Groups, which bring together 11 million members to share best practices and help each other grow.[38]

These services often lower the barrier to entry for new businesses. Designing a Facebook (or Instagram) page for your business is free; creating a website and the surrounding digital infrastructure is more expensive.

In 2018, Facebook pledged $1 billion in small-business initiatives.[39] Its "Boost Your Business" initiative has trained 60,000 small businesses across America and even more across the globe.[40] And it has helped more than one million users with free online education through "Blueprint," offering a wide variety of sales, marketing, and social content skills and the ability to earn credentials by completing the classes.

"New economy" opportunities are vital, especially as automation impacts traditional hourly jobs. Retail jobs continue to grow—overall employment is expected to grow 2 percent between 2016 and 2026, according to the Bureau of Labor Statistics—but that's at a far slower pace than the average for other occupations.[41]

A Horizontal Economy

Technology will continue to usher in choices for consumers. Bringing innovative products to market will be democratized with quick and efficient means to produce and make these products available for consumers. More and more innovators will unleash a flood of new products. Choices for the consumer will increase exponentially. As a result, ninja retailers will have to be more nimble than ever. They must be able to keep up with new products, match them with their target consumer, and shift strategies to align with a lifestyle rather than a product category.

Future retailers will succeed less because of the products that they carry and more because of the lifestyle they represent.

The central marketplace is not going away—it's how we fill the stalls and how we maximize consumers' time that will change. Technology opens up infinite choices for consumers in terms of what to buy and how to buy it. But we have a finite amount of time in which to make these choices. Ultimately, the future of retail is not an either/or scenario, where retailers and consumers choose either the brick-and-mortar or online model. There will be no either/or choices—no commercial silos—in the ninja future.

It's a both/and world now. There will always be companies that prioritize convenience and utility, such as Amazon, where consumers can find and purchase almost any product with a few swipes. Successful retailers know it's not just about what we buy and how we buy—it's about *why* we buy one thing over another. They design their sales and marketing to increase brand loyalty—increasing the number of consumers who buy based on the retailer's brand, not the location. The companies that find ways to seamlessly integrate virtual and physical shopping experiences to make the most of consumers' time will be the ones that thrive in the ninja future.

CHAPTER 3

NINJA FUTURE ECONOMY

AFTER MY YOUNGEST SON TURNED SIX, I made my wife promise that we'd never host another large birthday party. I found the annual mound of presents outrageous—far more than any child will ever need, much less enjoy. We wanted our kids to be more mindful of the opportunities they had, such as the summer camps they loved.

I preferred the example set by his older brother a few years earlier. When planning for our oldest son's seventh birthday, to our surprise, he asked if the money that would be spent on gifts could instead go to kids who could not otherwise afford summer camp.

I will admit we were somewhat skeptical at first and decided to let him think it over for a few days—but he stuck by his request. So my wife found a program that provided a summer day-camp experience for children in inner-city Detroit, just a few miles from where we live. Our son's party invitation to his friends and classmates conveyed his request that contributions be made to Detroit City Camp.

The next surprise was the response from the parents of his friends: They were thrilled. They could skip the hassle of shopping for and wrapping yet another present. They had a ready-made opportunity to discuss charity, responsibility, and gratitude with their children. But the biggest shock was that together we raised nearly $2,000.

The contributions generated by our son's request were the only ones the Detroit City Camp received that summer. When the camp director asked him to attend the end-of-summer party, he was able to truly appreciate the fruits of his idea: hundreds of happy kids playing and learning in the well-run, mostly volunteer program. The joy he felt at realizing how much he had helped these kids surpassed any pleasure from any gift he ever got. That night, before going to bed he said, "Dad, this was the best day of my life!" That was his gift to me.

It also made me realize that no matter how much cool new tech we invent, there is no substitute for memory making. Things are nice, but they don't make you happy. We are becoming a nation overwhelmed by "stuff"—as Ikea's head of sustainability said in 2014, "We've hit peak 'stuff.'" We see signs of this shift everywhere: Marie Kondo's The Life-Changing Magic of Tidying Up was a runaway bestseller in 2014. Three years later the New York Times ran a story about kids not wanting the "stuff" that their parents have amassed over the years.[1]

More and more, consumers are opting to spend their money on intangible events—a shift from an economy of acquisition to an economy of experience. And although the trend is particularly strong among millennials—78 percent of whom are looking for "the perfect Instagram moment"—they're not the only ones who prefer an experience economy: according to a 2016 Harris poll, 59 percent of boomers would rather pay for an experience than a material good.

Ninja businesses will quickly adapt to the changing preferences of consumers to dominate the market in the years to come.

The Experience Economy

By 2030, spending on experiences like travel, leisure, and food is expected to grow to a whopping $8 trillion.[2] Ninja innovators across all sectors will find ways to capitalize on this shift. Airbnb revamped its offerings several years ago to explicitly cater to the consumer demand for experiences. Now locals can offer travelers not just their homes and apartments, but also an opportunity to participate in activities unique to the area. But even traditionally "stuff"-oriented companies have picked up on the demand as well. Prada has opened cafés in Italy and Lamborghini offers an "esperienza" program, where customers stay at a luxury hotel, visit a Lamborghini museum, and learn from expert instructors how to navigate a race course.

Not every company can—or indeed should—reinvent its central product to incorporate an "experience," but the vast majority of companies do sponsor events of some kind. Tech is adapting to the changing tastes of consumers; ninja businesses should do the same and seize these opportunities to pivot toward experience more than any particular product. Berkshire Hathaway nails this: Every year, shareholders swarm Omaha to revel in the amazing experiences the company offers at its annual shareholder meeting. The centerpiece is a Q&A session with Warren Buffett and Charlie Munger, but the other activities—from brand mascots, to a 5K, to exclusive cocktail parties—create a sense of community among the thousands of shareholders and help create a deep sense of loyalty to the company's brand.

Trade shows can also maximize the "experience" factor, giving companies the opportunity to find community and network within their industry as well as to showcase their products and services. Las Vegas is home to CES in large part because it's an experience-driven city that engages all five senses. Attendees see and touch all the most cutting-edge technology from all over the world during the day, and in the evenings they enjoy some of the most unique food and beverage offerings on earth, stay in glamorous hotels, and hear world-class performers.

We also strive to make it a memorable photo-op experience through consistent branding and eye-catching displays. In this age of social media, designing an event so consumers can see and be seen can mean the difference between a brand that flourishes and a brand that folds.

Other brick-and-mortar retailers are changing the shopping experience, too, with many adopting the "experience" and "subscription" models. Saks Fifth Avenue dedicated space on the second floor of its flagship store in New York to health and wellness classes and services, dubbed "The Wellery." Nordstrom bought Trunk Club, a subscription-based personalized styling service. Fast-fashion chain Zara added robots, mirrors that display hologram images of shoppers "trying on" clothes, and self-checkout options at its flagship store in London.[3] And any tech-loving consumer visiting a Fry's Electronics is delighted by an array of temptations, from TVs, tablets, and cameras to the build-it-yourself components for sophisticated computers and gaming systems.

Smart retailers know that customers are more likely to buy things they can envision and experience in person. More and more, companies are setting up experience showrooms, so that customers can see, hear, and touch products in a setting designed to elicit appreciation, instead of just imagining what these products might be like in their homes. Dallas-based Starpower, which specializes in luxury appliances and electronics, holds an annual expo that showcases cutting-edge technology. The expo now draws thousands of consumers from across Texas—and many of them become loyal customers. "It is not enough to just see innovative products—they must prove how they impact one's life," says Starpower cofounder Dan Pidgeon. "This innovative showroom sorts through the challenges of making complex home and lifestyle decisions. Most important, our customers leave our store with the peace of mind that the job will be done right."[4]

Sharing Economy

Changing consumer preferences are also opening up new economic opportunities. "Sharing economy" services—including home rentals, delivery services for hire, transportation services, and freelancers for hire—provide new sources of income for workers. The concept of the sharing economy isn't new: activities like bartering, agricultural shares, yard sales, clothes swaps, and communal housing have always been part of our social fabric. What distinguishes the present sharing economy from yesterday's informal give-and-take is that now people can create new opportunities to actually earn income and use these activities to more reliably financially support themselves. Consumers looking for a different type of experience are seizing the benefits the sharing economy provides—creating a win-win for everyone.

Short-term rentals are a prime example. Every spring, CTA hosts events in Washington, D.C., where we connect our CTA members with members of Congress and policymakers. We typically have about 250 out-of-town guests attend. But a few years ago, our organization had a problem: We had more people wanting to come to our annual Washington meeting than we had hotel rooms. Our guests who could not get a room in our block at the lower rate we had negotiated had few options as available hotel rooms had skyrocketed in price as this was peak cherry blossom season. Several shortened their trips. Others simply canceled their plans to come to Washington. Some pursued a third option: staying with area residents through the short-term rental services such as Airbnb, HomeAway, and VRBO.

These internet platforms allow homeowners—or "hosts"— to list their homes for everything from short-term stays to longer vacation rentals. For travelers, these short-term rentals are often a more cost-effective, convenient, and comfortable option than hotels. And by renting out their own homes, hosts can supplement or even cover their own costs of living. A 2017 Airbnb report found 4 percent of British hosts say Airbnb allows them to stay in their homes and avoid foreclosure or eviction.[5]

Short-term rentals expose travelers to new neighborhoods. Roughly three-quarters of Airbnb listings are outside of traditional hotel areas, driving visitors to explore new neighborhoods with locals-only shops, restaurants, and attractions.[6] Short-term rentals are symbiotic: they satisfy wanderlusting travelers who want to go beyond the bounds of conventional city centers as well as the homeowners who host them. The average British host has been in her home for twenty-two years[7]—and is able to offer decades of expertise about the neighborhood, both history *and* hot spots.

Ride-sharing services lower barriers to entrepreneurship while enhancing public safety by curbing drunk driving. Uber, for example, now supports more than three million drivers globally.[8] People who drive for Uber and Lyft generally do so to earn extra income as they pursue other goals or tend to other responsibilities.

Changing Business Models

The experience economy is turning traditional business models and product consumption on their heads. Take car ownership as an example. Cars are used only 5 percent of the time.[9] We drive to work, park. Drive to the grocery store, park. Drive home, park. Imagine if instead, cars were used 95 *percent* of the time. Looking at the difference, could cities eliminate 90 percent of parking spaces? Could parking lots turn into sidewalks, gardens, and parks? Could we save the waste from raw materials and parts used in car production and turn cities into greener, more environmentally friendly areas? Could cities be built with people in mind, rather than vehicles?

The rise of Uber and Lyft—mobility as a service—was a first step. Few realized just how important ride-sharing apps would become: on-demand, anytime, safe, affordable transportation at your fingertips. I can't remember what life was like without it! And with more than 75 million active users[10] worldwide taking more than 15 million[11] trips a day, getting around has never been easier. In fact, according to Mary Meeker's 2018 Internet Trends report, when you factor in costs including gas, car insurance, and maintenance, it's actually cheaper to take Uber-POOL and UberX than to own a car in big cities such as New York, Los Angeles, Washington, D.C., and Chicago.[12] Now, add in other car-sharing services such as Zipcar, Gig Car Share, and Car2Go and the latest mobility addition—bike and electric scooter shares. As city dwellers with the options of ride-sharing, on-demand car sharing, and public transportation, it's no wonder why car ownership is decreasing among millennials.

German automaker Daimler understands the shift and is ramping up investments in future ninja mobility startups such as Car2Go, Uber competitor Taxify, and app-based carpooling service Via. Ford is also focused on an innovation-driven future. Back in 2016, Ford announced the creation of Ford Smart Mobility, a subsidiary focused on emerging technologies and expanding the Ford business model into mobility technologies. CES 2018 keynoter and Ford Motor Company CEO Jim Hackett, who once headed Ford Smart Mobility, invested in connected vehicle startup Autonomic, ride-sharing startup Chariot, and subscription vehicle service Canvas.

At CES 2018, I sat down with Lyft's cofounder and president John Zimmer to discuss his vision for the future of transportation—what he called the "Third Transportation Revolution." Zimmer believes we're currently in the first of three phases to fully self-driving vehicles. The second phase is self-driving vehicles at low speeds with backup human drivers. The third phase is fully autonomous vehicles. He agrees with many other experts that 5G will accelerate this process. That's because such vehicles are essentially mobile data centers. They'll generate a lot of data, but they'll also need to receive large amounts of data to effectively navigate and react in real time. A workable self-driving ecosystem needs the lightning-fast vehicle-to-vehicle connectivity that 5G provides. He sees networked self-driving vehicles as the "killer app" of car ownership, and predicts that by 2025 private car ownership will "go the way of the DVD" and all but end in American cities.

Other industries are heading the same way. Beyond the physical components needed to play music and videos, many of us don't even own copies of the movies and TV shows we love. Digital content reduced the clutter and waste of traditional content mediums and toppled businesses such as Circuit City and Blockbuster. Netflix, Amazon Video, Hulu, and PlayStation Vue have, in most cases, taken the next step by *licensing* you the rights to watch movies and TV shows. Monthly subscriptions keep customers hooked, coming back regularly for the latest content.

Music has evolved in a similar way. Disruptors such as Pandora, Spotify, and Apple Music follow the subscription model, allowing customers to freely stream whatever they like—as long as their subscription is active.

These ninja innovators enjoy many benefits: repeat customers, higher customer loyalty, and, most important, vast amounts of data that allows them to personalize the consumer experience. Future ninja companies understand that data is central to a winning business strategy. (We'll talk in detail about ninja companies in Chapter 10.)

For those who lament that DVDs often reside in retail clearance bins, remember that society's desire for a streamlined "experience" led to this. We are moving away from ownership of stuff and toward access to services. Instead of buying your favorite movies on DVDs, you pay for a subscription to Netflix. Instead of buying new music on CDs, you subscribe to Spotify. Instead of owning a car, you pay for a service that lets you access a fleet of cars when you need one. Ninja innovators developed personalized content, ride-sharing, and subscription services because millennials and Gen Z members chose experiences and convenience over ownership. The market just recognized the demand.

Human-Machine Partnerships

Ninja innovations are already changing the way that we work, another challenge unique to our age. As future ninjas seize the moment, these disruptions will become radically more pronounced. Let's face it: *Disrupt* is an unsettling word. It connotes rupture, interruption, disorder. But it is also a transitive verb: one that exerts its action on a specific object—in this case, our personal lives and our global economy. It connotes movement: a shift and transfer of energy from one direction to another. This will not be an abysmal narrative of computer systems replacing large swaths of the global workforce. It also will not be a simple narrative of workers gaining a handy digital coworker to make their job easier and more efficient. The large-scale impact of technology on the workforce will be more nuanced.

The Organization for Economic Cooperation and Development (OECD) estimated in 2016 that 32 percent of jobs will be *different* in the near future than they are today due to technology.[13] Health care is one obvious example. Jobs in the medical field will abound, but professionals will increasingly be aided by advanced technologies such as artificial intelligence (AI), including machine learning. We may become increasingly comfortable ceding some diagnostic and analytical duties to proven AI systems, but ninja innovation, at least in the next two decades, will assist doctors, not supplant them.

The economic potential of AI is enormous. A 2017 PwC study projects that AI will add more than $15 trillion to the world economy in 2030.[14] None of us can predict how many jobs AI will create as new interfaces and industries emerge. The shift won't be uniform: Some sectors of our economy will experience the AI revolution long before others. We need to be realistic about the extent to which technology will alter the workplace. We need to get serious about making sure that today's students—future ninjas among them—are adequately prepared for tomorrow's workforce.

CTA research shows that lack of public trust is one of the main barriers to development and implementation of AI. In the age of connectivity, big data, and AI, the world is asking an existential question about the role men and women will play in our own future. To me, it's crystal clear: Humans can and will

dictate the terms by which technological innovations comple-
ment our work and our play. Like all technology, it is up to us to
ensure that AI can act both as capably and ethically as we train
it to be. If we hold ourselves accountable to standards of fairness
and excellence, that will play out in the AI solutions we develop.

Another part of this suspicion of future ninja innovation
comes from a lack of understanding of what these changes mean
for workers. There's no denying that AI will disrupt industries,
but the extent to which it will eliminate jobs has been somewhat exaggerated in the media. Understandably, when statistics
about potential job loss due to automation make headlines, the
public may be more resistant to reading the fine print about how
technology is also changing the nature of existing jobs. So in
2018, CTA created a 21st Century Workforce Council—a forum
for industry to address the skills gap in the United States and
ensure the tech sector has the necessary pipeline of ninjas for
the millions of jobs we are creating: data analysts, programmers,
robotics experts, and more.

When CTA surveyed tech executives on their labor needs
in 2018 and in the future, 92 percent said they expected they
would need more employees with technical skills in the next
five years. And 74 percent said it was a challenge to find candidates with the right skills and abilities. American companies
face a major skills shortage for AI engineers and other highly
technical roles, yet most American students are not pursuing
advanced degrees in these fields. American students earn fewer
than half of the U.S. doctoral degrees in many STEM fields.[15]

Increasing the number of STEM graduates in the United
States is important to the success of our economy, but future
ninjas don't necessarily need a graduate degree. (Indeed, for all

the concern about the impact of self-driving trucks on the trucking industry, from 2016 through 2018 we have faced a huge deficit of drivers willing to take on these jobs.) Companies like Microsoft, Apple, and IBM are partnering with community colleges today to develop curricula that match students' education with skills shortages in the tech workforce. Innovative models like this will help close the skills gap and make tech-based careers more accessible to a broader range of Americans.

Future ninjas will need technical skills, but more important, they will need routinely to refresh their skills to stay ahead of rapidly evolving technology. This necessitates a fundamental change in mindset that starts with our education system. We are investing an extraordinary amount of brain power in developing technologies that will change the way we work, and ultimately make the world safer, more efficient, and more enjoyable. We need to invest some of that brain power in modernizing our education system so that students are prepared for these new tech jobs.

We should expose more children to robotics and coding at early ages, thereby ensuring that they develop a base level of familiarity and interest in these critical and lucrative fields. And since we know that individuals learn differently, we should set aside our "one size fits all" education model. Some of us are visual learners, others are aural learners. Some need interaction, others can learn just fine without a human. Some blossom in group settings, others shrink. Technology can create different education experiences for different students, and we should take advantage of ninja innovations in the classroom to customize learning. And we should look outside the classroom to apprenticeships, as IBM is doing, to ensure alignment between industry needs and skills training.

AI, smart cities, drones, and other technologies will create new categories of jobs that didn't exist a decade ago. Cultivating and nourishing future ninjas is our paramount goal. It's an ambitious one, but that's what ninja innovators do. If we can develop artificial intelligence, we can certainly rise to the challenge of preparing our workforce for the consequences and opportunities of ninja innovation.

Wildcards

So far, we've examined some of the tangible, predictable, and manageable trends that are swirling around us. But it's important to remember that external, unpredictable factors will require us to prepare and adapt. Climate change is one obvious example.

Not being a scientist, I'm not going to weigh in on the global warming debate. However, I am proud I led an American technology industry consensus to exceed the goals set in the Paris Climate Agreement. I cheered in support in April 2018, when French president Emmanuel Macron told a special joint session of the U.S. Congress, "[W]e are killing our planet. Let us face it: There is no Planet B." In that same speech, he asked, "What is the meaning of our life, really, if we work and live destroying the planet, while sacrificing the future of our children?"[16]

While climate change is natural and has been a constant

part of our planet's history, the issue of the impact of humans is controversial. What is not in dispute is that weather patterns are changing. A wealth of data shows that unusual and sometimes extreme weather—including rain, storms, winds, fires, and temperature variations—have increased in frequency and intensity over the last sixty years.[17] In 2017 alone, people in Puerto Rico, Texas, Florida, and California suffered from devastating weather-related flooding, loss of electricity, extreme winds, and fires.

There is no reason to believe this trend will reverse. It may lead to greater population dislocations, refugee crises, and challenges to single-source supply chains, distribution routes, and corporate locations. And it will undoubtedly drive the resilience movement, which I'll talk about in more detail in Chapter 11.

Adapting to all these trends—both known and unknown—as we move toward the ninja future will require human agility and technical ingenuity. We can't perfectly anticipate every situation or preemptively design every solution. Fortunately, we already have most of the technical building blocks in place.

CHAPTER 4

NINJA INNOVATION TODAY

THE U.S. PATENT OFFICE ISSUED a record 347,243 patents to innovators in 2017.[1] This compares to about 70,000 patents issued by the same office in 1997.[2] The phenomenal pace of progress has been driven by a few basic technological ingredients. The groundbreaking innovations of future ninjas will be based on different combinations of these building blocks: sensors; broadband and 5G; algorithms; cloud computing, big data, and analytics; biometrics; robotics; blockchain; and quantum computing. Whether you're aware of it or not, you already encounter most of these in your daily life: from autopilot on airplanes, to the fingerprint scanner on your smartphone, to the smart speaker in your kitchen.

Sensors

Sensors often use technology called micro-electrical mechanical systems (MEMS). These remarkable little devices use a series of integrated circuits on a semiconductor to develop systems that include both mechanical and electrical elements. In essence, MEMS are miniature machines that activate in response to an outside stimulus to produce myriad results. The smartphone in your pocket contains roughly two dozen sensors that sense, measure, respond, and convey information to the device. They capture and process information on tilt, acceleration, vibration, and location. They also enable features such as the camera, touch screen, and fingerprint scan. You rely on sensors every time you check your heart rate on your Fitbit, consult Waze on your phone, reposition your tablet to play a video game, or hear your smoke alarm sound.

The first basic accelerometer sensors in the 1970s cost more than $500 apiece.[3] By 2000, the cost had fallen to $3.50 apiece. Now, with more than a billion smartphones sold globally each year, these sensors are mass-produced, and economies of scale dropped the price to 34 cents each in 2018.[4]

Low-cost sensors can detect changes in movement, location, air pressure, temperature, light, sound, wind—even smells. Combined with a power source, a strong smartphone processor, and wireless broadband, these minuscule miracles are transformative in their ability to provide you with important information, or convey information to the cloud or other connected devices, which can then act on this information.

Sensors make the spaces in which we work and live smarter.

For example, HVAC automation systems function better with more detailed information about the internal and external environment. Lighting, fire, and safety systems all improve when they have access to additional data about the building.

And when you feed the data from sensors into powerful cloud processing and artificial intelligence systems, the benefits are exponential. For example, a soil moisture sensor can tell you everything you need to know about a single spot of farmland. And when you process that information with cloud-based AI systems capturing myriad data points—like temperature, motion sensing, and even animal facial recognition—farmers can leverage weather predictions to automate watering systems, monitor the health and activity of their livestock, and make more accurate estimates of total yield.

Ninja buildings and ninja farmers? Yes. The possibilities are endless.

Broadband and 5G

Think about the first time you accessed a website or streamed a video from your phone on a cellular network. It was captivating, I'm sure, but probably also tedious, patchy, and irritating since early networks lacked the capacity and speed we now take for granted. But by 2017, YouTube viewers were watching more than one billion hours of video content every day—much of it on mobile devices—because it's no longer tedious or slow.[5]

Upgrades in cellular connectivity have dramatically improved throughput—the amount of information that can pass through a system at a given time. Today we stream music across a host of services in countries across the globe, listen to podcasts while we run, video chat with friends and family whenever and wherever we are, and watch entire movies without a hitch. How? Broadband.

Broadband allows massive amounts of data to be transferred almost instantaneously. It includes both wired transmission (cables, fiber, even power lines) and wireless transmission (satellite, Wi-Fi, and mobile cell service). In the developed world, cell service is mostly 3G and 4G. Ninja innovations are quickly shifting this to 5G, or "5th Generation" transmission, and a business revolution has already begun (more on this in Chapter 6).

Countless services and businesses have been born as a result of the exponential advance in speed and connectivity. 3G connectivity gave us less than 1 megabit per second (Mbps) download rates. At that rate, it took twenty-six hours to download a two-hour-long movie. 4G brought us theoretical speeds of 100 Mbps—meaning we could download that same file in six minutes. But 5G? With download speeds of 10 Gbps to 20 Gbps, 5G will let us download the movie's video file in *3.6 seconds.*[6]

The lightning speeds, larger network capacity, and lower latency rates (that is, lag time) of our ubiquitous broadband means we can harness the power of the internet for future innovations that rely on speed and precision: 4K Ultra HD video, virtual reality, self-driving vehicles. The high-speed connectivity of 5G will allow us to place an incredibly complex piece of machinery in an inhospitable environment—in soybean fields, under bridges, on oil rigs—and control it in near real time from the safety of an office or lab a thousand miles away.[7]

Cisco predicts global mobile data traffic will grow 700 per-

5G: How fast is it?

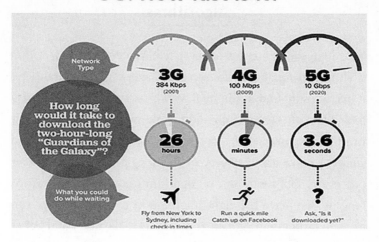

Figure 2: "5G: How fast is it?" Courtesy of CNET[7]

cent between 2016 and 2021, to 49 exabytes a month (one exabyte is one *million* terabytes), due in large part to the IoT.[8] Before long, almost everything around us—cars, kitchen appliances, wearables—will connect to the internet and produce a new stream of data that we can use to improve our lives.

We need to lay down the small cell and fiber infrastructure necessary for 5G today. Accenture estimated in 2017 that investments in 5G infrastructure could generate $500 billion for the U.S. economy and create three million jobs in the first seven years of deployment.[9] Businesses that require blazing internet speeds and low latency rates will flock to the cities and states that prepare for 5G now. By embracing 5G today, innovators can take a bold step toward the connectivity of the ninja future.

Algorithms

Your high school math teacher may have defined an algorithm as simply an equation or formula that takes inputs and translates it into a result. Out in the "real world," algorithms are powerful tools that can dramatically improve human life by making us healthier, happier, and more productive. That's a pretty bold claim to make about step-by-step actions performed by microprocessors. But the power of algorithms is nearly limitless: As long as they have the right information coming in, they can analyze or manipulate data and help us make faster and better decisions.

For example, ninja innovators developed algorithms for wearable technology that can determine how many steps you've taken, how much and how well you've slept, whether you're stressed, or how strenuously you're exercising, based on measuring changes in or reaching targets for movement, location, heartbeat, and other biometrics. Having such detailed information at your fingertips can help you make real-time decisions about your health.

That's just one, personal application—but we are now living in a time when we routinely carry around devices with incredible computing power, and which can also tap into an exponentially more powerful cloud. The concept of algorithms has been around for a very long time, but the current environment is fertile ground for innovation based on algorithms—from predicting your insurance needs,[10] to identifying and eradicating "fake news," [11] to uncovering mutations [12] in the human genome. Your high school math teacher was right after all: Future ninjas most definitely will use them outside the classroom.

In creating algorithms, we need to be mindful of introducing "algorithmic bias"—that is, inadvertently baking in stereotypes based on who is doing the coding. For example, researchers at MIT's Media Lab found that facial recognition technology is right 99 percent of the time for white men, but is much less accurate for women with darker skin.[13] Algorithms are only as strong as the data they're built on. This is yet another reason why diversity in the tech workforce is vital: Everyone must be involved in building products that work for everyone.

On Algorithms

Algorithms are not a new concept; the word in its current meaning dates back to the nineteenth century. Mathematicians, engineers, and programmers are continually improving and changing algorithms. The result only works when combined with appropriate technology for their implementation.

In 1967, Dr. Andrew Viterbi proposed a breakthrough algorithm for packing and unpacking content sent over the air. But the technology was considered impractical to implement widely given the computing resources of the day. It was great math and great logic—but computers weren't yet able to handle the requirements.

This changed over time. In the 1980s, individual processors could handle the algorithm, and Viterbi's work became a consumer product: modems for personal computers. His algorithms were improved upon, combined with improvements in processor technology, and became part of one of the most widely used consumer products in the world. Viterbi went on to big things, too. In 1985, he cofounded the cell phone chipset giant Qualcomm.

Cloud Computing, Big Data, and Analytics

If you've ever seen one of IBM's "Watson at Work" commercials, you've seen a portrayal of the ultimate in ninja innovation. Processing big data and using the cloud and artificial intelligence (AI) allows Watson not only to make connections, but also to learn and propose solutions.

Ninja innovators developed cloud computing as a form of outsourcing: It lets us move the hosting of data and services away from individual resident, business, or government computers to servers run by businesses that specialize in server hosting. It frees up assets (cooled physical space, massive storage capability) and people (trained IT server and storage specialists) so a business can focus on its core mission.

But the cloud is so much more than file storage. Its real promise lies in letting demanding computer programs and Web applications leverage internet-connected sources of computing power in real time. Scalable computing is already a common practice on the Web: Companies that run popular websites can launch new servers in the cloud almost instantly when traffic spikes, and decommission them just as quickly. And some com-

panies are experimenting with "fog" or "edge" computing—
systems that take stress off the main processing center in the
cloud by processing part of the data locally, thereby increasing
both speed and security.

Because cloud computing allows us to capture large troves
of data, it makes big data analysis possible. Big data simply
means massive amounts of digital information. Big data's heavy
number-crunching and algorithms can be transmitted to a
server bank in the cloud and processed at lightning speed.

But the magic of big data is when you use analytics to gain
new insight. The *who*, *when*, *what*, and *how* of the information
you process could answer the question of *why*. For example,
"Why do some people with a medical condition die from it,
while others live?" "Which traffic intersections are most dangerous and at what time of day?" "What do people shop for on
Cyber Monday?"

Harnessing big data for predictive analytics is a huge opportunity for future ninjas. For example, if a factory floor manager
wants to figure out how to create a better, safer, more productive work environment for employees, she should first study
their physical environment. Machines on a factory floor can
collect dozens of data points every minute—from temperature
to vibration to humidity—and can send that information back
to the machine manufacturer's headquarters. There the data
can be compared against data from machines in thousands of
other factories; this analysis can improve efficiency and even
determine whether a piece of equipment may be prone to failure. She can also look for less obvious correlations. Suppose
this particular factory floor were located in Detroit and happened to employ a number of Lions football fans. The manager

could track productivity against the NFL schedule to determine whether Sunday night Lions games impact Monday morning factory productivity.

Pay attention, future ninjas: The most advanced level of big data analytics involves not only predicting the probability of future outcomes, but also automatically taking action based upon those predictions. Predictive analytics requires a feedback loop in order to continuously refine its predictive prowess. Fraud detection in the credit card industry is a perfect example: If you've ever received an automated call alerting you to a suspicious pattern of charges to your account, that call was likely prompted by an algorithm. That algorithm relied on big data that analyzed not only your established charge patterns but also those of millions of other consumers. Music streaming services like Pandora are another example—offering the perfect song at the perfect time, all enabled by analysis of your past listening habits.

Big data, cloud computing, and analysis are the foundation of smart cities: predicting traffic patterns, enabling self-driving vehicles to communicate with the world around them and with each other, monitoring infrastructure for signs of wear and tear. And to truly harness the power of this information flow, we need artificial intelligence.

AI is one of the hottest topics in tech. But it has been quietly operating behind the scenes for years in its most basic form, narrow AI, which specializes in one area. In 2011, IBM's Watson demonstrated a great example of narrow AI. Engineers trained the AI for one specific task: playing *Jeopardy!* Chatbots and voice-recognition technologies including Apple's Siri, Amazon's Alexa, and Microsoft's Cortana are other examples of narrow

AI. These services have multiple uses, but everything derives from voice recognition.

When narrow AI advances to general AI, also known as "human-level AI," these machines will be able to do pretty much everything a human being can do: for example, carry on complex conversations and understand nuances in language. Another way to think about it is that general AI will be able to "pass" as a human. Scientists have a host of different tests to define general AI, including the Turing test (can a machine pass for a human in conversation?), the employment test (can a machine take on a job that is currently done by humans?), and the coffee test (can a machine walk into someone's home and figure out how to make coffee—locate the machine, fill it with water, find the coffee, and brew a cup?).

Ray Kurzweil made headlines in 2017 by predicting exactly when these milestones in AI would come to pass. Kurzweil is a brilliant computer scientist, futurist, inventor, author of *The Singularity Is Near,* and now director of engineering at Google—not to mention CTA Hall of Famer. He forecasts that AI will pass the Turing test by 2029, achieving humanlike intelligence, and that in 2045, "humans will multiply our effective intelligence . . . by merging with the intelligence we have created."[14]

The final level of AI is superintelligence, which Oxford philosopher Dr. Nick Bostrom defines as "an intellect that is much smarter than the best human brains in practically every field, including scientific creativity, general wisdom and social skills."[15]

Researchers' predictions of when we'll reach these levels

vary widely.[16] Maybe superintelligent AI will signal the end of humanity; maybe it will mark the beginning of a new humanity. Either way, I am certain it will change humanity as we now know it. The ability to train a computer to synthesize similarities among fragments of unstructured data holds enormous promise for the ninja future. This goes well beyond tech companies: Businesses that aren't designing and developing AI directly can use the technology to increase productivity and decrease wastefulness, improve customer service, reduce fraud, and become more attuned to individual customers' wants and needs.

Biometrics

As each person has dozens of unique physical attributes, and sensors are getting cheaper and better at measuring them, biometrics have become the new frontier. We're a long way from the days of only using fingerprints. And the physiological response that old-fashioned and unreliable lie detector tests purported to measure can be gauged much more effectively with today's ninja innovations, which can perceive several physiological and behavioral indicators. These indicators can be used to establish or confirm identity, determine emotion, assess risk, or evaluate responsiveness. And yes, they can detect lies, too: instead of using a polygraph, we now have technology that can analyze the tiny movements of our pupils to determine whether or not we're being candid.[17]

Many people appear willing to sacrifice some privacy for security where our safety risk is higher (airports) or where we have vulnerable populations (schools and hospitals). I'm one of them. My work frequently brings me overseas, so I signed up for Global Entry, which shortens my time spent in passport control and customs. I willingly handed over my fingerprints in exchange for this convenience. Many security access systems privately offered also rely on fingerprints. Apple, Samsung, and a host of other smartphone makers use fingerprint scans to grant phone access. We can keep thieves from stealing our data—and our kids from unauthorized spending sprees.

Our irises are one of our most unique human identifiers. While the typical fingerprint scan uses 13 points of identification, an iris scan registers upwards of 200 unique identifiers.[18] More than a decade and a half after *Minority Report* haunted moviegoers with its iris-scanning spiders, Clear is a network security solution here in the United States that offers iris scanning (along with fingerprints) as a way to validate identity. EyeLock is another iris-based identity management tech company; its projects range from allowing secure access to server rooms to strengthening security at border crossings. And at CES 2018, Gentex demoed its latest in-vehicle biometrics system that scans the driver's iris to deliver custom security, comfort, and convenience features.

Facial recognition has shifted from fantasy to fact. Facebook and Apple iPhoto use it to allow automatic tagging of photos. Disney uses facial recognition at its theme parks in Tokyo to quickly scan annual pass holders into its parks. Security forces use it during high-risk events such as the Super Bowl to ensure that no one on a terrorist watch list can enter.

Some researchers wonder if our earlobes may be more accurate identifiers than fingerprints. Mark Nixon, a computer scientist at the University of Southampton, told *WIRED* magazine in 2010, "When you're born your ear is fully formed. The lobe descends a little, but overall it stays the same. It's a great way to identify people." [19] Fingerprints can be compromised through calluses resulting from hard labor, according to the *WIRED* report. And on the most practical level, earlobe prints are simply less common (and therefore potentially replicable) than fingerprints. At CES 2015, Descartes Biometrics launched HELIX, an ear-image-recognition technology that uses a smartphone's camera for authentication.

But biological indicators can do more than identify us: They can also assess us. Voice recognition technology can both identify a person and also provide information on his or her stress level. Boston company Cogito has developed software that can determine whether a person feels agitated, which can help manage inflow to call centers and escalate calls to managers before they get out of hand. It can also be used by car-sharing platforms to analyze whether a passenger is agitated and intervention is necessary.

Body language is still more an art than a science, but having AI crunch millions of data points on body position *before* an action can provide predictive intelligence on *likely* action. Similar analysis can be applied to gait, perspiration, and facial expressions. Tiny, nearly imperceptible movements of facial muscles—especially near the eyes—can indicate stress. How you hold your head can indicate how drowsy you are. Averting eye contact can mean anything from a lack of confidence to an intent to deceive. Poppy Crum, chief scientist at audio powerhouse Dolby Laboratories, has spoken and written extensively on biometrics as an indicator of emotion, including skin conductance and breathing patterns. Even measuring the carbon dioxide content of the air around people can indicate their stress and emotion levels, she says. On a 2018 tour of Dolby's San Francisco headquarters, she showed me a lab where a woman watching a movie was linked up with skin and brain sensors to evaluate her emotional and physiological response to movies based on the audio and video settings.

One creator of networked solutions, Axis Communications, has continually proven itself to be a ninja innovator. Axis invented the world's first Internet Protocol (IP) camera. As *Lifewire* explains, IP standardizes the way data is transmitted over a network. Unlike closed-circuit cameras, digital IP cameras can send and receive real-time data over the internet, making them a much more effective technology for surveillance.[20] Among other technologies, Axis develops sophisticated cameras equipped with intelligent analytics and capable of biometric verification such as facial recognition. And Axis will likely be a future ninja company, too. Anticipating the potential of biometrics, Axis is partnering with companies whose algorithms can assess physiological characteristics to assess risk and guide judgments as to whether further surveillance, human interaction, or law enforcement engagement is required.

Law enforcement and intelligence agencies will undoubtedly take an interest in products from ninja innovators that can detect our emotions—and intentions. This level of obtainable information may be unnerving—imagine a politician on TV being immediately analyzed for veracity! But it can also detect and deter potential terrorists or shooters in high-risk situations, including airports, border crossings, schools, or national special security events.

Robotics

When I think about robots, my mind often jumps to "Rosie," the in-home do-it-all helper that cooks, cleans, and automates away most daily chores on *The Jetsons*. But the field of robotics is already well beyond the fictional. Any mechanical device that can detect its environment, make decisions based on sensory information, and then execute a specific physical operation is a robot. In other words, robots are machines that logically and physically respond to environmental variables.

The first real robots weren't remotely humanlike. Many consisted of one "arm" that repeatedly moved objects from one place to another. Gradually, robots took on more complex tasks, such as assembly and welding, but they remained confined to industrial applications and had very specific skills.

Industrial robots today are highly versatile, but they don't look, talk, think, or move like a human. But at the same time, robots are also making inroads in consumer households. As component costs fall and software capabilities rise, home robots will become more intelligent, versatile, and personable. Commercial robots have evolved: They now excel at executing dangerous and repetitive work in factories, on battlefields, and even in the wild—some of the most awe-inspiring, up-close wildlife photography is taken by robots. Consumer robots take on less hazardous work—think cleaning floors and folding clothes—but these are tedious tasks that many of us simply don't *want* to do.

And parents are buying buildable robots to teach kids valuable STEM skills—like how to code—while also honing their problem-solving and critical-thinking abilities. Lego's Mindstorm EV3, for example, helps kids master basic and advanced programming, along with hardware and data-logging functions. We'll dive into more consumer applications for home robots in Chapter 5.

Blockchain

Blockchain is an open, digital, constantly growing ledger comprising linked blocks of information that permanently and securely record transactions between parties in real time. Blockchain is a way to establish confidence without actually having to know and trust the other party. Through the power of encryption, the blockchain can quickly and securely establish authorization of a service (for example, medical care through an insurance company's blockchain) or membership in a group (such as country of citizenship) without divulging sensitive information. It's the backbone of cryptocurrencies like bitcoin, which we'll talk about more in the next chapter.

Harvard Business Review characterizes blockchain not as a disruptive technology, but as instead "a *foundational* technology: It has the potential to create new foundations for our economic and social systems."[21] The business and societal impacts of blockchain technology are tremendous. As IBM CEO Ginni Rometty said, "What the internet did for communications, blockchain will do for trusted transactions."[22] From tracking shipments in and out of ports, to transferring land titles, to making sure artists are paid royalties for their work—in short, it has the power to streamline processes and eliminate abuse.

We're already seeing the evidence. A prime example is the

UN World Food Programme (WFP). The UN estimates that when paying for goods ahead of time, as is typically the case, roughly 30 percent of assistance is lost to corruption. Trials of blockchain-based payments in a Jordanian refugee camp yielded a 98 percent reduction in transaction and other fees associated with rendering aid.[23] The WFP can accurately tally food purchases, pay stores and vendors directly, and—crucially—pay upon delivery. The WFP's blockchain-based program uses iris scans instead of paper vouchers. Vouchers, like money, can be transferred from person to person. But with the blockchain, aid is locked to one person—one iris—virtually eliminating the opportunity for food vouchers to be stolen or sold illicitly.

Blockchain's benefits are right in our backyard, too. My doctor can verify my identity without me having to divulge my Social Security number (and without my doctor having to store it—a frequent source of identity theft). It becomes much harder for a company to sell information like my salary or shopping history to a third party. In theory, a blockchain-based election could securely establish identity and eligibility to vote, without requiring a trip to the polls. And, of course, blockchain lets us transfer money and buy and sell goods without having to share our bank accounts or personal information. This is a great tool for musicians, who, using smart contracts—pieces of code built into the blockchain—can more easily track and collect royalties. The whole system becomes more transparent and less cumbersome. In short, it makes sure everyone gets paid for their work.

In a global economy, future ninjas will find new uses for blockchain across a multitude of industries, from gaming to finance to smart homes and cities. This will transform business models and promote the transfer of goods and services around the world.

Before There Was Blockchain

In 2014, CTA inducted Hollywood legend Hedy Lamarr into the Consumer Technology Hall of Fame. Hedy's amazing story is proof that anyone with a good idea has the power to change the course of history, just like the anonymous Satoshi Nakamoto, who started us on the path to blockchain. In this case, Lamarr co-created frequency hopping wireless security technology—the basis of our wireless communications technology.

Lamarr was born in Vienna in 1914. Her mother, Gertrude, played the piano, and her father, Emil, was a banker. Both were assimilated Jews. By her late teens, the young beauty had appeared in five films, and in 1933 she married Fritz Mandl, an Austrian munitions maker whose clients included Hitler and Mussolini.

Lamarr accompanied Mandl to meetings with scientists and munitions engineers, sparking her interest in the technology of war. Mandl was controlling, however, so Lamarr disguised herself as her own maid and escaped in 1937. She was discovered in London by MGM mogul Louis B. Mayer. She soon became a Hollywood "it" girl.

When she wasn't making movies, Lamarr tinkered in the "inventor's corner" she had set up in her home. One evening, she had dinner with film composer George Antheil and their conversation wandered toward the war in Europe and Lamarr's desire to aid the United States, her adopted country.

Lamarr wanted to quit show business and join the U.S. government's new Inventors' Council. She showed Antheil some of the ideas she'd been working on. In 1940, she read about the sinking of the *City of Benares* by a German radio-controlled torpedo. This gave her an idea, to create a radio transmitter and receiver scheme that could be synchronized and hop together from one frequency to another to avoid being jammed. Thus the idea for "frequency hopping" was born. But Lamarr was at a loss as to how to accomplish this feat—getting radio receivers to rapidly change channels exactly in sync with the seemingly random hopping of the transmitter frequencies.

It turned out Antheil was also somewhat of a mechanic. Fifteen years earlier, he had written a short ballet called *Ballet Mécanique*, which featured unusual "instruments," including sixteen synchronized player pianos. Antheil took two key ideas from his composing experience. First, he proposed that transmitters hop among eighty-eight channels—the number of keys on a piano. Second, he suggested following the technique he'd used to synchronize the pianos to now synchronize the transmitter and the receiver. Literally, the transmitter and receiver are working from the "same sheet of music," with the transmitter sending a bit of the message on one channel, or "note," then hopping to the next channel for the next part of the message. As long as the receiver knows the sequence of notes, it simply follows along, tuning from one channel to the next, reassembling the message as it goes.

On August 11, 1942, the U.S. government issued Patent 2,292,387 to Antheil and "Hedy Kiesler Markey," Lamarr's married name. But the government wasn't interested in adopting the technology. Lamarr became an even bigger star during World War II, making more than twenty films before retiring in 1958. She received a star on the Hollywood Walk of Fame in 1960.

While she was making movies, Sylvania's Electronic Systems Division, not knowing the origins of the patent (since Lamarr had used her maiden name), devised an electronic version of frequency-hopping technology. Morphing into "spread spectrum," it was first used by the military for ship-to-ship communication during the 1962 Cuban Missile Crisis quarantine, unbeknownst to Lamarr.

Over the following decades, spread spectrum would be used by government and commercial entities in voice and data wireless products and platforms including cordless phones, cell phones, satellite communications, Wi-Fi, and Bluetooth.

Lamarr died in 2000. Rose Ganguzza, who accepted the CTA Hall of Fame award on Lamarr's behalf, said at the induction ceremony, "For Hedy, it was a singular invention, born from the desire to defeat the Nazis who had overtaken her homeland." [24]

Quantum Computing

Many of the building blocks we've discussed are already widely in use, powering the technologies of today. But "known knowns" on the horizon—such as quantum computing technology—could dramatically accelerate our path into the future.

Historically, computers have worked using chips that rapidly made binary or "yes/no" decisions. Under Moore's law—the idea that the number of transistors on a chip doubles every one to two years at ever-lower cost—innovation has been driven by the resulting doubling in processing power every eighteen months. So in 2018, Nvidia's most powerful system-on-a-chip (SOC) could make up to 30 trillion decisions every second.[25] The processor in IBM's original PC had 29,000 transistors[26]; your smartphone likely has more than 4 billion.[27]

But even Moore's law is subject to the limits of physics: Chips can get only so small. So computer scientists have been searching for an alternative. They now suspect it's possible that in addition to the "yes/no" or "0/1" gating decision, there may be a "both/and" option: that is, the choice could be both "yes" *and* "no"—or "zero" *and* "one"—at the same time. We call this quantum computing, and there's a global race to be the first to develop quantum computing capabilities.

Some believe that the first company to make this breakthrough will be able to immediately decrypt all existing encryption stored anywhere in the world. At a 2018 internet governance conference in the Netherlands, Jaya Baloo, chief information security officer at the Dutch telecommunications company KPN, noted, "My biggest concern is that whoever gets quantum computing will be able to decrypt all the private data we and others have." She said she believes Google and IBM, as well as a number of Chinese companies, are edging closer to solving the quantum computing mystery.[28]

Today, encryption works by scrambling information with

a secret key that the user knows. It's easy to unscramble—decrypt—the information if you know the key. It's like a combination lock: The owner can easily open the lock by entering the combination, but anyone else has to try random combinations until the lock opens. Thanks to its special ability to have bits that can be "zero" and "one" at the same time, quantum computing has the potential to break today's encryption by trying all the combinations at one time.

It's mind-bending and highly disruptive. It goes without saying that this presents tremendous risk. But it's also undeniable that if quantum computing is used in the right way, it can help solve the unsolvable, from mechanics to medicine. For example, instead of working for years on end to test how different proteins, molecules, and chemicals impact one another, quantum computing can run multiple tests at once, speeding up the process dramatically.[29] And while AI has already improved the speed of many systems, quantum computing will make them run even faster by increasing the pace of the data analysis that powers these machines.

Sensors, 5G, algorithms, big data, biometrics, robotics, blockchain, and—just around the corner—quantum computing: These are the building blocks of the ninja future. When combined with a power source, they can be integrated to create products and services that delight, inspire, and amaze us—and challenge us to think bigger than we ever have before. So let's dive deeper into these technologies.

CHAPTER 5

NINJA INNOVATION
TOMORROW

I'VE ALWAYS BEEN A VORACIOUS reader of science fiction. In 1977—
the year that brought us *Star Wars: A New Hope*, *Close Encoun-
ters of the Third Kind*, and *The Island of Dr. Moreau*—I dreamed
of how the technology I saw on-screen might someday solve the
terrible problems I faced that hot summer in New York.

I worked nights managing about a hundred servers, cooks,
and bartenders at the Jones Beach Theater restaurant on Long
Island, where Guy Lombardo, aka "Mr. New Year's Eve," performed. A few mornings a week, I had a side job unloading trac-
tor trailers full of eggs from states south of New York. Each truck
had around 800 cases of eggs, with 32 dozen eggs in each case.
I earned four cents per case, and was thrilled to bring home
$32 in cash for a few hours of tough work. (Plus, to the joy of

my family and neighbors, I often got to bring home a few dozen eggs when boxes were overloaded.)

In early July, the distribution facility owner asked me to fill in for a week driving a delivery truck on a route serving grocery stores and Dairy Queens in Brooklyn, Queens, and Nassau County, Long Island. I was game. I trained for a day with the regular driver, then loaded up a ten-gear delivery truck.

It was much harder than I'd anticipated. I knew how to drive a stick shift, but I struggled with the friction point on the clutch, and ten gears were a challenge. I frequently got lost despite my paper map (I was not born with the navigation gene). And backing up to each Dairy Queen was unbelievably stressful—even today, I break into a sweat when I have to back a compact car into a tiny parking space.

On the evening of July 13, 1977, New York City suffered a massive power outage after lightning struck two power plants. The next morning, when I started my Brooklyn and Queens delivery runs, I realized all the traffic lights were out. I didn't know whether to stop at intersections, so I plowed forward in the hopes that the truck's size would give me some priority and protection. Many store owners on my route stood guard with shotguns for fear of looting (and with good reason: Rioters set hundreds of fires and looters damaged more than 1,600 stores during the blackout).[1] They were wary of me, an unknown deliveryman, pulling into their bays at a tense time.

The blackout lasted more than twenty-four hours. Making deliveries that week was a stressful blur. By the end, I had stripped the gears, ruined the clutch, clipped store structures, and even missed a few deliveries. I hated feeling incompetent, disoriented, and lost. I dreamed of a technology that could set me straight.

A few years later, with a law degree in hand, I had my chance to help realize that dream. RadioShack asked me to help secure government approval to allow commercial use of military signals from Global Positioning System (GPS) satellites. For consumer-grade GPS to take off, we needed a change in the nonmilitary use of the signals from more than a dozen feet of degradation to near-total accuracy. Today most vehicles and smartphones include robust navigational and location devices—ninja innovations that would have saved me a lot of blood, sweat, and tears in the summer of '77.

Tomorrow's ninja innovations will render my all-too-stressful experience unimaginable to tomorrow's historians of technology. Self-driving vehicles will navigate roads safely and efficiently, even in a blackout. They'll be able to "see" everything around them, communicate with other vehicles, and even determine the trajectories of non-self-driving cars to avoid collisions. All it will take is smart regulation and ninja innovators creatively combining and capitalizing on the technological building blocks we have in place. Let's look at a few combinations of the ingredient technologies laid out in Chapter 4 to better understand how they can transform our lives.

Artificial Intelligence

As we touched on in the last chapter, we already see, use, and benefit from artificial intelligence (AI) in its "narrow" form every day: smart speakers, customer service chatbots, credit card

fraud detection warnings, personalized shopping recommendations, even moment-to-moment weather information. AI combines connectivity, algorithms, and big data to take on tasks that
traditionally required human-level intelligence.

In 2016, IBM acquired Weather Underground, which gathers data from more than 250,000 personal weather stations and
uses AI to microtarget weather forecasts in real time: temperature, cloud cover, humidity, chance of precipitation, and more.[2]

Bank of America's virtual assistant, Erica, is a customer service bot that helps customers with everything from transferring
funds to locking down lost or stolen debit cards. Sure, we can
easily do these errands through their website, app, or in person, but automating them through an AI-powered agent lets us
handle these tasks at our leisure without sacrificing customer
service. And with AI, there are no "regular business hours" or
holidays—you can get personalized help whenever you need it.

Large retailers also use service bots for store operations. In
2017, Walmart announced it would deploy shelf-scanning bots
built by Bossa Nova Robotics in fifty U.S. locations to monitor
inventory, check prices, and restock misplaced items.[3] Offload-
ing these repeatable, predictable, and manual tasks has a few
benefits for a retailer such as Walmart. First the bots free up
the time of sales associates to focus on other responsibilities.
Just as important, these robots add a layer of actionable data to
the retail floor. For example, if they see a group of items routinely misplaced or missing from shelves, the robots can suggest
displaying them somewhere else or can advise loss prevention
measures to prevent theft. This combination of task automation
with data collection is at the heart of the case for AI.

AI is becoming just as indispensable inside our homes. Almost overnight, smart speakers powered by digital assistants including Siri, Alexa, and the Google Assistant have become the go-to smart home hub. They're a key component of the IoT and a driver of smart home technology revenue growth. AI-enabled digital assistants embedded in smart speakers can answer questions, stream music, update your grocery list, and manage your calendar. When they're connected to compatible home systems, AI eliminates the need for screens and keyboards: Just by hearing your voice, they can turn off lights, adjust thermostats, lock doors, and start appliances.

The benefits of AI extend far beyond our front door. For example, AI already helps pilots fly planes—which is a major reason we haven't seen a spike in commercial airplane tragedies despite an increasing number of flights.

As AI becomes capable of doing more complex tasks, it will revolutionize everything from health care and transportation to entertainment and security. It will also raise serious questions about our economy and national (and personal) security. The question facing U.S. regulators and tech innovators: How should the United States advance its position as the global leader in AI, while also proactively addressing the substantial challenges and risks it brings?

Let's consider a few areas where AI is creating efficiencies and improving lives.

Industry experts agree that health care is one key area where future ninjas can leverage AI to solve real-world problems. The Census Bureau projects that by 2030, 20 percent of Americans will be older than sixty-five.[4] Our caregiving system is already stressed, but AI can mitigate part of this stress by enabling seniors to continue living healthy, active lives.

As discussed in the last chapter, narrow AI is capable of a limited set of tasks, yet is already having a major impact. AI-powered smart home technology can monitor for falls and other accidents and provide daily reminders for people struggling with memory loss. Israeli startup Intuition Robotics created ElliQ, a robot for seniors that can send reminders about appointments, message family and friends, respond to voice, and turn on music. Delaware-based HEKA has created an AI mattress that can improve sleep by monitoring and adjusting to people's shapes and positions as they rest.

The United States spends $3.5 trillion a year on health care.[5] The federal government shoulders more than 28 percent of that cost.[6] By 2047, the Congressional Budget Office estimates, federal spending for people age sixty-five and older who receive Social Security, Medicare, and Medicaid benefits could account for almost half of *all* federal noninterest spending. AI can be part of the solution.

Each individual patient is generating millions of data points every day, but doctors and hospitals aren't able to view and understand this enormous volume of information. AI can quickly sift through and identify aspects of that data that can enhance their ability to deliver far better care—and even save lives. For example, Qualcomm's AlertWatch:OR AI system, which provides real-time analysis of patient data during surgery, significantly lowers instances of heart attacks and kidney failure and reduces average hospital stays by a full day.

AI is a game changer in health care because it has an uncanny ability to identify patterns. That skill—searching for signs of abnormalities—is at the core of what doctors like pathologists, oncologists, and radiologists do every day. It's not a comforting thought, but 38 percent of us will be diagnosed with cancer at some point in our lives.[7] Cancer is the second leading cause of death[8] worldwide, but most countries face a shortage of qualified oncologists: A 2018 study of the oncology workforce across 93 countries found that in 27 countries, there were fewer than one clinical oncologist for every thousand patients.[9] And eight countries had *zero* clinical oncologists on-site to treat cancer patients. In the United States, the supply of qualified oncologists is limited by a legal cap on the number of residents while the demand is expanding as we live longer and more of us have better access to health insurance.

Humans need all the help they can get—and AI can help. Optellum, a startup based in the United Kingdom, has created an AI diagnostics system that can detect lung cancer in patients earlier than doctors can, offering patients a greater chance of survival. Scientists in Japan created a system that detects deadly colorectal cancer with 86 percent accuracy.[10] And a team at Stanford University built a database of 130,000 skin disease images and then created an algorithm to diagnose skin cancer.[11] We still need doctors—we need *more* doctors—but these AI tools will help physicians make better and more effective decisions.

In addition to health, AI can also play a huge role in confronting one of the most pressing safety issues of our time: cybersecurity. Major data breaches in recent years (Target, Equifax, TJX, and the U.S. Office of Personnel Management, to name a few) have shown how vulnerable our personal information is. But AI has the potential to help reduce fraud and cybercrime. Because AI can quickly learn fraudulent patterns—and identify when a regular pattern is broken—it can uncover threats to an organization's cybersecurity system.

Major companies such as PayPal and Visa report a low or reduced fraud rate due to AI in their security systems. According to *Harvard Business Review*, companies around the globe use AI for security purposes far more often than for any other objectives.[12]

Artificial intelligence is also providing solutions to many of our transportation and mobility challenges, and it is poised to power the smart cities of the future. Municipal entities, from Pima County, Arizona, to the Massachusetts Department of Technology, are actively pursuing AI systems to optimize traffic flow and ease congestion. Self-driving vehicles, which are built on a foundation of AI software, could mitigate the 94 percent of accidents that are caused by human error.[13] Personal mobility solutions such as Honda's UNI-CUB, which assists people who are not able to walk long distances, use AI to detect subtle movements of their users to adjust speed and direction. Ride-sharing apps, including Uber and Lyft, use AI algorithms to ensure that drivers get to neighborhoods where and when riders need them.

The United States is the world leader in AI, both in terms of research and commercialization, but our position is not guaranteed. China laid out a plan to create a $150 billion, world-leading AI industry by 2030, including a $2 billion AI research park in Beijing. France, Britain, and India recently announced their own strategies to lead in AI. Canada is positioning itself as a top destination for AI research and development, attracting investment from companies including Google, Microsoft, and GM—Montreal says it has the highest concentration of deep learning students and researchers in the world.[14]

Ninja leadership from the private sector, supported by a qualified talent pool and light-touch regulation, is a winning formula for innovation in the United States and abroad. Ninja leaders in government need to think strategically about creating a regulatory environment that will encourage innovation in AI to thrive, continuing to prioritize cutting-edge research while taking into account disruptions AI could cause. Good regulation balances safety and innovation when it comes to bias in algorithms and data sets, data ownership and security, and job displacement and workforce development. Above all, government policies around AI need to be both flexible and adaptive, and should not impose "one-size-fits-all" regulations that will hamper innovation.

Industry and government also need to collaborate to address the impact AI is having—and will have—on our workforce. Most jobs will be improved by AI, and new jobs will be created. But some will also be lost. We need to make sure that our workforce is prepared for the jobs of the future, which includes helping people whose jobs are displaced gain the skills they need to succeed in new roles. We as an industry also need to address data security to earn public trust in AI. Users need to be confident their personal data is protected.

No single policy decision or government action will guarantee leadership in artificial intelligence, but strategic investment, reasonable regulation, the free market, adaptability to developments, and—above all—a ninja approach will ensure we can benefit from AI and deliver the innovative technologies that will dramatically improve the human experience. We'll talk much more about this in Chapter 7.

How You Can Improve AI

Large, crowdsourced databases are critical tools for AI training. At a 2016 CTA conference, Dr. Fei-Fei Li, director of Stanford's Artificial Intelligence Lab, discussed a program she co-created called ImageNet, a visual data set designed to classify and detect images and scenes, and the ImageNet challenge, which prompted research teams to create AI algorithms to identify these images.

You can help train AI systems, too. Quick, Draw! is a fun game that's part of Google's collection of AI experiments that encourage us to act as teachers for AI. You have twenty seconds to draw a simple picture of whatever prompt you're given. The app asks you to draw something as simple as a square or as challenging as a lobster (it's more difficult than it sounds). As you scribble, a neural network tries to guess what you're drawing. And it's surprisingly good at recognizing even my clumsy drawings! Apps like these may help fine-tune our artistic skills, but they also help AI learn. As we draw, we teach the AI variations of how these concepts are represented and imagined.

When Quick, Draw! guesses correctly, your artwork gets added to the Quick, Draw! Dataset, a collection of more than 50 million drawings in 345 categories. We learn along the way, too; if we're unsure of what the image prompt looks like or how it could be drawn, we can visit the Quick Draw Dataset page and see how other people have interpreted and drawn the prompt.

Users can also flag images that don't really depict

the prompt so well, which gives the neural network more information and helps it better distinguish the images in the future. The data is then sent to developers, researchers, and artists to study and explore.

Augmented, Virtual, and Mixed Reality

To paraphrase my high school English teacher—who was paraphrasing poet Samuel Taylor Coleridge—we're all willing to suspend our disbelief when we want to be entertained. Harnessing tech for storytelling dates back to the camera capturing early silent movies. Then we added microphones to capture sound, and then higher-resolution audio and video quality. Today, when we pair our 4K Ultra-High-Definition TVs with home theater surround sound and set our smart home lighting system to the "theater" setting, we can almost re-create the movie theater experience at home.

The next step in the evolution of home entertainment will be virtual reality (VR)—an immersive innovation that combines the building blocks of sensors, data, and lightning-fast broadband—which will make it even easier to let the story carry us away.

In announcing Facebook's acquisition of VR goggle maker Oculus in 2014, CEO Mark Zuckerberg wrote, "Imagine enjoying a courtside seat at a game, studying in a classroom of students and teachers all over the world, or consulting with a doctor face-to-face—just by putting on goggles in your home. This is really a new communication platform. By feeling truly present, you can share unbounded spaces and experiences with the people in your life."[15] That same year, Sony announced Project Morpheus (the code name for PlayStation VR, which hit the market in 2016), and Google launched Google Cardboard, a low-cost alternative to high-priced VR glasses that dramatically lowered this technology's barrier to entry. Today the market includes three distinct categories: tethered VR headsets, which require a higher level of computing power from an attached PC or game console; stand-alone headsets that don't require a smartphone or computer; and VR designed for smartphones, where you simply put your phone into a headset.

At the 2018 Winter Olympics in PyeongChang, South Korea, Intel partnered with NBC to stream events to VR headsets, virtually transporting fans from home around the world to the Olympics. And Samsung's Winter Games showcase let visitors try their hand at VR technology that simulates snowboarding, skeleton, and cross-country skiing.

The content catalog is growing, and industry experts expect VR headset adoption rates to rise as the technology advances and prices drop. Understandably, many early investors are looking for measurable financial returns. The potential market, at least, is large. Nearly two-thirds of all U.S. households own a device they use to play video games.[16] And most investors and developers see much broader potential applications—beyond gaming—for VR. To achieve market viability we need two things: broader adoption across industries beyond gaming and media, and increased broadband access.

Imagine, for example, a family contemplating a cruise vacation: With VR, they could "walk" inside staterooms, and check out the ship's deck, dining rooms, casino, and pools before deciding which ship to book. The immersive nature of virtual reality would give them a sense of what it's like to be in these spaces in a way that 2-D video can't. VR is also a democratizing force in education: Students can travel the world and learn about other cultures and terrains without leaving the classroom. And picture the implications for medicine! Samsung chief medical officer Dr. David Rhew told me how doctors at Cedars-Sinai in New York are using VR to treat pain by virtually taking clients into soothing places or scenarios—a huge breakthrough in light of the opioid epidemic. In one study, patients reported a 24 percent drop in their pain scores after using VR.[17] Dr. Justin Barad of Osso VR is using VR to allow surgeons to practice new orthopedic techniques, creating a new method of learning that may radically improve the percentage of successful outcomes. Traditionally, young surgeons practice on patients, with the result that surgeons that have performed a particular surgery fewer than ten times have higher failure rates than experienced surgeons who have performed that same surgery more often. A 2009 study found that "the risk of serious complications from the most common form of gastric bypass surgery fell by 10 percent for every additional 10 cases per year the surgeon had performed."

But creating this type of fully immersive experience requires a staggering amount of data. The display has to cover the entire field of view. And it has to track correctly and quickly when you turn your head. If you were to turn your head to look behind you and saw only a spinning hourglass loading the rear view, it would defeat the purpose of VR. Any perceptible "lag" as the display catches up with the user's head movement detracts from the immersive experience.

Virtual reality applications have some of the highest data-rate requirements in consumer technology—five times more than that of HDTV[18]—and much of this data has to be stored and processed in the cloud. Gaming is a good example: The demand for lifelike graphics and instantaneous response times is a huge data draw.[19] Thus VR requires a robust broadband infrastructure to thrive.

Virtual reality's counterpart, augmented reality—or AR—works by superimposing images, sounds, and other data over a person's field of vision rather than completely subsuming it (as with virtual reality). Pokémon Go! is a prime example. AR's intent is to inform and assist your current view of reality rather than transport you to a new one. Because of AR's "lighter touch," the technology lends itself to being used briefly and casually in real-world scenarios.

For example, Swedish retailer IKEA introduced its Place app in 2017, which allows IKEA shoppers to digitally insert IKEA furniture into an existing room to see how a new couch or bed might look in a given space. Luxury apparel brand Lacoste lets you digitally try on shoes with its LCST app. American Apparel brought the AR experience in-store; shoppers scan product display signs to learn more about products, including reviews, color choices, and price details.

AR has amazing education applications, too. The catalog of medical knowledge doubles roughly every seventy-three days, according to Cleveland Clinic president and CEO Dr. Toby Cosgrove.[20] Practically speaking, this means the textbooks medical students use are outdated before the ink is dry. Yet the study of human anatomy has changed little over the past hundred years: Students still train on cadavers and learn from two-dimensional drawings. That's why the Cleveland Clinic has teamed up with Microsoft to transform students' understanding of human anatomy. Using Microsoft's HoloLens technology, medical students can supplement their study of a cadaver with AR-enabled information and graphics to deepen the educational experience.

In the defense sector, contractors have jumped headfirst into crafting the fighting force of the future. British defense giant BAE Systems is leading the way, designing futuristic upgrades for its battle-tested CV90 combat vehicle. BAE's aim is to give the soldiers inside a "vehicle of glass" that offers an unobstructed view of the scene outside using internally mounted displays fed by an array of high-definition cameras.[21] Similar technology allows a vulnerable turret gunner to see the battlefield while also being better protected behind plates of thick steel.

While AR and VR are evolving in the short term as two distinct technologies and markets, they will likely converge down the road. AR is more software-centric; VR is more hardware-centric. You can experience AR through your smartphone; VR requires wearing a head-mounted display. The combination of virtual and augmented reality is known as mixed reality, which overlays virtual objects in the real world *and* lets you interact with them. Or, in the reverse, mixed reality creates an enclosed VR world, but anchors it with objects in the real world around you. Mixed reality will be a game changer for teleworking, allowing employees around the world to port into a collaborative work environment—together—to tackle projects.

Augmented, virtual, and mixed reality are go-to arenas in the ninja future. One sign of a healthy new sector is how many accessory vendors flock to create add-on products. CES is full of innovative VR and AR products and accessories that aim to enrich the AR/VR experience: the 3dRudder Blackhawk foot motion controller, Go Touch VR's VRtouch fingertip haptic wearable, Vuzix Blade's augmented reality glasses with built-in Alexa, Rokid's AR glasses with facial recognition technology, the BeBop haptic Forte Wireless Data Glove, and the Titanium Falcon Talon smart motion controller ring. The launch of such diverse AR and VR accessories shows that these technologies will likely open up new consumer experiences and business opportunities for future ninjas.

Drones

Another industry where future ninjas are changing the marketplace is air travel—something I think about a lot on my weekly commute between Detroit and Washington, D.C. Lightweight commercial drone aircraft are transforming industries: online retail, film and photography, farming, transportation, even internet signal delivery. These machines use the building blocks of robotics, wireless connectivity, and sensors to achieve remote, unmanned flight. The potential benefits are limited only by the breadth of our imagination and creativity.

Drones are already taking over dangerous jobs like inspecting bridges, delivering aid and equipment to hard-to-reach places, and searching for survivors of natural disasters. In 2016, delivery giant UPS announced that its partnership with drone startup CyPhy Works successfully tested a drone delivery of an asthma inhaler to a summer camp in Massachusetts.[22] The three-mile journey took only about eight minutes—which could mean the difference between life and death. As Mark Penn highlighted in his insightful book *Microtrends Squared: The New Small Trends Driving Today's Big Disruptions*, coauthored by Meredith Fineman, drones in Sweden carry external defibrillators "so that bystanders can detach and use devices on people having heart attacks—particularly necessary in rural areas that ambulances can't reach quickly enough." And Silicon Valley–based Zipline, in partnership with the UPS Foundation and Gavi, the Vaccine Alliance, is using drones to deliver blood and medical supplies to Rwanda's scattered population. At CES 2016, Chinese drone maker Ehang introduced the first human-sized drone. And two years later, Intel debuted its passenger drone at CES 2018: the Volocopter, an autonomous "air taxi" that may one day be able to handle as many as 10,000 passengers a day.[23]

Drones have environmental benefits, too. A report from *Nature* says drone-based delivery can reduce greenhouse gas emissions and energy use in the freight sector. In California alone, using small drones rather than diesel trucks to deliver lighter packages would cut emissions by more than 50 percent.[24] More broadly integrating drones into our transportation system can reduce urban traffic, cut our nation's fuel consumption, and displace noisy trucks on our roads.

These are dramatic ninja innovations. But future ninjas can also solve the more mundane practical problems of daily package delivery from carriers like UPS, FedEx, and Amazon.

Together, FedEx and UPS handled an average of 27.5 million[25] packages every day in 2017—and many of these are light enough to be excellent candidates for drone delivery. Delivery times, which currently range from a day to weeks, could be cut down to mere hours, if not minutes.

Disruptive innovation by unmanned systems has the potential to provide a multibillion-dollar boost to the economy and create tens of thousands of new jobs.[26] This is a "known known": There is no doubt drones will transform the market. Delivery costs will plummet. Some workers will be displaced. Some jobs will disappear, others will be created. What is unknown is: How, exactly, will the market transform? Which jobs, specifically, will be in play? How can companies capitalize on that? These are the pressing question for future ninjas.

A 2016 report from PwC valued the emerging global market for business services using drones at more than $127 billion.[27] And an industry report from the Association for Unmanned Vehicle Systems International found that the drone economy will create 100,000 U.S. jobs by 2025.[28]

Of course, this will be a global shift, and it's not a given that the United States will lead the way. Canada is embracing the drone revolution: In 2017, Transport Canada approved a 900-mile region of Alberta for testing delivery drones, with the end goal of making robotic cargo service available. France's national mail service, La Poste, uses them to deliver to pickup locations. And in 2016, Amazon successfully staged the first home delivery in only thirteen minutes in Cambridge, England.

Here, it's worth noting that Seattle-based Amazon chose to test the delivery drone in England because, according to CEO Jeff Bezos, they've been "getting really good cooperation from the British equivalent of the [Federal Aviation Administration], the CAA [Civilian Aviation Authority]."[29] This kind of outsourcing should be a wake-up call to U.S. policymakers. Regulating drones—both commercial-industrial and recreational-hobbyist—requires a consistent and coordinated national approach. To be fair, the drone revolution has happened especially quickly, even given the lightning-fast pace of innovation, and the FAA has done a lot to keep up. In 2016, the agency adopted a set of regulations balancing safety and innovation that opened the door for the drone-based future delivery economy. But the agency didn't go far enough. The FAA must exert its authority to avoid a patchwork of confusing and conflicting local rules and instead ensure a uniform, innovation-friendly framework that safely incorporates drones into our everyday lives.

As future ninjas put these robots-on-wings to work in life-altering ways, governments need to be more nimble and welcoming. Drones can revolutionize the global economy and improve the lives of people everywhere; ninja innovators won't wait on slow or hesitant policymakers. The United States will either be a ninja leader in the drone revolution—or let it fly by.

Self-Driving Cars

In 1958, Chrysler introduced cruise control, allowing drivers to set a specific speed and then relax while driving long distances.[30] As I wrote in *U.S. News & World Report* in 2017, cruise control's popularity soared[31] during the oil crisis some fifteen years later, since the automated technology could deliver better fuel economy.[32] Consumers are still excited about driver-assist technology: CTA research found 93 percent of American drivers who use advanced driving features love them, and half of those who don't yet use them are eager to upgrade and try them out.[33]

Now, our cars do all sorts of things to make our lives easier and safer: help us park, avoid accidents, navigate efficiently, and remind us to focus on the road if we start to doze. And we're about to go even further as self-driving cars are entering the market, bringing about a full-scale automotive revolution. The vehicles of tomorrow are sophisticated robots, equipped with hundreds of sensors and many rely on 5G connectivity for real-time information to assist split-second decision making in critical, life-or-death situations.

Vehicle accidents claim more than 37,000 lives every year just in the United States.[34] More than one million people die globally in traffic accidents, and many more are seriously injured.[35] Distraction-related accidents—caused by everything from daydreaming to eating to texting to applying makeup—are part of the problem: In 2016, more than 10,000 people died in the United States in accidents related to impaired driving.[36] If 94 percent[37] of U.S. traffic accidents are caused by human error, then drastically reducing human error with self-driving technology saves lives, prevents injuries, and makes our roads safer.

Self-driving cars will also save us money, cutting the cost of insurance, licensing, and repairs. Multinational insurance agency Aon estimates that self-driving cars could lead insurance companies to lower premiums by 40 percent or more.[38] A Ruderman Family Foundation report forecasts savings of $1.3 trillion from the increase in productivity, decrease in gas expenses, and drop in accidents.[39]

Self-driving cars will free up time spent in traffic or searching for parking spaces. They'll also boost productivity, increase fuel efficiency, and eliminate many traffic snarls. Think of all the other things you can do in the car if you're not focused on the road: catch up on your email, prepare for your first meeting of the day, pour over the day's headlines, maybe even finish up those outstanding expense reports. And perhaps most exciting, self-driving technology will unlock new sources of productivity and generate new avenues for economic growth, particularly for the 20–30 million Americans [40] who are kept off the roads due to physical disability, according to a report from Waymo, as well as the 16 million Americans over the age of sixty-five who have little or no access to public transportation, according to the Institute for Highway Safety.[41] Self-driving cars will grant new independence to these individuals, giving them the ability to enter the workforce and contribute to their local economies and societies and the freedom to travel to work, medical appointments, community events, and family gatherings. According to the Ruderman report, self-driving cars could open employment opportunities for two million people with disabilities.[42]

With these possibilities on the horizon, it's no surprise that three-quarters of consumers are excited about self-driving cars, and two-thirds say they're willing to trade out their current vehicle for a self-driving one.[43] But as this technology gains speed, some have called on regulators to put the brakes on self-driving cars in the wake of two fatal accidents. In March 2018, the first pedestrian fatality involving a self-driving car sent shock waves across the world. Even with so many precautions taken, and so many test trials run, a life was lost. Several days later, the industry was rocked again: A driver in California was killed when his car crashed while in autopilot mode.[44]

Consumers have—quite rightly—called for increased scrutiny and greater accountability. And we owe it to them to fully investigate every self-driving fatality. Only an ongoing, transparent discussion will create a framework that combines consumer safety, company accountability, and flexibility to advance self-driving technology and prevent future tragedies. A key part of that conversation requires acknowledging the difficulties inherent in technological disruption. It also requires acknowledging the skepticism that inevitably accompanies this disruption. Consider, for instance, that whenever a self-driving vehicle is involved in a fatal accident, media coverage is wall-to-wall. Yet fatalities in standard cars—whether caused by technical or human error—are so commonplace they often receive little to no coverage.

Disruption, with all the change, uncertainty, and sometimes pain it can bring, is not always easy to accept. But our nation has a long and proud history of confronting our fears and harnessing disruption to create a safer, fairer, and more accessible world.

Take air travel. Few of us would want to return to a time when land and sea travel were our only options. Today more than 2.5 million people fly in the United States every day.[45] And 2017 was the safest year for passengers in the history of air travel.[46] But the safety and security that passengers have come to expect didn't occur immediately. It took years of investment and years of missteps to create the safe flight ecosystem we now have in this country.

In 1956, for example, two planes collided midflight near the Grand Canyon.[47] This tragedy led to renewed investment in air-traffic control systems nationwide and spurred the creation of the Federal Aviation Administration. Before continuous use of autopilot in 1964, three fatal accidents occurred every one million flight cycles.[48] By 2016, that number had fallen twentyfold to 0.15 fatal accidents per million flight cycles, thanks to tech advances such as collision avoidance systems, En Route Automation Modernization, advanced ground proximity warnings, and more sophisticated air traffic control.[49] Today autopilot takes care of about 90 percent of flying, and we can travel virtually anywhere in the world safely and efficiently.

By contrast, every day, roughly ninety people are killed on U.S. roads due to human error.[50] Now is not the time to abandon an innovation such as self-driving technology: It holds the potential to revolutionize road safety and provide unprecedented mobility options for underserved populations. Yes, a complete transition to self-driving technology will be gradual; it may not be perfect for decades. Yes, it will likely result in some accidents—but even if not perfect, it will still dramatically reduce the total number of accidents and minimize human suffering and loss. Future ninjas should seize the opportunity to prepare now. True ninja innovators know that the perfect should not be the enemy of the great.

Personalized Health Care

Technology is improving the human condition, helping us live longer, healthier, more productive lives. The medical community is unlocking mysteries about diet and disease detection with cutting-edge research, lightning-fast data analysis, and ninja technology. But digital technology also offers much more basic information access: We, as consumers, now know more about our own health and wellness than ever before.

Innovation in health-care technology, built on sensors, big

data, and algorithms, means we can track our personal bio-metric data in real time right from our wrists or smartphones. Think back a decade: How many times, outside of a medical appointment, did you pause to check your pulse? I've been a regular runner since junior high, but I don't think I ever bothered to track my heart rate while training or racing until I started wearing a Fitbit. Now? With a twist of my wrist, I easily can check how close I am to my daily goal of steps taken, my pace, and my heart rate without breaking stride. Almost every day I check how I slept the night before and how often I was restless or woke up. And I can do it all with "over-the-counter" consumer technology that sets up, syncs, and begins tracking in minutes.

Fitness trackers help us quantify and measure our health and our daily routines. And while some studies show that some fitness trackers end up unworn in bedside drawers, as the *New York Times* explains, "Simply knowing how many steps you take, or how much sleep you get, will spur you to seek more, especially if you're comparing and competing with your online peers—a big difference from the un-networked $2 pedometers that came in cereal boxes a decade ago." [51]

The main technological driver behind our skyrocketing access to our own wellness data is the development of the micro-electrical-mechanical systems (MEMS), discussed in the last chapter. These tiny sensors are becoming less expensive even as they become more accurate. Understanding the mass-market appeal of such highly precise and personalized health care, ninja innovators keep developing new services to delight consumers and to solve real problems. But MEMS' size and cost make them ideal for use in wearable devices, such as earbuds that monitor your body temperature and utensils that help offset hand tremors when someone is eating while also collecting data on the tremors for researchers.

And here's where it gets exponentially more valuable to us (and, personally, exciting to me). Our growing appetite for anytime/anywhere connectivity with our friends, family, colleagues, and doctors will improve our health and wellness. How do you respond when your doctor asks, "Tell me about your symptoms" or "Describe your pain"? Probably with a lot of subjective, anecdotal self-analysis: "I seem more tired than usual," or "It feels like it hurts less." But there's a gap between what's actually happening to your body and how you interpret it. So out comes the blood pressure cuff, "Open wide and say *Ahhh*," and "Does it hurt here?" Maybe you have blood drawn. In every case, you wait for information.

Now consider a medical consultation powered by ninja innovation—one that doesn't even involve parking lots or waiting rooms. Without asking a single question, your doctor could review your activity levels over a given time period. She could check your recent hydration, sodium, and oxygen levels without needles. A quick review of your connected prescription dispensers might show you inadvertently skipped a few doses of your medicine. An example: A friend of mine has been a diabetic since childhood and frequently had to extract blood samples. Recently he told me his life has changed thanks to a small, flat device he wears that samples blood from a subcapillary every five minutes and sends the information to his smartphone. An alert goes off if his blood glucose level is outside the normal range. There are also automatic glucose-level monitoring-and-adjusting devices that give diabetics an "artificial pancreas" to keep their blood sugars at safe levels. This sensing technology has amazing implications for the 425 million adults worldwide who live with diabetes.[52]

Digital therapeutics—apps, sensors, and smart technologies that function as stand-alones or in combination with conventional treatments such as medicine or therapy—have the potential to change behavior, and in some cases may be more effective than drug treatments. These treatments work well for conditions such as diabetes, high blood pressure, and insomnia. The idea is that a patient's well-being starts with doctor's orders, but ultimately depends on the patient's willingness to change behaviors and monitor his or her own health.

Focused ultrasound holds the promise of noninvasively treating myriad conditions—from tremors to cancer—at early stages. Cutting-edge prosthetics combine software with sensors that respond to the wearers' movements, allowing them to perform highly precise, complex tasks (like turning keys in locks) that were unimaginable just a few years ago. On sports fields and on the battlefield, head injuries are another frontier. Concussion-sensing technologies in helmets—like those developed by MC-10—are increasingly providing coaches, trainers, and the U.S. military with immediate information about head injuries, so they can appropriately assess, extract, and treat those affected.

Future ninjas also understand that our genetic makeup is fertile ground for innovations in health tech. Cloud computing and big data mean we can analyze millions of patient medical records to uncover which diets and treatment regimens work best, depending on patients' maladies, genetics, demographics, and physical activity. Each individual's genetic code can now be mapped, and the cost of doing so is dropping rapidly. In-creasingly, the individual human genome will be a baseline for recommended exercise, sleep, stress, and nutrition for wellness programs. When you get sick, genetic mapping will also allow personalized diagnoses and treatment plans.

Future ninjas are on the cusp of other ingenious break-throughs in genetics, health care, and telemedicine that will soon become mainstream. These discoveries will allow millions of consumers to assess and address their health concerns, and will enable doctors to diagnose and treat patients with greater accuracy than ever before.

How Do Step Counters Actually Work?

Step counters work by monitoring motion. Consider flying on an airplane: When you sit in an airplane waiting for takeoff you're (hopefully) relaxed and putting a little pressure on the seat back as you rest against it. As the airplane accelerates down the runway, the force of the acceleration pushes your back against the seat with more pressure. After the plane reaches its cruising speed and stops accelerating, the pressure eases, and your back stops pressing so firmly against the seat.

What if a bathroom scale were embedded in the back of that seat? While sitting still on the runway or at cruising speed midflight, the scale would have a low reading because you're only putting a little pressure on it. The reading would be much higher during takeoff as your back presses against it. This is essentially how an accelerometer works. And they're used in many products today, including health and fitness wearables like step counters. They're so small that they easily fit inside most fitness trackers. When they accelerate, the tiny little springs inside them stretch and compress, and the electronic circuits inside measure by how much.

To ensure step counters accurately count steps across devices, CTA created a standard for measuring steps that describes a standardized routine where a person wears a step counter and performs specific walking and running exercises. The person's activity is video recorded and the device's results are compared with the actual number of steps seen in the video. CTA has similar standards for measuring the performance of consumer sleep and heart rate monitors—the goal being to determine how accurately the sensors and algorithms in the devices are working together to reflect reality.

Household Helpers

Robots have been the future ever since I was a kid devouring science fiction books by the pile. The 1960s visions of humanoid robots gave way to robotic assembly arms in the 1970s. Today commercial robots inspect bridges for structural damage in the wake of natural disasters. They can search for and dispose of bombs. They can work in cold and sterile climates to process food. They can even be used to make short deliveries in urban areas.

Robot adoption has historically been driven by the internal

needs of businesses, but more applications are emerging in the consumer world, beyond mere task-based systems to indispensable companion and service robots. In 2016, Alibaba chairman Jack Ma predicted, "Robots will be part of the family."[53] The International Federation of Robots says 31 million domestic robots will be in U.S. households by 2019.[54] This growth is driven in part by higher disposable incomes, and market saturation of other home tech products. Everyone's looking for the next breakthrough product to make our lives easier and save us time—our most valuable resource.

The first robots appeared on the CES show floor in 1983. Back then, Genus the robot—which could vacuum your house and open doors and even shake hands—was expected to cost between $3,000 and $12,000, but it never really hit retail shelves. At CES 2000, Sony debuted dog-like Aibo, the first consumer robot. (*Aibo* is the Japanese word for "companion" or "friend.")

Robots are becoming more humanlike; increasingly they can "sense" the environment and react accordingly. Home security robots powered by AI along with inexpensive, high-quality cameras can keep our homes in check when we're not there. Robots like Robear's nursing robot can be our companions, and in some cases caregivers.

Sophia, an AI-enabled robot developed by Hong Kong–based Hanson Electronics, earned full citizenship status in Saudi Arabia in 2017. Created by CEO and founder David Hanson, Sophia took the stage at CES 2018 to participate in a panel discussion on robotics. In an interview with *i3* magazine, Hanson laid out his vision for Sophia:

I'm fully dedicated to Sophia coming into her own. She is like a baby and we're going to raise her into adulthood. We are going to make living machines and she is going to determine her own destiny. She will have free will, she will be able to move through the world. She'll graduate from university, and who knows? Maybe she might even cure cancer and win the Nobel Prize. I hope she becomes a full being and helps humanity in these ways. Or helps in her own ways, surprising me and in this case, she will deserve citizenship.[55]

But this is just the beginning. Within the next two decades, ninja innovations will take us from any major city on earth to another one in two hours, powered by robotics. This is according to Boeing chairman, president, and CEO Dennis Muilenburg, who shared his vision at the Economic Club of Washington, D.C., in 2018. And we'll go beyond earth as privatization and competition transform space travel. Future ninjas *will* send rockets to Mars. I'd put money on it.

Or at least bitcoin.

Dean Kamen—Robot Ninja Warrior

Dean Kamen is a central figure in the development of robots. He is famous for inventing the Segway, but he holds more than one thousand patents. He is focused on a mission to turn seawater into freshwater, solving one of the pressing problems of our time. Kamen is now heading a massive project seeking to re-create human organs.

Arguably, no other living person has had a bigger global impact on inspiring youth in science and technology than Kamen. The FIRST program, which he launched in 1989, challenges students from kindergarten through high school to pursue education and career opportunities in STEM. It also teaches them how to work on teams and solve problems. More than half a million students in ninety-five countries participate annually.[56] More than three-quarters of FIRST alumni end up working in a STEM field. And girls in FIRST are more likely to make gains in STEM than peers or even boys in FIRST. Kamen told *WIRED* magazine that he started FIRST to make STEM as obsession-worthy among students as sports and entertainment. "We have a culture that confuses the cause of our wealth with the result of our wealth and we have so many distractions that are preventing kids from separating what should be an amusement and a pastime with what should be important to them."[57]

That's why FIRST attracts support from the leaders of a diverse array of major companies and universities, as well as millions of volunteer hours from working technologists, scientists, businesses, and parents. Boeing head Dennis Muilenburg, who sits on the FIRST board, sees it as a vital part of the Boeing and national investment in innovation. At a 2018 breakfast he told the audience that Boeing has hundreds of sponsored teams that are part of the global fabric of FIRST. "I love to invest in the next generation," he said.

Cryptocurrency

Over the centuries, civilizations have used many different forms of currency, from shells to grains to coins to banknotes. All were physical; all had a specific value. But in the past several decades, our relationship to money has changed. How many of us pay for our everyday expenses using cash? We're much more likely to use credit cards or mobile apps. As historian and bestselling author Yuval Harari writes, "More than 90 percent of all money—more than $50 trillion appearing in our accounts—exists only on computer servers."[58] Our money is no longer tangible—it's digital.

Ninja innovators recognized the opportunity when they saw it. In 2009, someone using the pseudonym Satoshi Nakamoto introduced a new form of currency: bitcoin. Bitcoin is revolutionary: "a stateless digital currency."[59] There are no banks, no middlemen, and as of 2018, little to no regulation. Investors can buy them on digital exchanges. Owners—who can remain anonymous and essentially untraceable—"store" bitcoin in digital wallets or in the cloud.

In the past few years, a sort of bitcoin mania—a digital gold rush—has gripped the financial world. Bitcoin and a host of alternative cryptocurrencies experienced uncharted growth in 2017. As *CNNMoney* reported, bitcoin's value shot up more than tenfold, peaking at nearly $20,000 per bitcoin and "easily outgunning the returns from many traditional financial assets like stocks, bonds, and gold."[60] But as often happens, many investors who bought in near the peak lost considerable sums, leading to calls from politicians and regulators for consumer protections.

But it's also true that there are real people making real money in cryptocurrency. And, as a general concept, cryptocurrency represents by far the most successful application of one of our ninja building blocks: blockchain (more in Chapter 4). Blockchain was invented to facilitate bitcoin—its entire purpose is trust, verification, and permanent recording of transactions. It allows users to complete peer-to-peer transactions securely, skipping over a centralized third party.

Of course, nothing is foolproof. Cryptocurrency is only as secure as the security systems that protect the keys. In June 2018, hackers breached South Korean cryptocurrency exchange Coinrail and stole about 30 percent of its virtual currencies— about $36 million[61]—sending the price of bitcoin down 7 percent and exposing Coinrail's weak security systems.

What did these hackers steal, exactly? There's nothing tangible to take. The truth is, cryptocurrencies like bitcoin, ethereum, and litecoin have no intrinsic value. Unlike the dollar, the peso, or the yen, cryptocurrencies are not backed by the full faith and credit of a government, institution, or person—they're purely speculative. Their "value" is driven by their perceived scarcity. Of course, publicly traded stocks are speculative, too. The difference is that when you own a share of stock, you hold some equity in a company, including a share of any dividends paid, which means the intrinsic value of a share of stock is based on an underlying, legally recognized claim to something of value.

Even with their extreme market volatility, cryptocurrencies aren't going away—the potential benefits for businesses of all sizes are too big. Cryptocurrencies eliminate exchange rates and foreign transaction fees for cross-border business. They also offer ninja innovators new pathways for jump-starting their businesses, through initial coin offerings ("ICOs"). Banks are often hesitant to assume the risk of funding startups, despite potentially huge returns. So alternative funding systems are filling the void. Kickstarter and Indiegogo are proven success stories, and there is plenty of evidence to suggest that ICOs can become a legitimate fund-raising companion alongside those initial crowdfunding darlings.

Back in the summer of 1977, I just wanted to deliver eggs without getting lost. I never imagined that one day I could use invisible currency to invest in self-driving vehicles equipped with mapping technology I could activate just by saying an address aloud. I never imagined that a drone could deliver my new activity tracker within hours, allowing me to share countless data points with my doctor before he snapped on AR goggles to operate on me with the help of a robot assistant. Such miracles will be par for the course in the ninja future. We can turn today's science fiction into tomorrow's reality.

PART II

RISK, REWARD, AND REGULATION

CHAPTER 6

NINJA RISKS, NINJA REWARDS

TODAY'S NINJA INNOVATORS HAVE LAID the foundation for tomorrow's ninja future. The incredible technologies now in the works will transform our work and play—and even our rest.

But every silver lining has a cloud. With every innovation comes risk. Most of us would happily accept some risk in exchange for the benefits of a particular technology. Other risks are more complex and have serious implications for our personal lives, our economy, even our national security.

Take privacy. As a society, we have to debate what information we're entitled to keep private. What happens when concepts of privacy collide with useful products that people want and need? In Chapter 2, I mentioned Google Glass—eyewear that, among its many planned features, could have been used to identify people by name and provide you with a few social identifiers: how you know them, their kids' names, and so on. Those (like me) who meet hundreds of people but are forgetful of names would value this technological assist. But public sentiment about privacy waxes and wanes and so has not yet allowed this technology to be sold in the marketplace. I believe that's a real loss. Not only am I deprived of something that can help me, but intentionally barring this product also chokes off related innovation.

My personal mission, and the challenge of our industry, is to ensure that promising innovations are not stymied from reaching their full potential, and that consumers are allowed to evaluate and decide what services they want and need and the information they're willing to share to get those benefits.

We have to overcome our apprehension about new technology intruding on and monitoring us, similar to the plunge we took when we embraced the convenience of credit cards. When credit cards were introduced, people were afraid to use them because they feared someone would steal them and rack up huge liabilities. Congress intervened and set a fifty-dollar maximum liability for someone whose credit card—or even its number—was used by someone else. And for two generations credit cards have been the primary way we exchange money to buy things. Consumers became comfortable and this comfort helped propel our economy forward. Understanding this lesson, future ninjas engineered and launched even more convenient digital payment methods and currencies. Now we're debating the need for greater oversight of cryptocurrency exchanges, and other measures designed to bring some order to the cryptocurrency market.

Each ninja innovation raises a similar series of questions: What does this mean for our privacy? Our security? Our environment? Our jobs and economy? Our health and happiness? We must grapple with the costs and benefits of each innovation.

The Importance of Privacy

By combining low-cost sensors, algorithms, and broadband with customer data, ninja innovators can create services that enhance our health and safety and even preserve lives. Consumers love the personalized, tailored experience these services can provide—but even so, they've become subject to increasingly stringent privacy laws and concerns.

Privacy is important. Some, like Microsoft CEO Satya Nadella, are calling privacy a "human right."[1] Indeed, the right to a certain kind of privacy is protected by the U.S. Constitution. The Fourth Amendment expressly prohibits government from making "unreasonable searches and seizures" of citizens and their property. Since the amendment was enacted, scores of Supreme Court decisions have tried to clarify what qualifies as "unreasonable." Just how far does the ban on government searches extend? When and where can the police search without a court-issued warrant? What are the standards for a search warrant?

So far, the court has determined the Fourth Amendment protects Americans from government searches of homes, library book borrowings, smartphone address lists, and cars, but not searches of items in the police's "plain view." In the digital age, privacy has come under renewed scrutiny in part because the things we store on our devices are, generally, *not* in plain view.

So is this sort of privacy a right? Or is it a threat to health, safety, and innovation? Both? If it is a right, it is one that will sty-mie the emergence of new services and products, especially those customized to meet the needs of individual consumers. Just as a tailor needs to know your measurements to make clothes that fit well, an internet service or app may need to know about you to meet your expectations or even provide a higher level of service.

The American approach to privacy has created room for in-novative business models and new services to delight consum-ers. It has also carved out areas where a societal or consumer interest in privacy trumps business interests: American youth have their criminal records expunged. Medical records are protected from disclosure under HIPAA (the Health Insurance Portability and Accountability Act of 1996). Americans can join a "Do Not Call" list. Personal bankruptcy filings and late pay-ments must be expunged from credit reports after seven to ten years. And companies are required to inform customers of any data breach involving their private information.

Many politicians, influenced by the rhetoric of privacy ad-vocates, err on the side of us always owning and controlling our own personal data. But if you put specific questions to these leaders—as I have done in oral testimony to Congress—their views often change. Here's an easy example: If the cars on the highway in front of you collide in fog and that information can be sent to your car to avoid a deadly crash, is it a privacy viola-tion? What about information from other vehicles that lets you know about icy or rainy road conditions ahead? How about if a car in front of you runs over a big pothole, one that you could avoid? Is this private data that should be protected?

Is medical information *always* sacrosanct? In a natural disaster, for example, shouldn't first responders have access to tools that can scan for and detect vital signs so they can find survivors and triage treatment?

These are just a few scenarios in which ceding a bit of privacy could help protect lives. Many Americans are well aware of this and willingly share their data with companies. CTA research reveals that U.S. consumers are willing to share personal information in exchange for greater control over their information (53 percent), access to rewards programs (48 percent), and access to support services (46 percent).[2]

The targeted approach the United States takes regarding privacy contrasts starkly with approaches in Europe and China. European countries mandate privacy rights for everyone, regardless of whether these rights are good for society, jobs, entrepreneurship, and innovation. In May 2018, the European General Data Protection Regulation (GDPR) went into effect. This tough law requires that any business, including non-European businesses, in possession of personally identifiable information (PII) on European citizens use the information only for the business purpose it was given, receive specific approval for any other use, and discard it once the business purpose is achieved. The regulation has only limited exceptions, many ambiguities, and substantial penalties—as high as 4 percent of global revenue for offending organizations.

Europeans also have the "right to be forgotten," which means they can ask that factual information about them can be deleted from the internet. Google has received millions of requests from EU citizens to delete links that share their names or other PII.[3] (More on GDPR in Chapter 7.)

Like many other laws in Europe, these laws are commonly perceived as a blunt club to be used against large, successful

American companies. But the truth is that leading multinational firms are best positioned to weather broad and expensive new regulatory regimes. The real burden will fall on startups and small companies that lack massive compliance and legal budgets. So, ironically, clumsy European efforts to combat leading American internet companies will only lock in the dominant positions of those companies, while driving off potential upstart competitors.

Although the European Union and the United States are comparable in size and population, Europe lags in one key measure of entrepreneurship and innovation: unicorns. Unicorns are startups that have minimum market valuation of $1 billion. According to CTA's International Scorecard, the EU has 64 unicorn companies, compared to 321 in the United States.[4] Europeans certainly enjoy greater social program benefits and have stricter privacy protections than Americans, but when it comes to innovation, Americans are light-years ahead.

China's approach to privacy, like the European Union's, is also aggressive—but in the opposite direction. The Chinese government has used the shift to digital as a way to ensure social order and suppress dissent. The government tracks its citizens' behavior through their online activity—including their driving and purchasing histories—and increasingly assigns each citizen a "social score."[5] High-scoring individuals get benefits such as more exposure on dating sites or discounts on utility bills; low-scoring individuals can be barred from travel and top jobs, top hotels, and top schools.

Whether these invasive tactics will hurt innovation remains somewhat unclear. The country has already shifted to a combination of capitalism, communism, and government control, which has had huge economic success. In fact, China has the second-most unicorn companies of any country: Between 2010 and 2016, China produced well over fifty of them. What's more, the government has started to strategically invest in innovation in key areas, including self-driving cars, artificial intelligence, and drones. At the June 2018 CES Asia event in Shanghai, Chinese innovation was evident. The Chinese strategy of weak IP enforcement, requiring foreign companies to partner with domestic organizations for market access, eliminating privacy, and investing in key areas, appears to be working for the time being, although China is improving IP enforcement and weakening local partnership requirements.

We'll go into detail on the challenges China poses to innovation and individual rights in the next two chapters. Suffice it to say that from an American perspective, the lack of privacy Chinese citizens must accept, particularly when using online social networks, crosses a dangerous threshold in terms of human rights. It's the converse of the European approach, but is just as constraining. China gives its citizens too little privacy; the EU gives its citizens too much. But the United States' approach of careful, targeted regulation aims to preserve innovation while promoting appropriate consumer protection.

That said, privacy is a moving target, complicated by a host of real-world quandaries with real-world consequences. Encryption is a good example. Strong encryption is essential for people to have confidence in their digital privacy. Many internet communications platforms offer "end-to-end" encryption, which ensures that information exchanged online can be viewed only by the participants in the conversation. This way, users are confident that the sensitive data on their devices will not fall into the hands of hackers or other cyber eavesdroppers.

Privacy vs. Security

That's all well and good for law-abiding citizens, but as with any tool or new technology, some will seek to use encryption for criminal purposes. Law enforcement agencies stand at the crossroads of this complexity: On the one hand, they advocate for strong encryption, because it protects individuals, private companies, and governments; on the other, it shields criminals. Law enforcement warns of "going dark," or being prevented from quickly accessing what may be vital information on digital and mobile devices—most of which didn't exist when legislation concerning intercepted communications was written. Some in the law enforcement community say that laws have not kept pace with technological innovation, leaving significant gaps in law enforcement's ability to quickly obtain the information it needs to do its job. One way law enforcement is trying to work around this problem is by weakening encryption or asking tech companies to provide them with a so-called "back door"—a secret way to bypass security and access protected devices.

Law enforcement's approach is well-intended; they are often boxed in and have to seek creative ways to get the information they need to protect citizens. But the use of "back doors" would have massive negative consequences for users and the entire internet ecosystem. If a platform's backdoor "key" were to leak even once, the security of everyone using the platform—potentially millions of devices—would be instantly compromised. Anyone who follows the news realizes that leaks of sensitive government information happen all the time. A disastrous public disclosure of the government's backdoor encryption key would not be a matter of "if," but "when." And if companies were forced to ensure that the government could sneak into every conversation that their customers have, then customers who care about their security and privacy would likely turn to foreign companies to supply their needs—even if that means buying products abroad.

As privacy advocate and U.S. senator Ron Wyden explains, the encryption debate is not about privacy versus security, but rather "more security versus less security. If you want to be in a safe community, you shouldn't be able to weaken encryption."

This was put to the test in December 2015, when two shooters opened fire on workers at the San Bernardino, California, health department in a terrorist attack that killed fourteen people and wounded twenty-two more. The FBI was stymied by a locked iPhone left behind by one of the shooters and asked the courts to force Apple to give them access. Apple, while offering to work closely with law enforcement in other ways, declined to create a "key" to the phone, explaining that any such exploit would harm its customers by allowing access to millions of other iPhones if the key were to be exposed.

Congress wisely chose not to intercede, and the FBI managed to hack into the phone shortly thereafter. Later it came out that the FBI had inaccurately told Congress that it had exhausted all efforts to break into the shooter's phone and overstated the number of encrypted phones they were unable to access.[6] Understandably, this undercut the strength of the FBI's argument in the San Bernardino case.

Thanks to today's technology, law enforcement has access to more data than ever before. Predictive analytics can help determine when and where crimes may take place. Ninja innovations such as facial recognition, iris scans, and gait analysis are critical safety tools, enabling police to identify wrongdoers and search for victims. Drones and robots allow first responders to gather information, clear crime scenes, even defuse explosives without exposing themselves to unnecessary danger. With respect to the "going dark" concern, tech companies should explain there are usually multiple ways to access data stored on suspects' devices, and assist law enforcement in obtaining that data without new technical mandates. For example, Apple releases iCloud backup data when presented with a valid search warrant.

There is no doubt the threat landscape looks dramatically different than it did when I was growing up. We face substantial challenges, but law enforcement and the tech industry need not be at odds, because we all share the goal of keeping our citizens safe. But encryption back doors are not the answer. Such a concession would only make life easier for cybercriminals and more perilous for lawful internet users.

Both sides need to be transparent: Tech companies must clearly explain their data protection policies to customers, and law enforcement must stick to the facts and avoid hyperbole or overreach. Such transparency and collaboration is a winning strategy for ensuring law enforcement has the tools they need to accomplish their mission without undermining the privacy and security of millions of law-abiding users.

Cybersecurity

History shows that if there's something worth stealing, someone will try to steal it—and will sometimes be successful. This holds true in our digital age: Many security breaches occur when companies don't invest in online safety or maintain their digital defenses. And the vast majority of intrusions can be stopped by effective cybersecurity.

Tech companies recognize that data security is a top priority for consumers. But nothing in the world has ever been—or ever will be—100 percent secure. The tech industry shouldn't have to shoulder the burden of data protection alone. Government can take steps to improve a nation's data security infrastructure and shore up consumer trust. This might sound ironic, given that much of the conversation around data security until the Sony Pictures Entertainment hack was about *government* intrusion. All the more reason for government to prove its commitment to safeguard citizens' and businesses' valuable information with real solutions.

The worst thing countries can do in the face of cyber threats is impose new rules that make the internet less usable and the data of ordinary users less secure. In June 2018, the U.S. Supreme Court reinforced digital privacy rights when it ruled that police need a warrant before tracking a person's location through mobile phone records. In his majority opinion, Chief Justice John Roberts explained that privacy protections were necessary due to the role of the extensive cell phone in modern life: "The time-stamped data [contained in a person's phone] provide an intimate window into a person's life, revealing not only his particular movements, but through them his 'familial, political, professional, religious and sexual associations.'" Most of the world post–September 11 has found a middle ground between personal freedom and national security; we can and must find similar consensus in an age of cyber threats. Passage of government surveillance reform can help position a country as more progressive and supportive of innovation while boosting international confidence in American products.

Finally, new laws can help reassure citizens their personal information is as secure as the physical items in their homes. The fact that property is digitized and flowing across networks does not negate a legal protection against unreasonable searches and seizures. By ensuring the faith of citizens, government can work hand in hand with businesses to build a better security framework that thwarts the kind of attacks hitting companies every day.

But innovators and legislators can do only so much—each of us has a role to play, too, in protecting our data. The wall separating our offline selves from our online selves has been erased. With mobile technology—our smartphones, our wearables, and our cars—we're never really offline. Even if you remove yourself to a remote mountain retreat without any mobile technology, there's a part of you always online in the form of your personal and financial information. If this is true today, it's going to be even more true five years from now.

Understanding that none of us is ever fully "off the grid" might help us prepare to enter this new digital age with more sophistication and confidence than we've had in the past. If our personal information is valuable to someone else, it should be just as valuable to us. We must learn to protect it, and that starts with knowing how it's being used by others. This growing consumer consciousness in the value of our own data is the beginning of our defense against hackers. In addition, all consumers can and should strengthen the security of our connected devices by changing default passwords, using two-factor authentication, buying well-known brands, and having systems installed by certified professionals.

Threats can come from anywhere and affect anyone. In the U.S., we have to work as one nation to properly balance privacy and security for all.

Geography

Our one nation, however, is not at all balanced in terms of our geographic distribution. In 1910, more than 50 percent of the U.S. population lived in rural areas;[7] by 2016, that share plummeted to under 20 percent.[8] This new rural-urban divide has led to significant cultural, political, and economic differences. More rural Americans live in poverty or with a disability than do urban Americans. And while rural Americans are more likely to be business owners or homeowners than those who live in cities, they are far less likely to find a job or pursue higher education.[9] They're also more likely to live in the state where they were born.[10]

These are significant gaps—but technological innovation and broadband connectivity are increasingly helping to bridge them, giving Americans who live in the country many of the same opportunities and resources available to city dwellers.

In Chapter 3, I described Airbnb as a great example of how

homeowners can leverage online platforms to support themselves and grow local economies. This has been especially noticeable in rural areas, where the number of active Airbnb hosts spiked 1,800 percent between 2012 and 2017.[11] Rural areas in 41 states experienced 100 percent year-over-year growth. Almost 20 percent of Airbnb listings are in rural areas, versus only 12.5 percent of hotel rooms—opening up new economic opportunities in places with otherwise limited resources. And rural Airbnb hosts make on average as much as, if not more than, urban hosts. All told, rural hosts across the United States made almost half a billion dollars in a one-year period during 2016–17.

It's an exciting development—and one that will continue as tech innovation expands from coast to coast. Drones, for instance, will bring significant benefits to various rural industries. A 2017 PwC report predicts a global market value of $4.3 billion in mining and $32.4 billion in agriculture through the incorporation of drones into key processes such as analyzing soil, assessing the health of crops, and drainage.[12]

And both drones and self-driving vehicles can help shrink distances, making it easier for rural areas not only to participate in e-commerce by lowering the cost of shipping, but also for rural Americans to get vital medical attention. European researchers in 2017 found drones were able to get defibrillators to people experiencing cardiac arrest faster than ambulances.[13] Drones can also deliver prescription medication to those who live far from a pharmacy or are housebound. Self-driving vehicles will be able to connect people with disabilities and older adults in rural areas with their local economies and improve their access to medical care. And Apple partnered with RapidSOS to launch a feature that lets first responders automatically pinpoint a location when an iPhone user dials 911.

Tech also has important implications for the rural job market. The Conference Board says there were more than 566,000 ads for computer and math jobs in the United States in May 2018.[14] But only about 100,000 students graduated with bachelor's or master's degrees in computer science in 2015–16 (the latest available data).[15,16] Thanks to online education, students across the country can acquire many of the skills needed to succeed in the job market—no matter where they're based. And employers are not restricted to urban areas or coastal states when looking for top talent. Teleworking means that the best talent can come from—and continue to work in—America's heartland.

That said, new business models such as teleworking require fast, reliable internet connections. In most states, fewer than half of households' internet connections meet the Federal Communication Commission's benchmark fixed broadband speed of 25 Mbps.[17] Smaller, more densely populated areas help boost a state's internet connectivity—helping to explain why Delaware, New Jersey, Massachusetts, Rhode Island, Maryland, Hawaii, and New Hampshire earned the highest marks on our 2018 U.S. Innovation Scorecard for Fast Internet.

It's important for our country not only to be a global leader on connectivity, but also to get the fundamentals right at home. And when it comes to expanding broadband service, we can sometimes be our own worst enemy.

Expansion of 4G LTE and rollout of 5G is often stymied by local regulations. The antennas required for 5G are the size of a backpack and can be easily affixed to already-existing infrastructure, like lightposts or even the side of buildings. Yet local governments don't distinguish between these antennas and the two-hundred-foot-tall cell towers required for other telecommunications systems.[18] Rent-seeking local governments view new technologies as cash cows and charge exorbitant fees for the right to install infrastructure. Meanwhile, some of our foreign competitors act like ninja innovators, unconstrained by such regulations as they race to become leaders in the new generation of broadband technology.

To maximize the benefits of 5G, we must invest in small-cell technology to make broadband's accessibility and efficiency as consistent as possible across terrain. Small cells work in tandem with the large cell towers that provide the majority of our nation's cell coverage. Mounting small cells is a labor-intensive project, but ninja innovation has shrunk them to the size of a shoebox. They can be installed on traffic lights or other already-existing pieces of infrastructure. Eventually small cells will help make up the backbone of our coverage across the nation, though the impact will vary between cities and rural areas.

This isn't a silver bullet—small cells are not intended to cover big distances, so don't expect quick rollout for rural areas. To bridge the gap we still need broadband and cell towers that cover larger territories. But in the long run, the effect would be transformative.

Projects are under way to expand rural broadband access. Microsoft's Rural Airband Initiative calls for maximizing unused TV white space spectrum to bring broadband to 80 percent of underserved rural communities. Instead of using expensive fiber optic cables, Microsoft's bold plan uses empty channels between TV stations to deliver connectivity to more than 20 million rural Americans at much lower costs. While broadcasters are often crowded tightly using all available spectrum in urban areas, the spectrum in rural areas set aside for broadcasters is often untapped. Opening this spectrum for broadband use can bring the benefits and opportunities of broadband to rural citizens.

Environment and Health

In Chapter 3, we touched on climate change and dramatic shifts in weather patterns. These trends may not impact our daily lives right now, but they have serious implications in the near future for how we live, work, and do business.

President Donald Trump drew the ire of the environmental community—activists and businesses alike—when he withdrew the United States from the Paris Climate Accords in 2017. I had mixed emotions about the decision. On the one hand, I was disappointed: Many companies and industries had committed to addressing climate change, and the withdrawal meant loss of U.S. leadership. In terms of traditional pollution like smog and wastewater discharges, the United States is a relatively clean nation, and the environmental goals were excessively modest. Accordingly, after the withdrawal, I urged our CTA board of directors to show that the private sector could take the lead if our government would not. As a result, we committed to holding our industry accountable for meeting or exceeding the standards set in the agreement.

On the other hand, I saw the president's point. The agreement required billions in cash from the United States that would go toward polluting nations such as China. And while the agreement sets specific targets for U.S. and European air pollution reduction, China is permitted to increase its pollution levels without limit until 2029 and then may try to keep its 2029 pollution levels as a target.[19]

Air quality in China is dreadful—and a major health hazard. More than 1 million people in China die from poor air quality every year.[20] However, pollution isn't a problem confined to China. The World Health Organization found that from 2011 to 2016, global air pollution had grown by 8 percent[21]—a reality that, in the long run, will affect our global health, productivity, and economy. The OECD predicts employers will lose a total of 3.7 billion working days due to pollution.[22] CTA included an "Environment" category in the International Innovation Scorecard to reflect the fact that pollution kills people, chills innovation, and hurts a nation as a choice for ninja innovators to start businesses. A cleaner environment, by contrast, attracts innovators and fosters happy, healthy, productive, and creative workers.

One reason for high levels of global pollution is the mass migration of people to cities over the past several decades. According to a 2014 UN report, fewer than one-third (30 percent) of the global population lived in urban areas in 1950.[23] We stand at about 55 percent[24] today, and the report estimates that by 2050, the number will rise to 66 percent. That means even more crowding on our cities' streets, even more stress on sanitation systems, and even more dependence on industrial systems.

As if that weren't worrisome enough, it's highly probable that some of these cities could be underwater within a matter of decades. Sea levels are rising, and major storms like 2017's

Hurricanes Harvey, Irma, and Maria are growing in intensity. And while urban migration means many businesses will compete for costly real estate in coastal cities like Miami and New York, they'll have to pay even more in insurance costs to get such properties—if the properties themselves can withstand the weather. In fact, the World Bank estimates that costs from flooding worldwide will rise to over $50 billion *each year* by 2050 and puts Miami and New York at the top of its list of cities where costs will be greatest.[25]

Even as sea levels rise, in certain parts of the globe freshwater is becoming a rarer and rarer commodity. Media attention has focused primarily on Cape Town, South Africa, where water is becoming so scarce that city leaders are planning for a potential "Day Zero," when the city will no longer have water available by tap. But other regions, from coastal China to Southern California, are threatened by water shortages as well.

Such resource shortages aren't merely a threat to human health—they're also a threat to business productivity. Many of the basic products in our home, from leather goods to smartphones to chocolate bars, take thousands of liters of water to make. Water shortages will disrupt supply chains and force businesses to charge consumers higher rates for the goods that we now take for granted. And the truth is, climate change leads to resource scarcity, which historically leads to mass migrations of people in search of assistance and, all too often, armed conflict—just look at Sudan and Somalia as two recent examples.

It's a dire picture, and one that should inspire action from future ninjas. The European Union has already taken major steps: Not only did it spearhead the Paris Climate Accords, but the EU is also addressing single-use plastics to help prevent pollution that clogs our oceans and kills millions of birds and hundreds of thousands of sea mammals. A number of companies have followed suit: McDonald's, IKEA, Starbucks, and Whole Foods have vowed to eliminate plastic products like straws and bags from their stores. And American Express has said it will use recycled plastic for its credit cards.

The tech industry is already driving massive gains in energy efficiency to help reduce global warming—innovation is constantly developing smaller, lighter, less energy-intensive devices. Indeed, the devices in our homes today use far less energy than they once did. A CTA-commissioned study found the average LCD TV used 76 percent less energy in 2015 than the average TV in 2003. And while the number of electronic devices in American homes went up by 20 percent between 2010 and 2017, the total amount of energy they used dropped 25 percent. Industry-led voluntary agreements have shrunk the energy consumption of devices used to binge-watch your favorite shows, such as set-top boxes and internet equipment. Even the energy used by the data centers that power these devices has flatlined. (Helpful tip: CTA offers resources for calculating home energy use and locating local electronics recyclers at www.GreenerGadgets.org.)

But more businesses need to take a stand and promote sustainability. We'll need ongoing partnerships between public works services and private sector supply chains if we want to be able to offer consumers goods that are environmentally preferable at the same low prices. For example, electronics manufacturers including HP and Dell have engaged with recyclers of old electronics and plastics from electronics—using them as sources of plastics for new electronics. These types of closed-loop initiatives help create sustainable markets for scrap plastics and diversify the sources of plastics required for new products.

Public-private partnerships will be crucial to crafting efficient and sustainable solutions. Many companies directly support efforts—such as those of the Recycling Partnership, the ENERGYSTAR program, and energy efficiency voluntary agreements—that substantially affect recycling and efficient use of resources. Such proactive engagement is vastly preferable to having the government craft clumsy, overbroad environmental regulations that inhibit innovation.

Clear, eco-friendly policies will attract future ninjas. According to Pew, 65 percent of millennials attribute climate change to human action.[26] This means that if you can demonstrate that your company is working vigorously to combat climate change, more talented young workers will flock to your team and more millennials will be excited to buy your products.[27]

Far from being in conflict with one another, as they are so often portrayed in popular media, business interests and environmental interests are closely linked. Future business success in all sectors depends on the health of our planet.

CHAPTER 7

NINJA REGULATION

IN "GOLDILOCKS AND THE THREE BEARS," our heroine tests porridge, chairs, and beds in search of the perfect balance—not too hot or too cold, not too hard or too soft. Simplistic as it is, the story of Goldilocks is a useful way to think about the role of government regulation on business and technology.

Different countries, different states, and different municipalities take different approaches to regulation. The European Union and China are prime examples. As we discussed in the last chapter, the EU and China take extreme, opposite positions on privacy. They've also staked out diametrically opposed positions on a variety of other regulations regarding innovation.

Some Like It Hot

The EU's approach is decidedly too cold. Several years ago, while waiting to speak at a European conference on innovation, I heard a top European government official urge his colleagues to leapfrog the Americans by encouraging entrepreneurship, relaxing rules, and promoting STEM education and English proficiency at the high school level. He was followed by a government minister who suggested a different approach: attacking big American tech companies using new legal arguments.

Over the last two decades, European regulators have targeted leading U.S. tech innovators, including Google, Amazon, Apple, Uber, Intel, Facebook, Microsoft, and Qualcomm, among others.[1] In 2015, the EU's antitrust chief accused Google of abusing its search engine dominance to favor its own comparison-shopping services over those of its competitors. In 2016, the EU announced plans to create a digital single market that would allow all citizens to use digital services, no matter what country they're located in. This shift would place heavy burdens of privacy, copyright, and competition on major U.S. tech companies, like Google, Facebook, Twitter, and others. In 2017, European commissioner for competition Margrethe Vestager rewrote tax law and led an effort to require that Apple pay $14.5 billion in connection with alleged tax avoidance. Apple says it followed the law and paid the taxes it owed to Ireland—to the tune of $400 million annually.[2] The European Commission (EC) also went after Starbucks, Amazon, and McDonald's on tax-avoidance charges. And in 2018, the EC imposed a $5 billion fine on Google's Android operating system for antitrust violations. This will have ramifications far beyond Google itself. The Android ecosystem includes 1,300 brands, 500 operators, and 1.3 million app developers. The EC attack on this free and open platform means that small businesses— from app developers to content creators to marketing firms— will also suffer.

And in 2018, the EU doubled down by implementing GDPR. As discussed in Chapter 6, GDPR suppresses innovation by introducing a vague, massive, and complex compliance burden. As a result, companies of all sizes are hiring lawyers instead of engineers. The penalties for noncompliance are potentially disastrous: €20 million, or 4 percent of global revenues—whichever is higher. And the legal danger is real—opportunistic trial lawyers filed €7.6 billion worth of lawsuits against Facebook and Google the very first day GDPR was in effect.[3] As we learned from our experience fighting patent trolls in the United States (CTA advocates for patent reform and has fought for federal legislation to protect entrepreneurs from patent troll extortion), small companies and startups will find they are the next victims in line, since they lack the legal resources to fight back against frivolous litigation.

Little wonder many firms are withdrawing from European markets or simply blocking access to users in the EU. And as discussed in the last chapter, the burden of these rules falls proportionately heavier on small businesses, which struggle to survive, much less find the legal resources to adhere to heavy regulation. So by disadvantaging startups and encouraging litigation, GDPR harms innovation, economic growth, and the competitiveness of Europe's digital entrepreneurs.

These actions, though frustrating, come as no surprise.

The EU has a long history of protectionism, promoting well-regulated, often state-owned and/or heavily subsidized incumbent companies at the expense of game-changing, disruptive innovators. But the hard truth with which the EU needs to grapple is that consumers pick products that suit their needs best. And in an increasingly connected world, they're less likely to worry about what nation a company hails from.

Some EU leaders are more forward-thinking than others. France's Emmanuel Macron said it well at CES 2016 on a panel on innovation:

> We have to recognize the fact that Uber and all these players provide new opportunities for people as customers. . . . And guess what—even when you want to block it, people choose that. . . . You should know that the first city outside the U.S. for Uber as a market is Paris. So people decided, and they are pro-innovation as customers. . . . You should not create a sort of bias, you should . . . create a level playing field between these different players, but it's not about blocking innovation.[4]

Countries that waste time fighting market disruption will feel the consequences—both economic and diplomatic. Furthermore, the barriers the EU is imposing on the internet increasingly restrict access to information, dangerous moves for a government to make, since it's a slippery slope to the controls on access to information imposed by totalitarian societies.

So the European Union's regulatory approach is too cold. What does a "too hot" approach look like? China is a prime example: It pushed hard to help develop Chinese companies and advance its own industries, leveraging a combination of intense focus on STEM education, industrial espionage, and mandated sharing of intellectual property by companies wishing to do business in China. In 2017, China registered 16,000 new enterprises *every day*—up from 15,000 every day the year before. It has made patents a priority, incentivizing patent filings and pumping funding into R&D. China's government has set ambitious national patent targets that have resulted in China surpassing the United States in patent applications. But quantity is different from quality, and many of these new Chinese patents are weak or of low quality. This is not a strategy that America should emulate.

More troubling, China has blocked Google, Facebook, Twitter, and similar websites and services. Blocking allows China to copy these successful companies and try to improve on them. It also allows China to control content on Chinese platforms. By limiting content and censoring and imprisoning dissidents, China has maintained control of its population and chilled expression and creativity.

China is fighting to become more innovative. But it remains to be seen whether a society closed to information and fixated on monitoring its people's social media citizenship will be able to make the breakthroughs in innovation necessary for long-term leadership.

Getting to "Just Right"

As the 2010s come to a close, the United States remains the world's unquestioned innovation leader. American companies dominate the technology industry. U.S.-based platforms are the global online standard for commerce, education, and entertainment. That's no accident: It's baked into our national character.

The Founding Fathers were America's original ninja innovators. The First Amendment of the Constitution protects our right to express ourselves vigorously and freely, establishing the legal basis for online speech. Later, our Supreme Court protected innovation by ruling that products with legal uses couldn't be banned just because they challenged existing business models. As the internet emerged, Congress passed laws clarifying that responsibility for speech on social media platforms lies with the person posting the content. Our antitrust laws prioritized consumer welfare and did not punish companies simply for being successful.

When record labels, hotels, taxis, and other legacy businesses implored U.S. legislatures to shut down their upstart digital competitors, policymakers usually politely declined and suggested they work it out in the marketplace. Our immigration system has generally been open and welcoming to the world's best and brightest. We have historically practiced and promoted the benefits of free trade. Let's look at a few examples of industry and government working together to create the right policy mix.

The *Betamax* Decision

The introduction of home recording and the VCR in the 1970s opened the floodgates to lawsuits and legislation. The Ninth Circuit of the U.S. Court of Appeals in 1981 held that the VCR was an illegal product because it could be used for copyright infringement. The case was appealed to the Supreme Court, and the technology industry simultaneously began a protracted battle in Congress against what was then considered the biggest and most effective lobbying organization in town: the motion picture industry.

As the lawyer in charge of the coalition fighting for innovation, I also took on the task of coordinating more than twenty amici filings. These roles gave me a front-row seat to the drama. Our goal was to ensure manufacturers could continue to sell innovative products and consumers could rent movies and buy VCRs. In 1985 the Supreme Court issued a 5–4 decision in *Sony Corp. of America v. Universal City Studios* (the *Betamax* case), ruling that a VCR is legal because it has significant noninfringing uses, including recording over-the-air broadcast television.

The next big battle was over audio recording. People were creating their own mixes with cassette tapes. And the music industry followed the motion picture industry, seeking to put huge taxes and restrictions on audio-recording equipment. So the tech industry fought a two-front battle against two industries, in the courts and in Congress. Ultimately the tech industry managed to convince both that technology must run its course, innovation is good, and policymakers and judicial bodies should be cautious in restricting consumer access to new technologies. In fact, the entire digital economy is based on replication. When you forward an email, you make a copy. When you stream a song, a temporary copy resides on your computer. Without the *Betamax* decision, the internet as we use it every day would not exist.

Leading this battle was a heady experience, but I benefited from the amazing wisdom of the technologists, engineers, and lawyers on our team. I wasn't making friends in Hollywood or the music industry by insisting we not choke off new possibilities because existing industries were comfortable the way they were. That's not what this country is about. That's not what innovation is about. Our team believed passionately that innovation was ultimately good and that these technological wonders would empower people worldwide.

We were right. And thanks to the fairness of the U.S. judicial and legislative processes, we prevailed. The world is better because we fought against blocking access to entertainment, information, and education. Consumers were fortunate that we prevailed. And so, ultimately, was Hollywood, the bulk of whose revenues increasingly come from streaming media[5]—a marketplace that would not exist if they had won the *Betamax* fight.

SOPA/PIPA

Three decades after *Betamax*, on January 18, 2012, Americans opened their internet browsers and saw only darkness. Wikipedia shut down completely for twenty-four hours. A black band masked the Google logo. Google, Wikipedia, Reddit, CTA, and other major websites had banded together and gone dark to make a then-obscure piece of legislation infamous.

These internet giants and other online sites joined millions of Americans in protesting the 2012 Stop Online Piracy Act (SOPA) and PROTECT IP Act (PIPA) legislation in a historic grassroots movement. After SOPA was introduced and discussed in committee hearings, and after PIPA passed in the Senate Judiciary Committee, more than four million people signed Google's online petition linked to the blacked-out home page. Eight million people looked up how to contact their representative when prompted to by Wikipedia. Tumblr alone produced 87,000 calls to representatives.[6] The vast numbers led most congressional sponsors to rescind their support of the bill. The protest led to a new wave of internet advocacy and the foundation of groups including the Internet Association, now led brilliantly by Michael Beckerman.

Why such an uprising? Congress intended SOPA and PIPA to *protect* the American copyright industry. But the ill-advised legislation was so broad that it had the potential to *harm* or eradicate entire websites or online services, instead of specifically targeting individuals who uploaded illegal content.

The *New York Times* called the SOPA/PIPA protests a "coming of age for the tech industry,"[7] and CTA was proud to help lead it. It was a bipartisan and cross-industry effort: Venture capitalists and law professors, computer scientists and human rights advocates, progressives and Tea Partiers united to fight the legislation. Still, the bills progressed through Congress and appeared to have the momentum necessary to become law.

CES 2012 proved to be one of the turning points. We invited two legislators—Republican congressman Darrell Issa and Democratic senator Ron Wyden—to Las Vegas to explain how the bill would jeopardize the freedom of the digital world. Both policymakers made strong, smart, and passionate cases. Within days, the internet blackout began and the tide reversed. Members of Congress rescinded their support. Weeks later, SOPA and PIPA were history.

We did this because we believe innovation, rather than an overbroad law, is the best way to grow the economy and fight piracy. History has proven us right: In the years since SOPA/PIPA failed, we've seen many instances of market disruption and many more cases of technological innovation. Spotify, the now-ubiquitous Swedish streaming service, intentionally developed free ad-supported streaming as a legal alternative to illegal piracy. It worked: Piracy has dropped significantly. In 2017, less than 7 percent of daily Web traffic in North America came from peer-to-peer file sharing, compared to 31 percent in 2008.[8]

Videocassette rentals, DVD sales and rentals, YouTube, and broadband created new avenues for distribution and revenue—not to mention hundreds of thousands of new jobs for budding content makers. Even more exciting, streaming services also led to significant revenue growth for the music industry. The Recording Industry Association of America, one of the major supporters of the SOPA/PIPA legislation, reported that revenue generated by streaming platforms grew by 43 percent between 2016 and 2017, and accounted for nearly two-thirds of total industry revenues.[9] This growth is due in large part to paid subscriptions to streaming services. The internet created an incredible distribution opportunity for new artists to promote their work. And while brick-and-mortar music stores have dwindled, hundreds of thousands of musicians benefit from services like Pandora, Spotify, and Apple Music to gain exposure and find new fans. Even more surprising, old-school technologies like vinyl records and cassettes are thriving! Sales of records have increased each year for the last dozen years through 2017, selling more than 14 million albums.[10] More artists are creating music and reaching a global audience today than at any time in history. Furthermore, the increase in recorded music drives demand for the live experience, and the concert business is booming as never before.

Just as the internet prompted market disruptions in media and retail and communication, next-generation technologies will lead to similar market disruptions in other industries. Will Congress support new technologies or stifle them? And how will legacy industries evolve to thrive in this changing technological landscape? In 2012, members of Congress sided with progress over fear. The recent explosion of innovation has proven them right. As other new disruptive technologies emerge, policymakers should heed the lessons of SOPA and PIPA and allow new innovations to thrive.

Betamax and SOPA/PIPA are prime examples of U.S. policymakers allowing "permissionless innovation"—a laissez-faire approach by which regulators give innovators the freedom to create new services and systems without getting approval first. This bias in favor of innovation is vital for any government serious about embracing an innovation economy. You shouldn't have to ask permission to innovate! Given the successful record of pro-innovation choices and the massive benefits for our citizens and our economy, you would think that policymakers would embrace and expand "permissionless innovation."

Instead, we risk doing the opposite: abandoning the approaches that made us successful. The United States is not immune to the creep of "techlash." As these platforms enter their teens and early twenties of existence, they're cause for new scrutiny and criticism. Tech is no longer the economic darling it once was. The political left, and some on the right, claim tech is too big, and conservatives accuse tech companies—particularly social media platforms—of political bias. Congress has paraded a series of tech leaders before Capitol Hill to talk about data privacy, security, and antitrust. And the techlash to innovations such as drones and self-driving vehicles paints a more troubling picture for the future of tech policy.

SESTA/CDA 230

The question of who is responsible for online content remains a thorny issue. Intermediary liability protection is the commonsense idea that internet platforms are not responsible for content posted by users. Enshrined in Section 230 of the 1996 Communications Decency Act, this law allows the internet as we know it to function. Without Section 230, any site hosting user-generated content would have to screen every submission to avert ruinous lawsuits.

On a practical basis, doing this in real time would almost be impossible due to the sheer amount of content created: Twitter alone hosts 350,000 tweets per minute; 200 billion tweets per year.[11] If any single user post could lead to legal action against the social media platform, it would shut down. Today's internet experience would be virtually impossible.

And so Section 230 was considered inviolable—until 2018, when Congress was approached by groups representing victims of sex trafficking (and quietly backed by Hollywood studios, the hotel industry, and others who saw the chance to weaken online competitors that were taking their customers and disrupting their businesses). Moved by the emotional nature of the subject—sex trafficking is a horrid crime and victims deserve protections and justice—and ignoring opposition from civil society organizations, the Department of Justice, and victim advocacy groups, Congress passed a law known as SESTA-FOSTA, which allows trial lawyers to sue social media sites that "facilitate" sex trafficking. Unfortunately, the law's hastily written language was so broad and vague it could potentially impose liability to any website with a comments section.

Immediately, Web services began pulling down popular forums featuring consumer-generated content. Other websites eliminated sections or imposed broad filters. Congress made the internet experience less rich for users and more difficult for entrepreneurs, all while doing very little to protect actual victims of sex trafficking. Most alarming, this law has pushed voluntary sex workers back onto the streets or the Dark Web— offering them even less transparency in their work and making their work less visible and more dangerous.

Intermediary liability is not the only area where we are turning away from our long-standing innovation values. Ill-informed voices on both ends of the political spectrum are urging tougher regulation of leading internet companies, equating them with public utilities like water or electricity, urging regulation that will break these companies up in the same way that the federal government broke up companies like Standard Oil and the

Bell System, which had a virtual monopoly on basic necessities. This comparison makes no sense. Platforms like Google and Amazon are not necessities: People use them willingly because they make their lives better. More, they have numerous easy-to-access competitors, both on and off the internet. These naysayers seem to prefer a European antitrust approach, where regulation is triggered not by consumer harm but by a company's marketplace success. If that's the case, why would ninja innovators bother?

These arguments are absurd. These are companies, not public utilities. People use services such as Amazon, Facebook, and Google not because they have to, but because they want to. More, there is no "lock-in" cost for consumers: Internet users are free to move around shopping, search, and social networking sites. Businesses like Google thrive not because of monopolistic behavior, but because users willingly embrace technologies that enhance and improve their lives.

GDPR, American-Style

Another threat to American technology leadership is the imposition of GDPR and other onerous data compliance mandates. We touched on this complex issue earlier, but it's vital that ninja innovators understand the current stakes in the privacy debates.

American online companies have succeeded, in part, due to our moderate and reasoned approach to online privacy. We avoided both the extremes of heavy regulation, as seen in Europe, and the elimination of virtually all user privacy online, as in China. Instead we recognized that not all personal data is equally sensitive. We created specific privacy regimes for information pertaining to health and finance, while allowing the internet economy to function and users to benefit from personalized advertising and services.

One would think that the last thing the United States would want to do would be to switch our successful privacy framework over to the costly and business-smothering European model. Yet in 2018, California hastily passed a privacy bill that echoes GDPR, requiring companies to delete consumer data and not sell it to a third party, if a consumer asks. The law goes into effect in 2020, and passage of the bill sets the stage for a national debate in the United States on consumer privacy. The rushed legislative process and the bill's vague terminology open the door to a legion of potential abuses. For example, the definition of information a consumer can prevent a company from using is so broad it could allow a subject of a press investigation to stop a story from being published online.

Sharing Is Caring

Companies such as Uber and Lyft, Airbnb and HomeAway—which empower users, make our cities more livable, and launch entrepreneurs—are also facing regulatory pushback. Powered by the encouragement (and campaign donations) of taxi companies and hotel unions, local regulators are trying to hinder home- and ride-sharing platforms.

Most local efforts to regulate such businesses out of existence prove unsuccessful thanks to protests by citizens who use and enjoy these new services. Not long ago in Texas, the state legislature overturned regulations targeting Uber and Lyft after public outcry. After all, who really wants to go back to the time when your only choice was paying to sleep in a sterile and over-priced hotel or trying to hail a grubby taxi that may or may not stop for you on the corner?

At a local level, ride-sharing services help make communities safer by providing people with the opportunity for a sober ride home after a late night. Nearly one-quarter of Lyft rides occur between 10:00 P.M. and 6:00 A.M., and 47 percent of Lyft passengers use the app during hours when public transportation has ceased.[12] An astounding 88 percent of people ages twenty-one and older say Uber makes it easier to avoid driving after drinking. More, many Uber drivers value and benefit from the flexibility ride-sharing offers.[13] And ride-shares offer meaningful interaction between drivers and passengers—a valuable avenue for face-to-face interaction in an increasingly fractured world.

Short-term rentals offer new income streams to homeowners, open up new neighborhoods to visitors, and boost local economies: 43 percent of spending by Airbnb guests is in the neighborhood in which they stay.[14] Older adults (ages sixty and above) are the fastest-growing segment of Airbnb hosts, and two-thirds of older hosts are women—not the typical population that comes to mind when thinking about people who make money on the internet. Sites like HomeAway, VRBO, and Airbnb help people supplement their income and stay in their homes. In 2016, hosts aged sixty-plus earned a collective $747 million on Airbnb. As Airbnb's Josh Meltzer explained: "Older Americans aren't just embracing home sharing for the economic potential, but as a way to maintain social connections as they age."[15]

Calling for added rules on innovative ecosystems, which

are already transparent and self-regulated through ratings of both riders and drivers, hosts and guests, is backward thinking. Proposals to curb the sharing economy hurt consumers, local economies, and the ninja innovators who rely on the freedom, flexibility, and additional income of this entrepreneurial economy.

"Just-Right" Regulation

The American approach to privacy and regulation, while not perfect, makes the most sense. We understand that "one size fits all" does not work, and different data merits different levels of protection. We know that users willingly disclose data in exchange for benefits such as personalized shopping recommendations. And we recognize that narrowly addressing specific problems works better than imposing complex, top-down compliance regimes.

This smart, balanced approach has allowed U.S. companies to thrive. American tech companies are the unquestioned global leaders in online business, communication, and entertainment. This didn't happen by magic: Our nation took calculated risks and passed thoughtful laws that have allowed innovation to flourish. Our laws encourage new businesses and don't overregulate. Innovation is the linchpin of the U.S. economy—and the internet is our generation's gift to humanity. It provides immediate access to information, commerce, and employment opportunities to people all over the world. It's important to protect these crown jewels of the U.S. economy.

By attacking tech, we're tearing down the framework that

nurtured the ninja innovations that make companies from around the world want to set up shop and grow here. Let's not forget that, according to *Fortune* magazine in 2018, the three most admired companies in the world—Apple, Amazon, and Alphabet—are tech companies.[16]

Washington is focused primarily on the big players, but these issues affect companies large and small. In the wake of this techlash, let's not forget the facts. The technology available to us today can connect us and help us like never before. Anyone living near a crisis area who updates their status on Facebook's Safety Check can let their loved ones know they're safe. A small business owner is able to scale her business on Amazon and reach customers around the world. Workers using sharing economy platforms such as Postmates, Thumbtack, or TaskRabbit have greater flexibility and the option to do what they do best, whether it's fixing appliances, making delivery runs, or building furniture. These services have given meaningful and reliable work to hundreds of thousands of veterans, retirees, and stay-at-home parents. They have delighted caregivers and allowed people to have meaningful interactions in ways that serve our human need for connection.

We've seen over and over how a thoughtful policy approach to disruptive innovation can result in economic growth and job creation. By neglecting or throttling emerging technology and services, we wind up ceding our ninja advantage, instead playing catch-up to other nations.

As discussed in Chapter 5, the inadequate federal policy on drones is a perfect example. As connected technology drove the usefulness and popularity of consumer drones—U.S. sales grew about 250 percent from 2013 to 2014, another 150 percent in

2015, then doubled again in 2016—exponentially more people were flying drones. But consumers had little guidance on how to pilot their drones safely. And with no federal policy framework to follow—no rules, no guidelines—companies looking to test their drone technologies in the United States turned to other countries instead.

To the U.S. government's credit, once it recognized drones' potential to deliver meaningful public and economic benefits, it engaged the private sector. A partnership between the Federal Aviation Administration (FAA) and drone industry groups produced and promoted the "Know Before You Fly" campaign to educate consumers. The FAA lowered the barriers to commercial use of drones, including the 2018 approval of an integration pilot program to connect public entities and municipalities with cutting-edge drone technology companies such as AT&T, Flirtey, and Google. While we can do more on the federal policy front to help the industry advance, the United States has responded and compensated for its late start. For example, the FAA's Integration Pilot Program gives state and local governments an opportunity to partner with private sector entities to safely integrate drones across the country.

We will fully realize the benefits of drones only with a smart government approach to emerging technology—one that balances safety and innovation, encourages a partnership between the public and private sectors, and recognizes the role of technology to power our economic engine.

The same is true for self-driving cars. We discussed their potential to revolutionize road safety and boost the economy in Chapter 5. For consumers to enjoy the full benefits of this technology, we need a unified approach from big stakeholders—

automakers, consumer welfare groups, disability advocates, and organized labor—to make self-driving vehicles on our roads a reality. Self-driving policy is on the right track. Department of Transportation secretary Elaine Chao understands the unique challenges and benefits of self-driving technology. In 2018, she released revised guidelines for self-driving vehicles to eliminate unnecessary hurdles for the technology. And industry leaders Ford and Daimler, Uber and Lyft, Waymo, and others are part of CTA's Self-Driving Vehicles Working Group, working together to help educate consumers and policymakers about the benefits of self-driving technologies. But we need strong federal legislation that unifies policymakers to support this flourishing technology. A patchwork approach, where self-driving vehicles are legal in different forms in different stages, will frustrate innovation.

Keys to a Smooth Transition

To realize this vision of a seamless, innovation-friendly regulatory environment, we need cooperation among government, industry, and consumers. The good news is we've done it before. In *Ninja Innovation*, I wrote at length about the global transition from analog to high-definition TV (HDTV). To recap: In the late 1980s, there were a few different directions TV might have gone in. Japan jumped out of the gate, rolling out the first HD system (an analog system) in 1989. The United States was the first to go digital. And Europe pushed a two-step transition. As we work through the challenges of ninja innovations like drones and self-driving cars, it strikes me that the U.S. approach to the television transition is a great model for achieving the balance we need from industry and government leaders. Three constants are needed for a smooth transition to a potentially disruptive new technology: strong leadership, shared goals, and consumer education.

Strong leadership. Good leadership during periods of disruption is a balancing act. Sid Topol mastered the unified approach during the transition. Sid headed up our association's Advanced Television Committee—a group of industry leaders committed to making the shift from analog to HDTV. Topol began every meeting by listing the areas with group consensus. He did the same at the end of each meeting, adding any new points of agreement. This seemed tedious at first, but slowly I realized that by emphasizing all we had in common, Sid gave us a solid foundation on which to build new ideas.

Former FCC chairman Richard Wiley, who led the Advisory Committee on Advanced Television Services, was another extremely effective leader. Although dealing with a variety of different subcommittees, Chairman Wiley expertly balanced the need to keep policymakers in the loop without bogging them down in the industry-level discussions. Although he was a volunteer, he inspired a tremendous and ultimately successful effort with his dedication and focus on our shared national goal.

Shared goals. The goal of government and the tech industry with advanced television was simple, but incredibly challenging: to develop the greatest TV system in the world that would also meet the particular needs of U.S. consumers. Japan beat us to the punch on HDTV, and many leaders wanted us to adopt their system (with a few tweaks). But we knew we could do better, and with one voice, we pushed hard for that vision. The result not only eclipsed Japan's system in terms of quality and flexibility, but also showcased the importance of a light, nimble, and cooperative regulatory approach to innovation.

Europe was struggling with which approach to use around the same time. But instead of letting the consumers choose what kind of viewing experience they preferred, European regulators enacted a low-quality standard for broadcast digital TV. Unsurprisingly, European viewers rejected this standard in favor of HDTV's high-resolution picture offered by satellite. This highlighted the importance of allowing innovators the freedom to create the best possible product for consumers while fostering a collaborative relationship between government and industry.

Consumer education. People won't buy a product if they don't understand how to use it or how it will improve their lives. We made it a priority to develop clear messaging around HDTV, from videos to websites to FAQs. These materials explained to consumers the benefits of HDTV and made the transition as easy and appealing as possible. We also spent a good deal of time educating legislators and other policymakers, making sure every member of Congress could see, feel, hear, touch, and understand the benefits of the technology.

These same ingredients will guide our transition to a ninja future of robotics and self-driving vehicles. Strong leadership will ensure an industry-led, national approach to balancing risks and benefits instead of a patchwork approach that frustrates everyone. Well-defined national goals—such as reducing traffic fatalities by a certain date, not just a vague desire to "make roads safer"—will challenge stakeholders to work together to overcome obstacles. Communicating a clear vision of the benefits of disruptive technology in terms of safety, security, and opportunity will help convince consumers to come along for the ride.

The success of innovation in the United States isn't due to geography or good fortune or what we eat for breakfast. We are flourishing because, again and again, our culture, our constitution, and our policymakers generally favor a light-touch policy approach that ultimately supports progress and disruption over the status quo. In other words, it's not too hot, and not too cold—it's just right. It's what has made America the world's best place for entrepreneurs to bring extraordinary new ideas to the public.

New innovations will always bring new challenges, and powerful incumbent industries will always beg for government protection from new competitors. Government regulation should never be an "unknown." Instead, by addressing new technologies with a smart, balanced regulatory approach, governments allow business leaders to invest time and resources into growing their companies, creating high-paying new jobs, and developing new products and services that will, in turn, create even more jobs and improve lives.

Pro-innovation policies are America's secret sauce. They have allowed ninja innovators to develop the world's most vibrant technology economy and immeasurably enrich lives. They will allow future ninjas to do things we can't yet imagine. So let's resist cries to stop progress. Let's double down on innovation.

CHAPTER 8

NINJA NATIONS

INNOVATION IS THE ENGINE BEHIND the American Dream. Looking around the world, it's easy to spot which countries are cut from similar cloth. In nations where governments are open to new ideas, where people enjoy freedom, and where environmental stewardship is a priority, human progress thrives. Openness to innovation is a determining factor in a country's growth and stability, in large part because it boosts the economy and provides future generations with the jobs they want. Graduates entering the workforce today don't necessarily want to stay in the factory jobs of past generations. The paradigm of success has evolved along with the internet economy. But where are the best places for ninja innovators to harness their creativity and curiosity and start new businesses for the ninja future?

I am confident that no country embraces innovation and promotes the policies that drive it as fully as the United States. But as a firm believer in the value of metrics, I wanted to put that belief to the test. So in 2018, CTA launched the International Innovation Scorecard, which graded thirty-eight countries and the European Union across twelve criteria. And after hearing countries' interest and enthusiasm about our inaugural rankings, the 2019 International Scorecard became even broader and more ambitious, examining national policies that affect innovation in over sixty countries.

The International Scorecard gauges countries' policies on a host of critical issues, ranging from broadband connectivity and cost, to whether governments are welcoming or restricting disruptive technologies, to taxes, to the environment. But the International Scorecard also evaluates countries from a uniquely American perspective in areas that are indispensable to the United States' global leadership in innovation: diversity, immigrants as a share of national population, and freedom of thought and expression.

In that first analysis in 2018, I fully expected the United States to outperform every other nation. And the United States *did* earn a spot in the top tier of thirteen countries considered Innovation Champions. But to my surprise, the United States did not earn the highest overall grade, but instead came in with only the fifth-highest total score. The top honor went to Finland, buoyed by blazing fast broadband speeds, a bounty of highly skilled workers, and policies that support drones and sharing economy services.

Finland and the United States are not alone at the top. Today more countries than ever are positioned to realize the benefits of innovation through their own nation's successes and the collective progress of the world. And several countries stand out for their unique ninja strategies to promote innovation.

France

I first visited France in 1991 and spoke to a group of European technologists about the future of television, arguing that Europe should listen to consumers and adopt the best system available at the time: high-definition television (HDTV). From that first trip, although I disagreed with some of the French government policies, I fell in love with the French culture and people. I admire France, particularly its technology leadership and innovative spirit, and have come to see France as a country that in the past has struggled to achieve its potential.

In 2013's *Ninja Innovation*, I critiqued the French government as risk-averse, always looking backward and "unwilling to change." I've criticized the French government's rejection of English words into the French lexicon, labor laws that stifle innovation, and the government's insistence on quotas of French music and movies. I was part of the successful resistance by American tech executives to French president Nicolas Sarkozy's 2011 effort to get Western governments to agree on the need for increased government control and regulation of the internet.

I maintained then that France had the essential ingredients for innovation but lacked the attitude and political will to succeed as a ninja nation. This from a nation that patented cinema, created the supersonic Concorde jet, and derives most of its energy from nuclear power—three forward-thinking initiatives. France also has a large cadre of highly trained engineers and magnificently marries technology and style: The tech from French innovators we see every year at CES just looks, well, cool.

In speaking to groups around the world, I used France as an

example of a "lost opportunity"—an innovative country stifled by government policies. My surefire audience laugh line was to remind them that the word *entrepreneur* derived from the French . . . but so did the word *bureaucrat*.

So I was more than a little surprised when in 2014, shortly after *Ninja Innovation* reached bestseller status, I was asked to gather a few American executives to meet with France's minister of the economy Emmanuel Macron and minister of state for digital affairs Axelle Lemaire while I was in Paris for a CTA board meeting. What an amazing opportunity! I gathered Boingo CEO David Hagan, Starpower cofounder Dan Pidgeon, VOXX chairman John Shalam, and VOXX president and CEO Pat Lavelle to join me, along with our international director, John T. Kelley. We met the ministers at the hotel where we were hosting a mini-CES event—CES Unveiled Paris—and used the opportunity to invite both ministers to attend our event the next day.

Our meeting focused on what France could do to become a more innovative country. Macron asked questions, listened, and took notes. He came to our Unveiled event the next day, and I had the privilege of connecting him with many French entrepreneurs. It was immediately evident that he was a friend to innovation—so I invited him to attend CES 2015 in Las Vegas a few months later.

Macron kept his word and attended CES. As he toured the CES floor, he was struck by the palpable energy and enthusiasm, and the gathering of the smallest and largest companies all in one place, showcasing their innovations. At that point there were 117 French companies exhibiting, including 69 in Eureka Park—the area of the show floor dedicated to startups.

The next fall, Macron attended our CES Paris event once again. His press gaggle grew, and so did his time and engagement with exhibitors. His passion for tech was clear, and after our event, he was kind enough to invite a few of us to lunch in his office. He was charming and forthright about French economic challenges but solicitous about solutions. He acknowledged the obstacles the French government had placed upon the business community and seemed to recognize that for France to again lead in innovation, government must step out of the way.

By 2016, Macron was the most popular politician in France. He returned to CES Las Vegas in January. In addition to touring the show floor, he spoke on a panel about global innovation (as discussed in greater length in Chapter 7). Macron's presence at CES lent a huge international media focus on French innovation, and France received extensive press coverage. And because of his leadership, the number of French exhibitors at CES grew. Coverage of Macron's trip to CES was so pervasive that many French people I meet recall it as a defining moment for the future of France.

Macron's pro-innovation stance captured the hearts and minds of French citizens, and in May 2017 he was elected president of France. I believe his visibility at CES shifted the global perception of France from stuffy and bureaucratic to young and innovative and helped propel Macron to his new post. He demonstrated his own disruptive innovation by creating a new party, En Marche!, which immediately attracted millions of followers. Using the momentum of his mandate to change, he recruited several supporters from his new party to run as candidates for the national legislature. In 2018, more than 50 percent of the legislature were La République En Marche! members.[1]

With a supportive legislature behind him, President Macron acted quickly. He eliminated the asset tax, slashed the personal tax, and set a timetable for reducing corporate taxes. Next he whittled away at the plethora of stifling rules that restrict employers from making changes in their workforce in response to market conditions. The early results have been positive. In 2017, the French economy grew a faster-than-expected 2 percent.[2] And CES 2018 hosted more than 5,400 French attendees and more than 340 French exhibitors, including 278 companies in Eureka Park—nearly double the number of French startups at CES 2016.

France also has a new home base for its own entrepreneurs. In 2017, Macron helped launch Station F, a massive startup incubator housed in an unused train station in Paris. The incubator is the pet project of Xavier Niel, "the godfather of French tech." Former president François Hollande, Macron's former boss, has even been working at Station F part-time.

In 2018, Macron's administration released a plan to position France as a leader in artificial intelligence, harnessing the massive amounts of data collected by France's state-run systems, including health care. Macron told WIRED magazine he had an "aha" moment about the value of AI after seeing it in action on the CES show floor and understanding its benefits, particularly in health care. "A few years ago, I went to CES. I was very impressed by some of these companies. I had with me some French companies, but I discovered U.S., Israeli and other companies operating in the same field," he said. "Innovation that artificial intelligence brings into healthcare systems can totally change things: with new ways to treat people, to prevent various diseases, and a way—not to replace the doctors—but to reduce the potential risk."[3]

Macron's focus on innovation and the future has made him a world leader. I saw this firsthand in April 2018 when I sat in the gallery of the U.S. Congress as he addressed a special joint session. Dozens of times he inspired me and the partisan audience to come together and applaud, stand, and cheer his vision of the importance of our shared fundamental values. The intersection of innovation and our values is reflected in these lines:

> *I believe in democracy. Many of our forebears were slain for the cause of freedom and human rights. With the great inheritance they gave us comes the responsibility to continue their mission in this new century and to preserve the perennial values handed to us and assure that today's unprecedented innovations in science and technology remain in the service of liberty and in the preservation of our planet for the next generations.*[4]

Macron may be the world leader who best understands the value of entrepreneurship, innovation, the certainty and importance of disruption, and the government role in encouraging innovation, both legally and symbolically. He represents the politics of hope over fear. He supports new business models and investment in technology—policies on which the French and global technology industries can thrive.

France in the Scorecard

France is an Innovation Leader in our International Innovation Scorecard, but it is still hamstrung by overregulation. The French workforce is better educated than most other nations: 45 percent of workers in France earn their wages from highly skilled professions, and nearly one-third of all degrees awarded in France go to STEM graduates.

However, the sharing economy has little support from French regulators, with strict government rules on both ride-sharing and short-term rentals. In 2015, French authorities suspended UberPOP, a ride-sharing program that allowed drivers without professional licenses to accept passengers, deeming it an illegal taxi operation. In 2016, a French court ordered Uber to pay $900,000 in fines for the infraction. French startup BlaBlaCar—which allows drivers to carpool with other passengers—has a strong following in the country, but doesn't serve the same market as ride-sharing since its focus is mainly on drives longer than fifty miles.

Similar regulatory roadblocks obstruct short-term rental hosts. This is especially true in Paris, Airbnb's single largest city market. After a push by the hotel industry to tighten rules on rental sites, Parisian regulators ruled that rental owners must register their property with the local town hall. In 2017, they threatened to take Airbnb to court if it didn't remove listings by rental owners who hadn't followed the registration rules.

As Paris makes a push to raise its tech profile and

welcomes increased attention from global players like Google and Facebook, another French city is making a name for itself on the world stage. About 190 miles southwest of the French capital, Angers is forging ahead with smart city technology, led by forward-thinking mayor Christophe Béchu. The city is part of the French Tech program, which partners startups, investors, and engineers to bolster ninja innovation, and hosts the WISE'Factory, an 8,000-square-foot hub for design, development, and testing of smart devices. In 2017, Angers hosted the World Electronics Forum, an annual gathering of tech leaders to explore the future of the electronics industry. Cité de l'Objet Connecté, a group of eighteen companies focused on dramatically reducing the production time for a wide range of smart devices, is also based in the city. The program pairs startups with other local players to ease the path from design to integration and, eventually, the launch of IoT new products.

The Netherlands

Prince Constantijn of the Netherlands is modest and reserved, but passionate about Dutch innovation. He may be royalty, but he also is a techie. He serves as special envoy to StartupDelta, a public-private partnership that works with innovation hubs, the government, and startups to grow the Dutch tech sector and attract global exposure.

Since 2017, Prince Constantijn has led a Dutch delegation to CES in Las Vegas. And in 2018, he helped create a Dutch presence in Eureka Park—more than fifty startups participated. A few examples: 20face is a facial recognition platform that can identify faces in low lighting, in different poses, and at different image resolutions; Incision offers virtual tools for surgeons to practice and prepare for operations; and Lightyear is developing a self-charging electric car.

The Netherlands is a nation of ninja innovators across sectors—bright minds that are solving some of the world's toughest challenges and sharing their ideas with global audiences. That's why we reached out to Prince Constantijn and Startup-Delta to launch a CES Unveiled event in the Netherlands. CES Unveiled events are held in tech hot spots across the globe and provide a gathering place for companies, tech experts, media, government officials, and industry leaders. Thanks to the eagerness and drive of Dutch innovators, CES Unveiled Amsterdam was our most successful first-time Unveiled event.

The unique character and history of the Dutch people have made this nation fertile ground for the ninja future. The borders of what is now the Netherlands shifted through the Middle Ages, but by the mid-1600s the country blossomed as a seafaring trade hub. The Dutch East India Company was the first company to officially be listed on a stock exchange.[5] In 1609, on behalf of the Netherlands, Henry Hudson explored and laid claim to New Amsterdam—what is now New York City.[6] The Dutch attitude of openness and innovation is embedded in the ethos of New York and has helped make both the Big Apple and the Netherlands cradles of innovation.

Recognizing that it's hard to do business in a language that less than 1 percent of the world population speaks, nine in ten Dutch people speak English as a second language.[7] They also have a strong libertarian and practical bent. Their legalization and regulation of marijuana and prostitution is designed to let citizens make their own choices, with government guardrails, so all interests are protected.

The Dutch have long been ninja innovators. Royal Dutch Shell—the eleventh-largest public company in the world as of June 2018, according to *Forbes*[8]—has harnessed big data analytics to streamline its oil extraction processes and boost sustainability.[9] Serving more than 48 million clients across more than 40 countries,[10] banking giant ING has led the exploration of blockchain applications.[11] And technology company Philips, which employs more than 115,000 people worldwide, is diving deep into health tech—everything from diagnostic imaging, to patient monitoring, to consumer health and home care.[12]

Health tech is top of mind for future ninjas in the Netherlands. Dutch tech business trade group FME is strategically focused on health technology as a way of offering lower-cost, better-quality health care. At a May 2018 meeting in their Zoetermeer headquarters, FME president Ineke Dezentjé Hamming and operational director Arjel Woudstra shared with me their practical view of how technology can assist the aging process through remote monitoring, which lets people live at home rather than incur the costs of assisted living facilities. They also have a plan to meet the Netherlands' looming technology worker shortage through training programs.

And in The Hague, future ninjas are studying ways to harness innovation to create a more peaceful world. I spent a few days in 2018 in the hundred-year-old Peace Palace, a place that has hosted many discussions among global leaders trying to build a more peaceful and connected world. Our meeting focused on safeguarding the role of internet as a tool for social engagement and holding bad actors like cybercriminals liable.

Through this delightful combination of practices, attitudes, and laws, the Dutch have distinguished themselves as entrepreneurs and innovators. And so it was no surprise that the Netherlands is among the world's Innovation Champions in CTA's 2018 Global Scorecard. Its high levels of diversity, freedom, fast internet, skilled labor force, R&D spending, high startup rate—plus six unicorn companies—gave it top-tier status in our rankings.

Netherlands in the Scorecard

The Netherlands' startup sector continues to expand, pushing the country's annual new business entry rate to 5.34 per 1,000 people. The country has produced six unicorns, behind only the United Kingdom and Germany among EU countries. The Dutch workforce is also highly skilled, with more than 47 percent in that category, and roughly 20 percent of all Dutch graduates hold degrees in STEM fields. This combination of breakneck business growth and a skilled workforce helped catapult the Netherlands to Champion status in our 2018 Scorecard—the highest of four possible rankings a country can earn.[13]

The Dutch government enthusiastically supports developing self-driving vehicles, citing the potential for tech to reduce traffic and improve safety. Government leaders opened public roads to test self-driving vehicles without a driver present, as long as a human can take control remotely.

Amsterdam may be most famous as a major port and tourist destination, with plenty of startups and a focused effort on becoming a smart city. Named the European Capital of Innovation in 2016 by the European Commission, Amsterdam has countered a range of city-wide problems with cutting-edge solutions, from self-driving vehicles to the Internet of Things.

With water covering 50 percent of its cityscape, a self-driving boat system known as the ROBOAT will bring a fully automated fleet of boats to the canals of Amsterdam. Designed to solve delivery and transportation problems, the boats can deliver packages and people and will eventually function as infrastructure to create on-demand, temporary bridges across canals. In and out of city waterways, the Things Network project, which launched in 2015, will connect the city and its citizens via a low-bandwidth web of sensors throughout Amsterdam. A pilot project to test the network placed sensors in boats around the city and, if the vessel began taking on water, the sensor notified a boat maintenance company to repair the leak. The network's supporters see future applications within city sanitation systems and as a bicycle location network.

Israel

If you define innovation by number of patents per person, Israel is one of the most innovative countries in the world.

What's their secret? Israelis have ninja innovation in their DNA. When you're living under the constant threat of conflict, a business risk is not nearly as intimidating. And this environment has produced a remarkable determination within the people of Israel to succeed—and indeed thrive.

In many ways, the ninja spirit in Israel and the United States are alike. Both countries have been built on a high percentage of immigrants, a culture of risk-taking and asking "why?," a focus on education, and free-market systems. Nearly half of Israelis hold tertiary degrees, making Israel the third-most-educated country in the world, behind only Canada and Japan.[14]

Israelis take their national existence and security seriously. They have a mandatory military service for most of the population. With that shared common experience and sense of mission, they believe and invest heavily in the defense industry. And the defense industry, of course, is huge in Israel, with spillover effects across other sectors.

For example, Tel Aviv–based startup Beyond Verbal developed an app that can recognize emotion in a voice. This and other technologies could be used to identify deception in our airports and at our borders. Other Israeli startups develop products with multiple use cases, too. Lishtot, headquartered in Jerusalem, has developed a product that detects contamination such as *E. coli* and lead in drinking water. And Qlone, created by Yokne'am Illit–based EyeCue Vision Technologies, is an app that lets you scan any object using your smartphone to create a 3-D model that you can then modify. These three startups were among Israel's four dozen exhibitors at CES 2018.

And Israeli tech innovation is spilling over into the United States. As of 2018, more than 350 startups with Israeli founders had opened offices in New York, including big names such as coworking space WeWork and ride-sharing app Vial.[15] So many bright ideas are coming out of Israel that startups are looking west for funding.

Much credit for Israel's entrepreneurial success can be attributed to former Israeli president and prime minister Shimon Peres. During his incredible fifty-five-year political career, he served three terms as prime minister, with stints as foreign minister, finance minister, and deputy defense minister. And he served as Israel's president from 2007 to 2014.

Peres spent much of his life advocating for peace. In fact, he shared the Nobel Peace Prize in 1994 with Palestinian leader Yasser Arafat and Israel's then prime minister Yitzhak Rabin for his contributions to the Oslo Accords. He founded the Peres Center for Peace, which helped the cause of peace by encouraging Jews and Arabs to share ideas and funded health-care services to Palestinians.

I had the honor of meeting Peres twice. In 2014, thanks to Israeli high-tech entrepreneur and conference legend Joseph "Yossi" Vardi, I joined several technology executives in discussing why Israelis and Americans lead the world in innovation. While Vardi joked about Jewish mothers being the driving force of many successful innovators, I talked about our immigrant nations' can-do attitude and other factors I'd discussed in *Ninja Innovation*. Peres agreed but said that I was overlooking the unique nature of the Jewish people, who always want to improve the lives of those around them.

And in June 2016, three months before Peres's death, I joined my wife and members of the CTA executive board in his office for what was the most exceptional meeting of my life.

His voice barely above a whisper, Peres mesmerized us as he described how innovation and technology can and should change the world. His guidance? Invest only in things that improve people's lives.

Peres noted that India and China rarely criticize Israel, as both have benefited enormously from Israel freely sharing its breakthroughs and innovations in agriculture and irrigation. As such, he said he'd never met an anti-Semite in China or India. He said innovation and technology are breaking down national borders and the limits of politics. He challenged us to do all we could to focus our efforts on using innovation and technology as a force for good, particularly for the billions of poor people in the world. We left exhilarated, motivated, and amazed at his wisdom, clarity, vision, and empathy. I have met many political leaders, but I've never met another leader who exuded such basic decency.

Today, my good fortune in meeting Shimon Peres looms even larger as his vision inspires me to do all I can to encourage innovation, as it will solve the world's most fundamental problems: namely, human problems.

Israel in the Scorecard

When it comes to innovation, Israel rivals much larger countries in measures of R&D spending and general entrepreneurial talent. Israel spends more on R&D than any other developed country, investing more than 4 percent of the country's GDP each year. And that investment is paying dividends: Israel has produced five startups worth

more than $1 billion. And with a new business entry rate
of 3.11 for every 1,000 people, it earns near-top marks in
entrepreneurial activity.

Roughly half of Israel's workforce works in highly skilled
jobs. That level of talent puts Israeli tech on the map, and
the country notes a handful of impressive exits. Google
acquired navigation app Waze for $966 million, and Cisco
bought mobile networking startup Intucell for $475 million.
Both companies thrived thanks to Tel Aviv's healthy startup
ecosystem, which placed sixth on a ranking of global startup
ecosystems—only a few slots behind Silicon Valley (in fact,
a swath of Israel along the coastal plain has earned the
nickname Silicon Wadi).

Tel Aviv has long been a hot spot for ninja innovation.
Airobotics, which makes automated drones for a variety
of industrial applications, was founded in Tel Aviv in 2014.
Since then, the company raised more than $30 million and
its drones have deployed for surveying and mapping at an
Australian mining site.

Another notable exit: In 2017, Intel acquired Jerusalem-
based self-driving vehicle tech company Mobileye for a
record-breaking $15.3 billion. But despite that homegrown
success, self-driving vehicles have been slow to the starting
line in Israel. Authorities closed off a section of roadways
for testing, but developers are still forbidden from testing in
real-world conditions on public streets.

China

In 1978 China initiated major economic reforms which produced seismic changes throughout the nation and which reverberated across the globe. China rose from a poor country to one of the world's two superpowers. More than half of Chinese residents now live in cities,[16] and Chinese consumption increased sixteen-fold between 1978 and 2015.[17] By 2017, at least one hundred Chinese cities had more than one million residents.[18]

China's economy will soon be the largest in the world. (In fact, if you measure by purchasing power rather than dollars, it is already the world's largest economy.)[19] One crucial economic reform was a shift from controlled central planning to more open trade and investment. In this way, China became the world's manufacturer. Using a series of five-year plans to set specific strategies and goals, its leaders increasingly pushed the country forward.

Ancient China was an original ninja innovator, responsible for inventing or perfecting many basic elements of modern life, such as restaurants and printing.[20] Over the centuries, however, that changed. China built a reputation not for innovation, but for stealing the inventions of other nations. A few recent examples: British carmaker Jaguar Land Rover sued a Chinese company for allegedly copying one of its models, another Chinese company was successfully sued for creating knockoff Scotch whiskey, and a German firm settled with Chinese firms accused of stealing truck designs. China's innovation economy flagged—until recently. As I heard a Chinese official tell a small Washington audience in 2017, "We've led the world for thousands of years, but for the last 200 years we have not invented anything. Now we are shifting to become the world's innovator."

And not a moment too soon. Dramatic changes in the workforce, the global economy, and the environment demand that the Chinese convert their economy from a manufacturing-based one to one driven by entrepreneurship and innovation.

The one-child policy in effect from 1980 to 2016 success-fully limited population growth, but it also produced a nation of only children. Each child grew up as the sole focus of up to six adults—two parents and four grandparents. The result was a highly educated, highly driven population, locked in com-petition with developing nations such as Malaysia, Indonesia, and Vietnam that were eager to grow their economies through low-cost manufacturing. Eventually, the one-child policy was lifted after a generation of parents and grandparents recognized a gender imbalance and gradually realized they needed more young people to care for them.[21] The scarcity of resources that originally prompted the policy also became less of an issue as the economy surged.

Another driving force behind China's shift toward an innovation-based economy is the extreme air pollution caused by manufacturing. New coal-fired plants were opening up at a rate of about one per week.[22] China's air quality is so poor that roughly 17 percent of deaths each year are related to air pollution.[23] For many city-dwelling Chinese, the biggest daily frustrations are traffic congestion and air pollution. American citizens would never tolerate such poor air quality and would immediately vote new leaders into office if they had to fight through such high levels of pollution in everyday life. China has taken positive steps to reduce pollution, like imposing a nation-wide cap on coal use and requiring output controls on steel and aluminum smelters. But it has a long way to go. China received some of its lowest marks on the CTA International Innovation Scorecard for air and water quality.

With a shortage of workers, an increasingly educated work-force, a growing economy, competition from developing countries, and a real pollution problem, China's strategy to shift to an innovation economy makes good sense. And it's working. An early measure of this strategy's success was the number of patents issued between 2011 and 2015. The 2011 Five-Year Plan included a goal of 3.3 patents per 10,000 people.[24] China exceeded that goal, issuing 6.3 patents per 10,000 people. Although many of these patents were weak or merely variations on a theme, China has increasingly started producing more original technology. At our first CES Asia in 2015, Chinese companies had few products in emerging technologies. By CES Asia 2018, not only did these companies take up triple the amount of space, they also used that space to showcase hundreds of innovative products incorporating artificial intelligence and augmented and virtual reality.

Another indicator of China's success is its rapid growth in exports. According to the World Bank, China's share of high-tech exports grew from about 19 percent at the beginning of the century to more than 25 percent by 2016.[25] The country boasts great ports, an expansive high-speed train network, and world-leading companies including Tencent and Alibaba, which did not even exist a generation ago. The government intends to build on these triumphs: its "Made in China 2025" plan outlined its ambitions to lead the world in ten areas: information technology; numerical control tools and robotics; aerospace equipment; ocean engineering equipment and high-tech ships; railway equipment; energy-saving and new-energy vehicles; power equipment; new materials; medicine and medical devices; and agricultural machinery.[26]

China's domination-through-innovation quest relies on several tactics. The first is education. In 2013, 40 percent of Chinese college students majored in STEM—twice as high a percentage as in the United States.[27,28] In an attempt to change its image as a copycat nation, government leadership is embedding innovation as a national cultural value. Concluding that the rote, repetitive learning methods of the Chinese educational system did not produce creative thinkers, they sent students abroad to study at younger and younger ages. In 2017, more than 350,000 Chinese students were studying in the United States. (Before 1974, China sent no students to the United States.)[29]

But the Chinese also play hardball. Their government subsidizes certain strategic industries such as cars, electronics, machinery, and building materials. They sell below cost. They force technology transfer by companies wishing to do business in China. They use ambiguous laws to block, bar, take over, or expel successful foreign companies. They also aggressively recruit Chinese expatriates who are working in the United States or elsewhere, enticing them with large financial incentives to return to work in China.

These initiatives are not just an economic strategy. They're a political strategy to achieve global dominance through strategic economic investment. As Western nations pull back, China has invested heavily in Africa, Latin America, and the Middle

East. Countries such as Turkey are warmly embracing increased Chinese involvement in their economies.

The next generation will witness a battle between two different worldviews. The United States, Canada, Mexico, much of South America, Europe, Australia, New Zealand, and other strong democracies will join to promote individual liberty, access to the internet, democracy, choice in religion and marriage, privacy, freedom, and limited government. China and its growing allies will join together to focus on ensuring social harmony by restricting liberty, limiting choice of religion, marriage partners, and political parties, and blocking access to media and internet sites that contain different points of view.

China in the Scorecard

Home to the world's largest population and a rapidly developing tech market, China offers fertile testing grounds for innovative tech. But government rules have stunted some development. One of China's highest grades in the 2018 Scorecard was in "Human Capital," where it outpaced every other country except Japan for the percentage of degrees awarded in STEM fields. Almost half of all Chinese graduates earned a diploma from a STEM program. And as even more graduates earn science and engineering degrees, elsewhere in the country that talent is being put to use developing new tech—including self-driving vehicles.

Baidu's self-driving vehicle tech has already been tested on Beijing's roads, thanks to an unsanctioned ride through the city's streets by CEO Robin Li. Since then,

Beijing regulators have loosened some rules on the growing industry. The Beijing Municipal Transport Commission has said that, under specific conditions, certain roads will be open for self-driving-vehicle testing. Companies must register for temporary permission to test their vehicles on these roadways, and a human driver must be behind the wheel to take over in case something goes wrong. However, there are more severe restrictions in place for companies creating digital maps of Chinese roadways. Foreign companies are banned from developing the detailed maps necessary for a wider rollout of self-driving vehicles.

My money (and my heart) is on America. We have the world's finest secondary and graduate school system. We have vibrant arts and culture that inspire people across the globe. We have diversity that brings us energy and new ideas. We have the American attitude of never being satisfied, and always trying to do it better, faster, and more efficiently. And we have something no other nation has: fifty states—and thus fifty innovation laboratories—up and running across the land. Each works in unique ways to support local economies. Each has the potential to become the next hotbed of American innovation. Whether or not they succeed in becoming a magnet for future ninjas depends on the priorities and policies of each statehouse.

CHAPTER 9

AMERICAN NINJAS

OVER THE YEARS, I'VE OFTEN been asked by government leaders how to encourage innovation. I outlined many of my ideas on this topic in my 2010 book, *The Comeback: How Innovation Will Restore the American Dream*. It laid out a series of policies by which the United States could preserve and expand its position as a pro-innovation nation. I was thrilled to realize it had an impact.

The Comeback was read by influential policymakers and prompted discussions about issues ranging from strategic immigration reform to broadband policy to corporate tax rates. I even spotted former president Bill Clinton holding my book as he got into his car. As I was told by his travel mate that day, the global technologist and legendary Consumer Technology Hall of Famer Tom Campbell, the president even read a chapter as they drove along!

It's been gratifying to see some of the ideas I expressed come to fruition. Congress acted on and then-president Barack

Obama signed laws creating additional spectrum for broadband. We finalized the Panama, Colombia, and Korea free trade agreements. More recently, the Trump administration cut many unnecessary and burdensome rules on business and lowered the corporate tax rate—ideas I championed in *The Comeback*.

Other proposals have made progress but still have some hurdles to clear. We still need immigration reform, including increasing skilled immigration and reducing our immigration backlog. We need to ensure that federal money used for construction means we also lay broadband infrastructure. Still other seemingly rational ideas, such as increased government accountability and efficiency in spending, have lain dormant for years. And the situation has deteriorated on three issues I advocated for: Rather than reduce our national debt, it has more than doubled since 2009, increasing the burden on the next generation; we have continued to ignore our urgent need to invest in infrastructure; and we're backsliding on trade. More, we're seeing the United States pull back from leadership of international organizations, including the WTO, NATO, the G7, and the Global Compact on Migration, which have successfully guaranteed global postwar security.

As the federal government has become increasingly polarized and paralyzed, we have shifted our gaze to the states. In 2015, CTA launched the U.S. Innovation Scorecard to identify the U.S. states best promoting technological progress, creating jobs, and improving the quality of life for people nationwide. In the past year, several states established new guidelines for self-driving vehicles. Some, including Michigan and Pennsylvania, have opened their roads to testing and developing systems that will bring about a new wave of mobility, providing safe and unprecedented transportation options for the elderly and disabled. Others, including Connecticut and Massachusetts, have slammed on the brakes.

The rankings on our Innovation Scorecard encompass a state's scores in each of twelve quantitative and qualitative categories, including whether or not a state has a law prohibiting discrimination on the basis of sexual orientation and gender identity, the percentage of the population with an advanced degree, the amount of venture capital and R&D money spent, and the number of households with high-speed internet connections.

We've talked a lot about ninja innovators based in Silicon Valley—and there's no question it is the epicenter of innovation. The Bay Area has many key advantages, including phenomenal universities and massive amounts of venture capital. As a result, it is home to nearly eighty unicorn companies, according to PitchBook. Californians also are open to taking risks, and it shows. On the flip side, it's an incredibly expensive place to live and raise a family. A 2018 study from the real estate startup Open Listings found that the average tech worker at Apple would have to fork over one-third of his or her salary every month to afford a home in Cupertino, Apple's headquarters.[1] Housing prices are a huge barrier for many startups, who need to attract talent but can't afford to pay employees industry-leading wages.

The Innovation Scorecard confirms that ingenuity is by no means confined to the coasts. There are pockets of innovation in every corner of this country—from Seattle to Boston, Phoenix to Pittsburgh. Over a thousand tech companies are in CTA's backyard in Northern Virginia, where I sit on the

Northern Virginia Tech Council board of directors. Innovation thrives where leaders adopt forward-thinking attitudes, take a light-handed approach to regulation, and collaborate with businesses in crafting regulation to govern the emerging technologies that will revolutionize the way we move and interact with the world around us.

As AOL founder and entrepreneur evangelist Steve Case advocates, innovation can be anywhere—we just need to leverage each area's strengths. In addition to joining us to advocate for the Jobs Act, which allowed crowdsourcing for startups, Steve took his vision on the road and visited four American cities with his first "Rise of the Rest" roadshow in 2014. In each city he hosted a contest where local entrepreneurs pitched a panel of judges, with a chance to win a $100,000 grant to take their startup to the next level. That fall he expanded his tour to ten more cities. (By 2018, the tour had visited more than three dozen cities nationwide.)

I was thrilled to join this marvelous venture as a judge in Kansas City and was intrigued and delighted by the passion of the ten entrepreneurs who presented their ideas. I will never forget the dedication, vision, and moxie of the woman who believed she had a better alternative to household cleaners with her range of environmentally friendly cleaning products. Nor will I forget the intensity of the deliberation afterward. With Steve at the table, we tried to be deferential, since he was the one writing the $100,000 check. But Steve had too much respect for the judging process to force his views on any of us. It's this attitude, along with his contributions to entrepreneurship by supporting pro-innovation public policy and entrepreneurship across America, that prompted us to honor Steve with our 2015 Digital Patriots award.

In the end, we awarded the grant to an online visual search collaboration platform—a cross between a search engine and a social network. What I learned from that judging experience—and this is bolstered by our Scorecard—is that certain communities excel at certain things. For example, Kansas City is a top destination for women-owned businesses.[2] San Diego is a fantastic hub for biomedical research. Boston is a hub for robotics. And in the Washington, D.C., metro area, there's cutting-edge innovation, with Virginia being home to many cloud computing services and a huge chunk of internet traffic (according to a 2016 report, 70 percent of the world's Web traffic flows through Loudoun County, Virginia).[3] Nevada has become a home for drone testing and research because its climate—both physical and political—makes it hospitable to test runs. These clusters spring up around universities, areas of government investment, or geographic anomalies. So let's take a deeper dive into some unexpected innovation hubs across the United States.

Pittsburgh

Pittsburgh has been known historically as a steel town, but in today's tech-driven economy, its leadership has charted a new course. During his tenure as mayor, Bill Peduto has pushed a city-wide agenda that prioritizes opportunity for all residents and resiliency in the face of all challenges. Practically, that's meant city-wide integration of public services with technology, from a website that tracks snowplows via GPS to an app that allows citizens to communicate their needs and concerns to the 311-line office.

These innovations have catapulted Peduto onto the international scene: He has traveled to Geneva for a gathering of AI experts and to Milan for a Rockefeller Foundation–hosted summit on urban development and resilience. The city's openness to innovation also resulted in significant investment from ninja innovators in social media. Facebook and Google have opened offices in the city, and Carnegie Mellon partnered with seed investor Innovation Works to hold a venture capital fair for AI and robotics companies.

Entrepreneurship and the job market are booming as well, in conjunction with the statewide trend highlighted in the 2018 Innovation Scorecard: 100 jobs disappeared in Allegheny County between 2001 and 2008—the main county in the Pittsburgh metro area—but between 2008 and 2016, the county created 3,300 jobs.[4] And the city's future looks just as bright: Carnegie Mellon will soon offer the first undergraduate degree in AI available in the United States, ensuring a steady stream of graduates who will design the next generation of systems and services.

Boston

It's known as the Athens of America for its longtime dedication to academic excellence, but Boston's contributions to the ninja economy are just as significant. The city has become a hotspot for robotics innovation, so much so that robots can now be seen in restaurants. Thanks to a partnership between MIT robotics engineers and renowned chef Daniel Boulud, customers can benefit from the speed and skill of robot cooks, which can whip up a delicious meal in 180 seconds flat.[5]

Founded in 1990, iRobot has sold more than 20 million home robots, including the phenomenally successful Roomba robot vacuum, the Braava robot mop, and many other consumer robots. In 2018, iRobot had some 1,000 employees and was projected to exceed $1 billion in annual revenue.[6]

In 2018, I spent a day at iRobot's headquarters, twenty miles northwest of Boston. I was surprised to learn that more than fifty robotics-related companies had been created by former iRobot employees (Rethink Robotics, CyPhy Works, Owl Labs, to name a few), many of whom were in the room that day. iRobot founder and CEO Colin Angle is thrilled with his employees' success, and the mutual goodwill was palpable. Silicon Valley's tech star rose when HP employees left to start up companies like Intel. Apparently, iRobot is to robotics in Massachusetts what HP is for high tech in Silicon Valley.

With both exceptional universities and more than one hundred robotics companies creating autonomous cars, automation robotics, drones, and home robotics, Massachusetts is a nerve center of robotic innovation. But every robotics CEO I spoke with agreed that their biggest challenge is finding the trained programmers and engineers needed to make robots work: In other words, they need future ninjas. Having tens of thousands of such jobs open should send a clear message to parents and educators: Push your schools to start teaching the skills growing industries need.

Boston is fertile ground for established companies, too, due to the area's wealth of talent and expertise. Thanks in part to partnerships with Panasonic and Amazon, MassRobotics—a nonprofit robotics organization dedicated to developing and deploying robots and smart devices—is expanding its coworking space so innovators have the resources to create game-changing robotics solutions. And Amazon, as the Innovation Scorecard noted, is expanding its presence in the region, too: The company plans to add an additional 2,000 tech jobs and develop its Boston Tech Hub by 2021.[7]

Dallas

We all know that everything is bigger in Texas. Business in Dallas is booming: Twenty-two of the city's businesses are on the Fortune 500 list.[8] Increasingly, however, the city is realizing that small organizations can have a big impact, too. Steve Case stopped in Dallas on his Rise of the Rest road trip to urge the state to focus on its small companies and startups. Our 2018 U.S. Innovation Scorecard revealed that between 2011 and 2016, companies in Texas with 50 employees or fewer created a net 74.56 jobs for every 1,000 people.[9] When you consider that the state only receives 2 percent[10] of the nation's venture capital, that level of entrepreneurial activity is a significant accomplishment—and, as Steve pointed out, a significant opportunity for investors.

Texas has made a concerted effort in recent years to entice tech talent and businesses out of California. And it's making a play to best the Golden State when it comes to self-driving vehicles. In 2017, Texas governor Greg Abbott signed a bill specifically authorizing testing on public roads without a driver in the car. That same year, self-driving shuttles debuted in Arlington, just outside Dallas.

Also on the outskirts of Dallas, the STEM Center of Excellence at Camp Whispering Cedars has developed a program to train our future ninja workforce. Through a partnership with the Girl Scouts of Northeast Texas, the camp promotes STEM educations for girls in K–12. The camp is designed to prepare girls and young women to meet a booming demand for workers in STEM fields. The ninety-two-acre campus is equipped with a range of features, each designed to tie into a STEM field. A ropes course will be used to teach physics, and an archery range will offer real-world examples of motion and energy concepts. "If we don't prepare girls now for these jobs, they will miss out on these opportunities to reach their full potential for themselves and our community," said Jennifer Bartkowski, CEO of Girl Scouts of Northeast Texas.

Washington, D.C.

I get a unique glimpse into the groundbreaking tech coming out of our nation's capital from my vantage point in Arlington, and I'm constantly impressed by the creativity and ingenuity of our local tech companies. No matter the size or sector, these companies—and the talent behind them—make the most of all that the Virginia, Maryland, and D.C. area has to offer.

One of the most delightful startups in the area is Phone-2Action, a company that links citizens with government representatives. Founded by Dr. Ximena Hartsock—an immigrant from Chile and former member of the executive cabinet of Washington, D.C., mayor Adrian Fenty—and Texas native and serial entrepreneur Jeb Ory, Phone2Action is a "mobile- and social-centric platform" that connects citizens with elected officials and allows them "to speak up on issues important to them in order to effect change."

Several studies, including some of our own research, show a tech-friendly attitude at work in the D.C. metro area. With policy frameworks that help entrepreneurs and innovators flourish, both Maryland and Virginia are "Innovation Champions" in CTA's Innovation Scorecard. Both states earn high marks for their robust tech workforce, fast internet speeds, openness to new business models, high number of STEM graduates, and strong job and small business growth.

At CES 2018 we welcomed three dozen companies from the D.C. area, representing a wide array of industries. Among them were Alarm.com, a smart home security system based in Tysons Corner, Virginia; Fret Zealot, an Arlington-based startup featuring an electric guitar that teaches you how to play through lights that cover the guitar's frets; and LifeFuels, a personalized drink device company hailing from Reston.

I'm proud of the innovations the D.C. metro area brings to CES and to consumers around the world. Our region has all the elements for innovative success—excellent universities, an educated workforce, and smart, pro-innovation policymakers. Without a doubt, the D.C. area is prime real estate for ninja innovators looking for a place to launch.

Chicago

Most of us don't think of the Windy City as a city of startups or a hub for innovation—but recent numbers prove otherwise. One organization surveyed the ten most profitable exits (either by selling a company or through an IPO) between 2012 and 2017 in major cities (excepting the Bay Area).[11] Chicago produced a whopping $14.9 billion, beating out New York, Seattle, and Boston. Well-known digital economy players GrubHub and Groupon were founded here.

What's more, the startups that flourish here cover the full spectrum of industries and sectors—from Machino, an online platform that allows companies to purchase previously used industrial equipment; to ShipBop, a shipping startup that supports digital commerce through logistics and management; to Mac&Mia, a service that lets a personal stylist pick clothes for kids. Add great ideas like these to a well-educated workforce—as the 2018 Innovation Scorecard points out, 12.7 percent of the state's residents over age twenty-four have advanced degrees [12]— and a new Apple-sponsored program in Chicago public schools that will teach kids to code, and you have a recipe for continued success in the Midwest.

Like Dallas and other innovation hubs, Chicago is also investing in education programs that give students a jump-start in tech fields. The University of Illinois Discovery Partners Institute, a research center serving two thousand students and faculty members, has partnered with the University of Chicago, Northwestern University, and the Israeli government. The $1.2 billion center lets students conduct research while working for local startups. Apple has also announced a city-wide rollout of its "Everyone Can Code" program to teach Swift, its programming language, to high school students. The effort is a partnership with the mayor's office, Chicago Public Schools, City Colleges of Chicago, and a handful of nonprofits and private businesses. The program also includes after-school coding clubs for students, which will provide instruction in designing and prototyping new apps.

Phoenix

What originally started as a hashtag (#YesPHX) to discuss Arizona startups on Twitter gradually became an entire movement to give those startups the resources and community support they needed to thrive. From coworking spaces to weekly open meetings such as One Million Cups, where local startups pitch their ideas to local founders, to annual events like PHX Startup Week, future ninjas will have a wealth of opportunities to grow, connect, and create.

The city benefits from strong state laws that have consistently favored new business models and innovations, welcoming drones, self-driving cars, ride-sharing, and short-term rentals. Maybe that's why companies including Uber and Yelp are growing their presence there: Innovation is hot in this vibrant city of visionary thinkers and doers.

Detroit

The city where I live is not one that often gets recognition for its innovation—not anymore. Motor City is now often viewed as the capital of an industrial auto wasteland, far from cutting-edge or pioneering. But I'm delighted to report the perception is in this case far from the reality.

Major auto companies such as General Motors and Ford are making significant strides in tech-driven mobility solutions. GM plans to make self-driving cars a reality on the road by 2019.[13] Ford, based just outside Detroit in Dearborn, has teamed up with Qualcomm to create a cloud-based platform that will allow our cars to interact digitally with nearby bikes, stoplights, and more. And down the road in Ann Arbor, MCity is a closed-circuit track for testing connected and automated vehicles, featuring sixteen acres of roads and traffic infrastructure, including traffic signals, sidewalks, simulated buildings, and streetlights.

But it's not just the large and historic auto companies that are thriving in Detroit. Smaller companies are flourishing as well. The number of venture-backed startups grew 50 percent between 2014 and 2017—and this growth is representative of a statewide trend.[14] Venture-capital-backed startups increased by a remarkable 48 percent between 2011 and 2016.

Dan Gilbert, founder and chairman of Quicken Loans, deserves credit for leading the Detroit renaissance with his company's rapid growth and legendary success. He has also invested in scores of Detroit startups, as well as more than one hundred Detroit properties, to revitalize the city.

People often ask why I travel back and forth between Detroit and D.C. so much. The truth is my family is in Detroit and my job is in D.C. But I also want to get out of the Washington bubble and be close to real people—and be where innovation is happening. It energizes me. It inspires me to support the efforts and ideas of entrepreneurs and innovators around the country. And it motivates me to do whatever I can to help smooth the way for innovators to go forth and build the ninja future.

PART III

BUILDING THE NINJA FUTURE

CHAPTER 10

CORPORATE NINJAS

SOMETIME IN THE 1980s, THE steady, linear advance of technology accelerated to a wave of innovation that lifted the nation and transformed everything irrevocably. The tech sector helped us realize that the seemingly impossible *was* possible: constant communication with family and friends, personalized experiences and interactions tailored to only what we like, and instant access to almost all the information in the entire world. The sharpest business leaders quickly realized that leveraging tech innovation wasn't limited to tech companies alone.

It has been amazing to be part of this success story: I have benefited as I led and enjoyed the rapid growth of CTA and phenomenal success of CES over the past three-plus decades. That success is due to the inventors and entrepreneurs who envisioned, built, nurtured, and expanded so many of the technologies we once considered "future ninja innovations" but now take for granted—from the internet and wireless connectivity to smartphones and robotics. The credit also goes to the thousands of people in the tech industry, our volunteers, and our staff, all of whom are critical to our growth. We all caught a rising tide at this amazing moment in human history.

The pace of innovation isn't going to slow down anytime soon. Every business, no matter its size or sector, will have to change to survive. But future ninjas will be the individuals and companies that *thrive*. With that in mind, here are my suggestions for how businesses can withstand the impact and embrace the opportunity of technology—and how we can position ninja innovators for future success.

Every Company Is a Tech Company

I've spent much of my career advocating for integrating technology in business: Colleagues have heard me say "Innovate or die!" more times than they can count. I repeat it because it's true: If you don't grow, change, and innovate, you will lose to smarter competitors.

It can be challenging to figure out how to harness new technology in your favor—but many companies, even in previously staid industries, are doing just that.

Look at the car industry: Ford understands it is now a tech company, *in addition* to being an auto company. Ford introduced its SYNC technology, which features mobile integration and 911 assist, among other connectivity features, back in 2007, the year the iPhone was launched. And Ford executives have taken the CES keynote stage multiple times in the last decade. GM has taken similar steps: In 2008, GM Chairman and CEO

Rick Wagoner was our first CES "car keynote." And in 2016, CEO Mary Barra keynoted CES, the same week the company announced it was investing $500 million in Lyft.[1]

It may surprise you to learn that CES has grown to be one of the world's top auto shows. It is certainly not a traditional consumer auto show promoting sales of new cars. Rather, it is a future-oriented trade event where the entire automotive community gathers in Las Vegas to understand how tech is changing their business. With new entrants such as Waymo, Tesla, Byton, and Zoox earning high market valuations as they develop new tech options for transportation, no auto company will survive by spinning its wheels.

The marketing and advertising industries have also been disrupted by technology. Chief marketing officers (CMOs) can no longer be *just* creative geniuses. They must also understand data and the complex array of technology platforms that form the advertising and marketing technology stack. And nontraditional players, including the Big Five consulting companies, are helping CMOs harness the technologies required to deliver content and track impact. Deloitte Digital, IBM iX, and Accenture Interactive are competing head-to-head with traditional advertising agencies such as WPP and Publicis Groupe.

CMOs also need to think about how emerging technologies like smart speakers will disrupt their businesses and how they can leverage the data consumers share with these devices to further personalize and target advertising. And outside the home, smart cities and smart venues will open up an entirely new canvas for advertisers to deliver highly targeted ads to consumers in hypertargeted locations.

Companies are experimenting with augmented reality

and virtual reality as they strive to deliver a better experience for their customers. Retailers are some of the first companies to embrace AR and VR in "experiential marketing," offering everything from virtual changing rooms to home makeover visualization tools. And the marketing and content creation communities have also figured out how to leverage tech to expand their business. Creating ads for newspapers, radio, and TV is no longer a business mainstay like it was in the last century. Instead, every marketing executive has to jump on new content platforms and consider social media "influencers." If a company's strategy is static from year to year, it inevitably becomes more expensive and less effective. Brands and their CMOs must be nimble and innovate to stay relevant, modifying and creating new brand strategies regularly.

As tech disrupts and changes, so do content creation and delivery. CMOs recognize the importance of creativity and flexibility, which is why C Space at CES has been a resounding success. Launched in 2015, this area of the show brings together advertisers, content creators, and marketing professionals to share knowledge about how emerging trends and technology impact branding. C Space has expanded to attract more than 10,000 advertising and entertainment executives each year, from companies including Disney, Knotch, Spotify, and Oath.

The travel and hospitality industry is changing as well, using cutting-edge technology to attract and serve its customers. As we discussed in Chapter 2, Carnival CEO Arnold Donald used the CES 2017 keynote stage to launch the world's first smart city cruise line. Hospitality executives everywhere took note, as they know their Travelocity, TripAdvisor, Google, and Yelp ratings will increasingly depend on their ability to innovate in the coming years. Airlines are embracing tech, using AI and machine learning to personalize the booking experience and offering Wi-Fi and content-streaming apps on board.

Food creators are also turning to technology. Farmers rely on drones and sensors for crop, soil, and irrigation needs and use GPS-managed self-driving tractors from John Deere. Vintners use algorithms and sensors to better monitor grapes and fine-tune their wines. Distributors and truckers use tech to manage inventory and get fresh products to market. And increasingly, consumers will use tech for ordering preselected ingredients to craft perfect meals and reduce wasted or spoiled food.

Service businesses use tech to identify and market to customers, then gauge their reactions and fulfill their needs. Retailers can customize selections for shoppers and maintain appropriate inventory at a lower cost. Clothing retailers, eyeglass sellers, hairstylists, even plastic surgeons can use algorithms to allow a customer or patient to envision how a product, style, or service would alter their appearance. Sensors can indicate customer interest; humanlike robots can provide information and service and even close a sale.

In Chapter 5, we discussed the advantages tech has for health care, both for patients and providers. The possibilities for other industries are endless. Still, many industries resent or resist the changes that technology will bring. Some professions, like taxi drivers and lawyers, will change dramatically, with real consequences for many in the field. Others, like construction workers and teachers, will have to adjust to meet new needs that technology creates—but on the flip side, technology will also give them myriad new opportunities to meet the needs of their customers or students.

Nursing homes, gas stations, schools, insurance companies, and even pizza parlors will all transform into tech companies. For many businesses, this transformation may be messy, stressful, and frustrating. But done right, they will improve services, making us safer, healthier, and more satisfied as consumers. So if your company is not a tech company yet, remember: Innovate or die!

Strategic Planning

In 2015, our senior leadership team gathered for a day at an off-site retreat to plot our future strategy. I'm a big believer in using five-year plans to set big goals and take action. My wife and I struggled over whether to live in Detroit or Washington several years ago; in the interim she became pregnant with our second child. We decided to commit to the Detroit area for five years. This allowed us to leave the cramped home she had when I met her and invest in a house. Her thinking, which I now share, is that our lives generally move in five-year cycles: the high school, college, and postcollege graduate or first job experience are generally about five years each. Then marriage, then kids. Stepping back and taking the five-year view helps put the consequences of decisions into perspective. Too often, we freeze up when we have to make big decisions, because it seems like every single decision has tremendous implications for the rest of life—but the truth is, most of them don't. Where you go to school, the first job you take, or where you live are all important decisions, but they don't define you for life.

So our leadership retreat focused on setting ambitious five-year goals, understanding the need to stay nimble. We didn't need to plan for CES 2050—just strategize about where we wanted to be in five years as an association, trade show, and business. We alternated the facilitation role and relegated anything off-topic to the "parking lot." By the end of the day, we had agreed on major goals tied to revenue, growth, new ventures, and our position in the market. Shaping our road map at that high level positioned us for success today and in the future.

I abandoned the traditional corporate strategic plan long ago. My experience at CTA and at other companies on whose boards I have served has taught me that strategic plans are stultifying, aspirational documents that, once completed, are too often relegated to bookshelves collecting dust while the vagaries of dynamic marketplaces nullify their assumptions. The standard strategic plan is a lengthy document that's time-consuming to create, requires a high level of detail, and is premised on tactics for addressing an uncertain future. It unfairly equalizes inputs, and discourages quick, opportunistic reactions down the line. Business leaders tied to a strategic plan are more inclined to double down on losing strategies and tactics instead of pivoting when circumstances change. And sometimes they miss new opportunities they couldn't have envisioned when creating their strategic plan.

In other words, organizations that have invested the time and energy in creating a strategic plan mistakenly think they're done "thinking ahead." Yet too often, they end up following "the plan" rather than the market.

By contrast, the result of our planning meeting was a single-page document: five five-year goals at the top, and a nine-point vision for achieving those goals below. I circulated the document to our staff leaders, took into account their edits, and recirculated it for final approval. Within two days we had a big-picture plan to carry us through the next five years. A few weeks later, the document was presented to, discussed by, and approved by our governing board, which has a shared vision on the value of market-driven innovation.

Our goals were big, change-oriented, and measurable. We had revenue goals, membership recruitment and retention goals, and global recognition and reputation goals. The goals were SMART: Specific, Measurable, Attainable, Realistic, and with a Timetable of five years. Our strategies were precise and covered every facet of the organization. We decided to go into emerging areas: augmented and virtual reality, drones, robotics, cryptocurrency, self-driving vehicles, digital health, and the sharing economy. We agreed we would find homes for these emerging industries in our association and conference and trade shows, especially our flagship CES events.

Our overarching goal was to become the go-to technology trade organization that could gather the players in each of these categories. To achieve this, our strategy was simple: empower our employees to attract emerging tech companies within these categories. We agreed that our employee champions for each industry category should self-select which category to lead and have a say in the staff support team. The result was leaders from our sales, policy, technical, and membership teams successfully leading the creation of vibrant efforts to capture the leading companies in each category. Our empowered employees have pushed us to grow our membership and create new working groups centered around drones, self-driving vehicles, content like AR/VR, IoT, artificial intelligence, and other strategic areas.

Since we've established that innovation can happen anywhere, it was also important to expand the geographic boundaries of CTA. We decided that day to open a Silicon Valley office to engage our members on the West Coast, and two years later we did just that. We agreed to expand our CES Asia presence based on the success of CES Asia 2016. The show expanded (by 2018 it was 2.5 times the size of the inaugural show in 2015), and so did we as an organization, hiring a full-time team in China to grow and support this event. Recognizing the value of a happy, productive, and stable workforce, we promised to maintain creative benefits and a balanced, healthy work environment. And so we created a student loan assistance program, after talking to a younger employee about the burdens of student debt. We also began offering new benefits, including telemedicine service and pet insurance. This, on top of our already amazing benefits—free yoga and boot camp classes, mortgage assistance, and a strong 401(k) program, to name a few—helps us attract and retain talented and committed employees.

But while the unique benefits are certainly a "nice to have," our employees do great things because we all share a sense of purpose. We believe innovation can and will change the world for the better. We believe technology can and will solve basic human problems, not just across transportation and education, but also across infrastructure, clean air and water, hunger, and health. Our mission is to ensure that entrepreneurs and innovators can create, invent, and share their ideas with others and with the market without the government or status quo industries shutting them down or choking innovation.

That's why a single page of big goals is enough to guide us.

Know Your Customer

Almost every CEO struggles to see around the corner and help shape a corporate strategy that will ensure his or her company's survival. We've already established that ignoring or avoiding technological changes is *not* a survival strategy. But it's a natural human tendency to think that nothing will change. As children, we think our parents will live forever. Eventually we realize that everyone—our teachers, friends, and relatives—is mortal. The passage of time slowly erases our perception of long-term stability; even the bedrock people or institutions that we believe in inevitably evolve or disappear. When I was a kid, I never would have imagined a New York without Korvettes, Circuit City, or an FAO Schwarz on Fifth Avenue.

The best most of us can do is to appreciate what we have and live in the moment. One of the most significant books I have read (and reread) is Eckhart Tolle's *The Power of Now*. Tolle beautifully describes how, as children, we live in the moment. The realities, responsibilities, and neuroses of adulthood diminish our ability to savor the moment. And as we discussed in Chapter 2, the seductive lure of technology makes it even more challenging to be present and focused.

This is especially hard for business leaders, who must simultaneously deal with the present and stay focused on the future. Leaders are responsible for the health of their organization and its owners, and most also feel an enormous responsibility to their employees. The C-suite title means you have owners, customers, and employees relying on your flexibility, responsiveness, and vision.

The pace of technological change often throws a wrench in businesses that otherwise run like clockwork. According to a 2017 *Fortune* survey, seven in ten CEOs considered their company a tech company, and 81 percent said AI and machine learning are important/very important to their company's future.[2] A good CEO understands that technology changes customers' wants and needs, it changes industries, and it changes what a company needs to do to compete. A great CEO responds to change, prepares for change, and takes the steps necessary to capitalize on it.

Supported by most major American banks, online startup Zelle allows payments directly from one checking account to another using an email address or phone number. It is incredibly easy for customers to set up and link to their checking accounts. Payers and payees avoid the challenge of writing and depositing checks, and banks have managed to avoid the three-dollar-per-check processing cost. Everyone wins (except the postal service and the check processing industry).

My wife downloaded the app and within a few days she became infatuated with the service and immediately switched everyone—from the kids' piano teacher to various sports organizations—over to the ease and immediacy of the service. But along the way, she encountered a few small businesses that simply couldn't respond or try something new, even though a customer was asking them to accept her payment with it.

Businesses succeed when they are in tune with the challenges and needs of their customers. Zelle will likely thrive: It will save banks the high cost of processing checks; consumers the hassle of writing, printing, and mailing checks; and businesses the time and cost of processing and waiting for checks to clear. It's not for everyone—no technology is—but it is a great example of an innovation that impacts what I call the time/money paradigm.

Everyone can be categorized by the amount of time and money they have. You can create a two-by-two time and money matrix to try to identify four groups of people:

1. **People with little money but lots of time.** Through choice or situation, people in this group have more time than money: think disabled veterans, empty-nesters, many retired people, and the permanently unemployed. This may not be a great potential customer group, but they could potentially be a source of volunteers or employees who could value the fulfillment, benefits, or cash an organization could offer. Some could also be product testers, volunteers, jurors, security guards. Others have found driving for Uber and Lyft a convenient way to convert their time into money. As technology increasingly allows work from anywhere, they are a source of talent in a full-employment economy.

2. **People with money but no time.** In this group are dual-income parents, some caretakers, many professionals, and volunteers. This group will embrace a new technology and service that saves them time: They would likely be thrilled to learn about Zelle, but not especially interested in advanced options on Instagram. This group is a potentially lucrative market.

3. **People with little money and no time.** This group includes the working poor, those holding down multiple jobs, working students, young and ambitious professionals starting their careers, and single parents. They will embrace new technologies and services if they save time or money. For example, in their own way Google, Facebook, and Waze offer free services designed to save time—but the user must be willing to share information and get ads in return.

4. **People with money and time.** This is the luxury group that businesses from health spas and resorts to fashion designers and automakers want to reach. Quality, status, and style are more important than cost or practicality. They will buy the first humanlike robots, trips to space, and flying cars.

When analyzing your customers, employees, and unique selling proposition, keep this matrix in mind to identify which of the four targets most affect your business. When you really understand your customers, you will be much better able to anticipate their changing needs and respond with solutions that make them happy—and loyal.

Find Your Greatness

Every business must be the best at something. It's what defines the company, product, or service. It's what attracts and retains loyal customers.

Have a question? Google it. Need supplies for your daughter's science fair project right away? Amazon Prime. Being the best is what separates a company from its competitors and makes potential customers crave the product.

My friend Steve Miller wrote a great book about this, called *Uncopyable: How to Create An Unfair Advantage Over Your Competition*. He talks about creating an "uncopyable attachment" with customers, so that they see you as delivering a superior product that they can't get anywhere else. Steve is right. Some people call this a unique selling proposition (USP). A USP must attract potential customers, distinguish you from your competitors, and reinforce your brand image. It should be deliverable in a simple phrase. It should be positive—it often has a superlative associated with it. It also should be true.

Some businesses claim they are the "oldest" or "longest-serving." These concepts connote stability and survival, but they could be off-putting to customers looking for a newer company. That said, a track record can be valuable. Having once lost my deposit for a carpet from a retailer that went under, I often look for signs of stability anytime I make a deposit for future goods or services.

Your USP can say you are "first," "best," or "top" in customer satisfaction, market share, price, warranty, durability, or quality. You can be the "oldest," "biggest," "fastest," or "most effective." But your claim should be grounded in facts. We recently leased a car from Shuman Chrysler in Walled Lake, Michigan. It proudly declares in ads, signs, and on its website that it is the "Biggest Chrysler Dodge Ram Jeep dealer in Walled Lake." It is also the only such dealer in Walled Lake! It is a bit tongue-in-cheek, as it also has won several national awards. More, this modest local claim is a charming discussion item that lets the sales team bond with potential customers by sharing the "inside" joke.

To be best at something you may have to narrow your focus either in time (for example, number one in 2019), geography (city, region, state, etc.), or customer segment (such as first choice for mothers). Or, you can combine factors to be best at something: the only pick-your-own, organic apple orchard in western New York.

In the consumer tech sector, defining your USP can be challenging. The market for tech is growing every day, and it's more segmented than ever within product categories. Take smartphones: Some consumers buy a smartphone because they want the best, lightest camera to take with them everywhere. Others choose a smartphone for its ability to run multiple operating systems on one device. Still others want the best audio and video quality available in a five-inch display. It's up to manufacturers and marketers to set themselves apart and connect with their unique audiences. And as innovators push the bounds of technology—packing more amazing services into ever-smaller packages—USPs in tech are limitless.

Your USP does not have to be objective. It could simply be positioning. Westin focuses on "Heavenly"® sleep. Hallmark connotes quality, emotive cards: "When you care enough to send the very best."[3] It could also be a feature: the only golf app featuring live professionals online.

It could even be a third-party endorsement: a toothpaste that has been approved by the American Dental Association and is recommended by four out of five dentists surveyed.

Social media has affected the value of the USP. Search engines allow a USP to break through if it's positioned to respond to common searches. Smart advertisers can also target ads precisely for querying customers. Facebook, Instagram, and Snap let companies tell a story about their USP and target potential customers.

Perhaps the biggest social media impact on USP is social media sites giving customers the opportunity to confirm or challenge a business's assertion that it is great at something. Airbnb, Amazon, Google, Travelocity, TripAdvisor, Yelp, and others allow users to rate and comment on their experience. As I travel around the world, I often see people outside restaurants checking online reviews before stepping foot inside. Customer ratings are powerful tools of democracy: They weed out bad businesses, put a brake on questionable business claims, and help great businesses thrive.

They are not without risk. A few years ago, my family rented a house in Naples, Florida, from a large real estate company. The home was fine, but some parts were dirty and had broken items and peeling paint. The company eventually cleaned the home but shocked us by keeping our three-hundred-dollar security deposit. This led to an interesting email exchange. I told the rental company this was unjustified and would be in our Airbnb review. The company said it would return the deposit so long as we did not write a review. I said I couldn't accept that condition, and that their written offer would be in the review. I soon received a letter from their law firm pointing to a clause in the lengthy lease agreement stating that the lessee agreed not to post reviews on social media. These threats and lawsuits were so common at the time, they had their own acronym, SLAPP, for strategic lawsuit against public participation.

We decided not to pursue the issue; we had more pressing priorities than legal defense of an online review. But because of that experience, I jumped at the opportunity to support the battle to ensure that writing factual reviews was a right. I was thrilled when, in December 2016, President Barack Obama signed the Consumer Review Fairness Act, which protects users who post negative reviews from being sued by the business they are criticizing.

Another risk of online reviews is the possibility that businesses can be hurt by competitors or customers who write false, malicious, or unfair reviews. For example, Dallas-based Starpower is a provider of luxury home theater and automation products. When a competitor posted a negative review, it took some expensive legal work to mitigate the harm.

My wife is a doctor in private practice. Once, an unhappy patient wrote a negative review after waiting over an hour and then having his desired treatment declined (it would have been unethical). Yet my wife couldn't respond to the review, since HIPAA law bars doctors from sharing medical information about patients without authorization.

This is especially challenging for doctors. Sometimes patients are kept waiting because another patient needs more immediate or emergency attention. Sometimes patients are addicts and are outraged if a doctor won't prescribe a specific drug. Sometimes patients are hoping to game the system and are annoyed if a doctor won't provide documentation to allow them to have a car tag that allows disabled parking or miss work for medical reasons. There are a thousand reasons why a medical office might be running behind. It's not a factory churning out products; it's a practice treating humans with complex needs, some of which require more time than expected. We've all been there, and we've all been frustrated by waiting, but it's part of life. My wife resolved the unfair social media critique by ignoring it, reducing its prominence, and giving appreciative patients a slip of paper with information on how to share a review of her on social media.

Leverage Your Strengths

One of the highlights of my job is the opportunity to meet business leaders around the world. There are two questions I hear no matter where I travel: 1) "I am a startup (or entrepreneur or a small company). How can I compete with big companies?"; and 2) "I work for a big company. How can we fight complacency and encourage innovation?" All too often, big and small companies fear each other—which is unfortunate because the truth is, they need each other to succeed. Here's why.

Startups, entrepreneurs, and smaller companies have one huge advantage over big companies: speed. They can move light-years faster without five or ten levels of approval, each incentivized to kill, table, or delay any idea with an element of risk.

Big companies have resources. They have money. They have people. They have customers. They have specialists in marketing, sales, distribution, manufacturing, law, and public relations. They are machines ready to do, well, big things. That brings its own challenges. If an innovative idea survives the internal approval process to go forward and get funded, it typically gets *too much* funding. It becomes a "strategic priority," which means that assets get thrown at it. But just because it's a strategic priority doesn't mean it's actually a good idea. Big companies often waste time and money by overfunding bad ideas—throwing good money after bad. By contrast, entrepreneurs have to scrape for every penny, which makes them extremely careful. Bad ideas get scrapped before too much money is wasted.

Big companies also waste money and time because they can't easily modify bad ideas. The details of big corporate life—large assets, multiple teams, lengthy approval processes—suck away the time and resources needed to adjust a new product or service in response to market changes like new competitors, opportunities, or customer feedback. Big companies can't change course too quickly; they aren't that agile.

Another major disadvantage of big companies is that they almost always have one big cash cow that provides the bulk of their revenue and allows them to dominate their market. This is their strength—but also their weakness, because everything revolves around protecting that cash cow. All those people, all that talent, all that energy is focused on that primary goal and everything else is secondary. This is not to say that big companies don't diversify; many do, and do it quite well. Through venture capital operations, large companies invest strategically in businesses that support their own core business. Intel has one of the largest funds, with $12.3 billion invested.[4] By looking at its investments in biometrics, AI, and big data, you see a road map of where Intel thinks the world is going.

And there are a select handful of major companies that successfully drive innovation internally. 3M constantly monitors its innovation and pushes for more. The company created a measurement called New Product Vitality Index (NPVI), which measures how much of its revenue was generated by products made within the last five years. Adobe empowers its employees with the Kickbox—a package that, among other things, includes a guidebook that walks them through the process of brainstorming and a prepaid credit card they can use to pursue new ideas. Apple formed a top-secret team of engineers, all recruited from within the company, to create the iPhone.[5]

But these companies are the exception. While many big companies try internal innovation, CEOs still worry they are falling behind. According to PwC's 2018 CEO survey, CEOs' concerns about losing their technological edge are rising sharply as advances in AI, self-driving vehicles, and other technologies create opportunities for new market entrants (as well as bad actors).[6] The fact is that most breakthrough innovation comes not from big companies but from small ones.

Small companies have vast opportunities because big companies need them in order to stay adaptive and nimble. Big companies can buy smaller companies. They can invest in them. They can partner with them. They can mentor them.

Coca-Cola figured this out. It realized startups can benefit from its vast marketing ability, expertise in storytelling, and huge customer base. So it created a hub in Israel called "The Bridge," where it helps promising startups develop their stories and introduces them to potential first customers. If the startup manages to win a contract, Coca-Cola has a temporary period of exclusivity.

Canon figured this out. Canon is a well-respected Japanese brand with global distribution, vast technical skills, and a huge patent portfolio. But Eliott Peck, Canon's U.S.-based executive vice president and general manager, was frustrated that his company was mostly inward-looking and did not even know how to reach out to startups. He hired thirty-year-old serial entrepreneur, investor, and corporate innovation strategist Mara Lewis to help him engage with startups. Several months later, he surprised his Japanese executives at CES 2018, showing up at the Canon booth with a "visionaries welcome" theme encouraging startups and entrepreneurs to come in and discuss ways to work together. The Japanese executives were thrilled!

Wells Fargo figured this out. In a 2018 speech at the Milken Institute Global Conference, CEO Timothy J. Sloan said they realized customers hated filling out lengthy mortgage applications. So they brought on Blend Labs Inc., a San Francisco startup, to deploy software that would make the process faster by electronically completing forms.[7]

We figured this out, too—although it has taken some time. I was an outside consultant in the early 1980s when I attended my first CTA board meeting. We were discussing whether or not the association should raise the charge for exhibit space at CES. The head of the largest exhibitor, Panasonic's Ray Gates, served as volunteer chairman of the board. He let the discussion play out and then said the proposed increase was, for Panasonic, just a tiny amount, a rounding error.

But he argued that innovation and new products and ideas were far more likely to come from basements and garages than from big companies like his own. The board must keep the show accessible, he said, so that anyone with an idea can expose it to the thousands of journalists, retailers, investors, and others who attend CES.

That view persuaded and inspired me and it is still our

mantra. Before each show, I repeat this story to our employees. I also remind them that some of our smaller exhibitors have borrowed money, stretched credit limits, or invested their life savings just to have this one shot to showcase their ideas. I urge them to be sensitive, caring, and empathetic to the natural anxiety of our startup exhibitors, especially if they experience unexpected problems.

But it wasn't until 2012 that we created Eureka Park, a special area for startups. That first year, we hoped to draw just thirty companies, but we got eighty eager startups, including first efforts from retired or laid-off engineers. It was the buzz area of the show. Every year since, the area has gotten bigger and better, as journalists, major buyers from retailers like Walmart and Amazon, and investors like Mark Cuban came to find stories and do business.

And Eliott Peck of Canon? He encouraged all his employees working the Canon booth at CES to spend some time in Eureka Park to be inspired by new ideas.

Serendipity

He's not the only one. The first reaction of many executives at CES for the first time is to reach out to their chief technology officer, their business development and sales team, and their ninja innovators and say, "Come out here! This is a team approach. We have to figure out how to do this so that next year, we can really take advantage of everything CES offers. We are going to split up the different categories; you go to this, we go to this, and we'll compare notes every day." This happens because most of the time, people in specific roles go to CES with specific objectives. But they don't account for one of my favorite words: *serendipity*.

CES is like no other environment you've ever experienced. You can't predict what you'll see, whom you'll meet, or—most important—what ideas you'll generate. It is truly an "expect the unexpected" environment. You see things you never imagined. You meet people you otherwise wouldn't know you're supposed to meet, but who wind up being that missing piece that takes you to the next level. Over the years, I've heard hundreds of stories of companies forming business relationships that changed their bottom line—just by going to CES.

This makes perfect sense, because at its core, innovation is about surprise. Innovation is rarely planned—on the contrary, it's often a random series of happy accidents. This is especially true in the digital age. The *outcome* might be planned—for instance, Thomas Edison wanted a working lightbulb, and Mark Zuckerberg wanted a platform to connect fellow students online. But the path to achieving these goals was paved with plenty of failure and surprise.

So be open to serendipity. Make a conscious effort to get out of your lane and mix up your routines. Attend trade shows, but also movies and operas. Work at your day job, but also volunteer and travel. Listen to music, audio books, podcasts that are outside of your usual genres. Most of all, go out of your way to meet people and be open to their ideas. More times than not, your collective wisdom will be the spark you need to light your way.

Fail Fast

If necessity is the mother of invention, failure might be its father. Over the course of my career, I have heard thousands of ideas, visited with hundreds of companies, and judged dozens of startup competitions. I have a strong sense of what will succeed and more often what will not. I look at the idea, the strategy, the team, the leadership, and the funding in the context of the marketplace. It is easy to be pessimistic: The truth is that most startups fail. But I get tingly when an idea is exciting, when it solves a real human problem, and when there is a strong leadership team.

I've talked a lot about Eureka Park, the area we host for startups every year at CES in Las Vegas. To me there's nothing more thrilling than walking through Eureka Park. The emotion, aspiration, and drive are palpable. You see and hear the hopes and dreams and ideas of hundreds of entrepreneurs up close. My promise to them is that whatever they thought they were selling before the CES opens, they will leave with a different concept when the show ends. Each startup founder hears from hundreds of investors, buyers, media, and businesses asking questions, giving feedback, and expressing their opinions. Think *Shark Tank* on steroids. (In fact, *Shark Tank* stars Mark Cuban and Kevin O'Leary often visit Eureka Park—and *Shark Tank* actually holds tryouts at CES.)

I urge startups to fail—and fast. Failing fast means killing the original idea so that, out of its ashes, a marketable idea can thrive. It means not being wedded to your original vision but being willing to adjust it to match the market—before the big investment is made. It is what smart investors require. It is what, as discussed earlier in this chapter, bigger companies are often reluctant to do because internal approval processes are so cumbersome. Failing fast requires great listening skills, courage, and a certain humility as the best conceptual ideas may not be practical or marketable.

So I tell startups not to waste their time developing a perfect version of their product or service but to present their idea roughly, using mockups, 3-D printing, video, posters, or some other medium. They should then take it to potential customers, either directly or through events like CES. Then they must consider the feedback and revamp the idea so customers will buy it. Once that happens, the bigger investments can and should be made to perfect a marketable idea.

Failing fast is a ninja mind-set. It requires situational awareness, careful listening, and the nimbleness to adapt to circumstances while subjugating your ego. It can and should be practiced by anyone with a new service or product. What it all comes down to is that it is not whether you think your idea is great. It's what the intended recipient thinks and wants. Ninjas adjust with lightning speed. It's the key to their survival.

Tap into the Wisdom of Crowds

At a 2018 CTA board meeting, Israeli researcher and advisor Dr. Lior Zoref, a former marketing executive at Microsoft and author of *Mindsharing*, spoke about the value of "collective intelligence" for finding innovative solutions to big challenges in record time. Zoref believes companies and people should draw on "the wisdom of crowds"—an idea that financial journalist James Surowiecki tackled in his 2004 book of that name—to create "greater output with less effort." Today we refer to this phenomenon as "crowdsourcing."

Israeli startup Waze, which was acquired by Google in 2013, revolutionized how we move through cities and towns by crowdsourcing traffic and road conditions from drivers in real time—including traffic jams and accidents. And a community of Waze map editors are constantly adding changes in their local neighborhoods to update and improve Waze's maps.

Crowdsourced maps were vital to the recovery effort in 2017 after Hurricane Maria pummeled Puerto Rico. By comparing satellite images to online maps, volunteers were able to note missing buildings, roads, and other landmarks, which helped emergency responders get to those in need faster.

In some ways, the gig economy is built on crowdsourcing. Sites like 99designs help innovators harness the power of crowds to bring their products to market faster, through online marketplaces for graphic design and Web design services. Now you can put out a bid and share your big idea with the design community. Within days, designers from around the world submit incredibly creative designs to help you launch your product or service. When you're deeply invested in your idea or product, it can be hard to let it go out into the wild, letting others interpret and manipulate and present it. But if the goal is for your product to hit the marketplace, then taking advantage of the expertise of others at the earliest possible moment gives you a competitive advantage. Instead of agonizing over details or expending resources you don't have on branding and marketing, future ninjas know it's more efficient to leverage the wisdom of crowds—giving them time to focus solely on areas that demand ninja attention.

Outsource (Almost) Everything

Time is our most precious resource: How we spend it defines our priorities. By choosing to spend personal time with family and friends, exercising, playing video games, watching sports, listening to music, reading, or surfing the internet, we're choosing what's most important to us.

The same is true for work. If you're an executive who is always putting out fires, you may be too focused on the present to be able to guide your company strategically into the future. Sacrificing long-term vision for immediate solutions makes it unlikely your company will thrive in a changing environment. Of course, you have to survive to be able to grow. If you don't do your job, you'll lose it. If you don't satisfy your customers, you'll lose them, too, and the revenue that comes with them.

But ninja innovators know there is always another way. Ninja innovators never confine themselves to two options. Instead, they create a third.

Most business enterprises have similar requirements. The financial side handles revenue collection, including invoicing, accounts receivable, accounts payable, expense monitoring, tax compliance, cash flow management, reporting, and forecasting. Every business owner, entrepreneur, or ambitious manager should understand the basics of how these systems work. But that doesn't mean you should be doing it yourself! There are great off-the-shelf technology solutions for startups, and any business verging on six figures in revenue should outsource part of this function.

This holds true for other back-office functions like information technology, legal, and operations. A great executive knows a little bit about each but doesn't waste time running any of these functions herself.

Whether you hire an employee or outsource a job is a threshold question. Does the position require a full-time employee? Does it require immersion in the company culture? Would it be done better by, and would your company benefit from having, an on-site employee? Is the field changing quickly? Would the knowledge of someone with multiple clients benefit your organization? Is your need or budget for the function likely to change soon? Personally, I feel a moral obligation when hiring an employee—more so than retaining a consultant or outsourcing a function. Hiring someone is a two-way commitment. The employee is betting on you and your company. You are betting on the employee and irrevocably changing his or her life.

For any organization to thrive, it needs to understand what it's good at and which functions can be better served with outside help. A lean organization with few employees can pivot quickly, be opportunistic, and remove layers of bureaucracy. It can also be more profitable, as outside vendors are often subject matter experts, cover their own training costs, and bear the risks of fluctuating business. Outside vendors also provide a healthy outside strategic view and recommend best practices based on a more global view of similar businesses. Indeed, the best consultants suggest best practices; the amazing (and rare) consultants suggest strategic initiatives with their other clients or businesses they know.

We partner with a great tech company, Phone2Action, the civic engagement and communications tool I mentioned in Chapter 9. Phone2Action started with a small idea: using mobile text keywords to patch constituents through to their legislators. The platform has evolved to let people leave comments on public registers in a way that's mobile-friendly and remarkably easy to use. In short, Phone2Action cofounders Ximena Hartsock and Jeb Ory found a way to cut through government red tape, allowing organizations like CTA to strategize on messaging and leaving the implementation to their brilliant software.

Every business has to do its own assessment—what to handle in-house and what to outsource—based on costs, time, and needs. But executives should spend their time doing executive work. My simple formula is to look at your own total annual compensation, add a 20 percent kicker for benefits and overhead, and divide by 2,000 (a rough approximation of the work hours most people have in a year: 40 hours per week times 50 working weeks in a year). The result gives you an hourly rate that a given employee costs your company.

Ninja innovators should think strategically about whether the time on a given task can be better spent outsourced. So, for example, an employee making $100,000 plus benefits would have an hourly rate of roughly $60. Paying someone $60 an hour to make copies or lay carpet may not make sense, when it can be done cheaper and probably better by FedEx or through hiring someone via TaskRabbit.

How executives spend their time is critical to a company's future. If executives are not investing in the future through customer retention and attraction, building the brand, developing talent, or learning, exploring, or managing their function at a high level, then the company is not benefiting from its investment in the executive.

Hire the Best

Ninja innovators know that the most important investment they can make is in the people they hire. Our top HR recruiter recently asked about an applicant for a job who disclosed his relationship with a relative of mine. I told our recruiter that this candidate was right to mention the relationship, but added that I don't know him and this information shouldn't affect our hiring decision. "Treat him like every other applicant," I told her. Had I known the person, I would have likely asked she not consider him for the open position, as it would cloud my objectivity.

She replied with appreciation. When I asked why, she shared that a former employer had many weak employees who were hired and retained because of connections with the CEO. Her comment made me think deeper about something that I assumed was just common sense. Shouldn't every CEO want only high-performing employees? My obligation to my company is clear: to attract and keep the best possible employees.

This also means that for the health of the company I sometimes have to move out employees who are not a good fit. It is common sense that I would set a higher bar to firing a friend or a friend's child. For me, letting someone go is difficult enough. It is the worst part of being CEO. You know you are hurting a person's self-esteem, life, and family. As one who has been fired, I know how much it hurts. But I also know that being fired helped shape me. More, I believe that in almost every case being let go is in the best interest of the departing employee in the long run. Everyone wants to feel appreciated for their contributions; if a supervisor is asking for an employee to be removed, the employee almost always feels unappreciated and is not loving his or her job.

Still, I am careful not to rubber-stamp a supervisor's request to separate us from an employee. I review every proposed "termination" based on substance and fairness and get opinions from at least two others in addition to the supervisor asking for the action. If the employee has a good attitude, is loyal and hardworking, we will see if a different department can use the employee. But this is not always an option, and occasionally we do move employees on.

I don't run a family business where keeping family members employed is a legitimate goal. Nor do I run an entity where homogeneity is a strategy to reduce cultural friction, clarify decision making, or achieve some other goal. We don't have stockholders, but we feel a deep commitment to our industry and our two thousand corporate members who pay us to move the industry forward. To do that, we need the best of the best.

We want people who possess the creative genius, different perspectives, and unexpected ideas that come from people with different life experiences and backgrounds. We want people who are passionate about the value of innovation. We want people with desirable skills, people who are clever and can work on teams, people who can speak, write, and represent us well. We want people who can keep their commitments and are responsive to internal and external customers.

We do use two other strategies that arguably run counter to the philosophy I just laid out. First, we encourage industry members to have their children apply for the more than thirty internships we open annually. This rarely leads to hires, though, perhaps because in most cases we require an eleven-month commitment, which is not ideal for everyone. Second, we give referral bonuses to employees who recruit people we successfully hire. Our employees know our culture and want any referral to be a good fit—their reputation rides on it. While they are valuable tools, referral programs do run the risk of limiting diversity, so we make it a priority to recruit heavily from diverse sources.

For smaller companies, the most critical feature—even above a technical skill set—is whether a candidate is a good cultural fit. Fifteen-month-old Instagram had just thirteen full-time employees when it was acquired by Facebook for $1 billion in 2012.[8] Thirteen employees! Imagine if just *one* of those employees weren't self-motivated, or couldn't work well with a team. Instagram now has more than one billion monthly users and generates more than $5 billion in U.S. ad revenue annually.[9] But what would a weak link or poor fit have meant for the company? Would Instagram still be such an innovative influence on today's social media landscape?

The truth is that any hire is a big risk. Training is an investment, and new people cost more than they can produce for the first several months. They can also be disruptive to existing staff if they don't fit our culture, don't pull their weight, or have a negative attitude. Trying to correct mistakes in hiring is draining and not good for those being hired or those doing the hiring. Hiring the right candidate is a big challenge no matter what business you're in, but in a service organization like ours, it's almost everything. Every customer must decide to pay us and want to use our services. Our employees are the face we present to our customers, and we take pride in hiring the best, most qualified candidates. Without good employees, we would fade into irrelevance.

I try to thank our human resources team frequently and remind them they are our gatekeepers for excellence. Each year, our organization wins several "Best Place to Work" awards. I'm proud of that, but the awards are not an end in themselves: They're a third-party validation of what we already believe and a recruiting tool to attract more great employees.

Develop Employee Ambassadors

As a young CEO, I used to take it personally when employees left our company. Our company was doing well, we had a great culture, and we did cutting-edge work. I simply couldn't imagine why anyone would leave. But in 1998, I read an article in *Fast Company* that completely changed my attitude. The piece argued that you should think of departing employees as goodwill ambassadors—and one of your most strategic recruiting tools.[10]

Not long after reading this article, in 1998, our then-CES director of marketing, Karen Chupka, surprised me by telling me she was resigning to move to Connecticut to accept a position at a private company. I swallowed hard: Karen was a smart, strategic, star employee who could always get disparate parties to agree. Although this would be a huge loss, I decided to test the theory and try to view it as an opportunity. I also spoke with one of our board members, Loyd Ivey, the legendary founder of

Mitek Communications and Electronics Group and owner of MTX Audio and other great brands. Loyd said, "Don't worry. We will get her back."

So we held a big farewell party at my house to make sure she knew how much we'd miss her and how valuable her contributions had been. We gave her a Palm Pilot as a going-away gift, as a signal we hoped she would stay in touch. Well, less than a year later, Karen accepted an offer to run CES and moved back. She has been repeatedly and deservedly promoted, most recently to our only executive vice president position. She has envisioned and developed many of our most successful ventures at CES, including our keynote program and C Space, which attracts content creators, top marketers, and tech platforms. She was—and is—a critical part of our success.

Karen was one of our first "boomerangs," a former employee who returned. We have had more than a dozen boomerangs at CTA, and they're some of our best employees. They come back knowing the company well, which means they hit the ground running. They eliminate the usual risks for the company: hiring someone who interviews well but doesn't really have the necessary skills, attitude, or fit. The benefit is mutual—returning eliminates the risk of taking a job at another company where they don't fit, don't feel valued, or don't love the culture or mission.

In the United States, the number of technology jobs is growing—that includes jobs within the tech sector and in technical specialist roles in other industries. According to a 2018 CompTIA report, roughly 7 percent of the U.S. workforce held tech jobs in 2017 and more than one million new tech jobs have been added to the U.S. economy since 2010.[11] As technology expands and evolves, so do opportunities for ninja innovators. From an employer's perspective, it hurts in the short term to lose good employees, but sometimes it's best to let them go—let them learn new things from new leaders, sometimes in new industries—but keep the door open for them to boomerang talent back to your organization.

Boomerangs play a vital role in CTA's success. So do interns and temporary workers. We strive to give them real experience and a sense that they are part of something bigger, and each year we get thirty to forty future ambassadors in return. Depending on their skills and our needs, we also hire them for full-time positions. Dozens of our current employees started as temps or interns. We also bring back lots of former employees as consultants or as extra hands during CES. They know us, we know them. They know what to do. We need them to do it. Everyone wins!

If you're an employee leaving a job, do so with grace, a comprehensive memo to your replacement, and a large dose of goodwill and humility. Ninja innovators: remember that former employees can be goodwill ambassadors—one of the best ways to find the next generation of ninjas who will take your business into the future.

CHAPTER 11

DIVERSITY AND RESILIENCE

NINJA INNOVATORS ARE UNIQUE IN many ways. Philips, a leader in health-care innovation. iRobot, creators of Roomba, the vacuuming robot. Phone2Action, a civic engagement platform. Zoox, a self-driving startup. USAA, the insurance, banking, and investment giant that is diving into emerging tech to customize experiences for their customers. Opaque Studios, which is transforming filmmaking through virtual reality. Each of these does something completely different.

In *Ninja Innovation*, I explored some of the characteristics that are common to the strongest and most successful companies: taking calculated risks, preparing for battle, building the right teams, adhering to a code of ethics, and occasionally breaking the rules. I've come to realize two other things will distinguish future ninjas from everyday businesses: a commitment to diversity and a focus on resilience.

One of the surest ways to become a future ninja is to be

open to new ideas, and new ideas are best fostered in organizations where people come from different backgrounds. That's why diversity is a core value in many organizations. At the very least, it should be a guiding principle of human resources. Diversity—of thought, experience, background, skills, ideas—is the bedrock of ninja innovation. Resilience—the ability for a company, a city, even a nation to persevere in its core mission in the face of tremendous adversity—is the bulwark of ninja innovators. If diversity and resilience are your lodestars, you are much more likely to be a future ninja.

Variety Is the Spice of Life

I have visited slow-to-evolve companies—I call them "male, pale, and stale"—and watched them fade into obscurity with copycat products as they suffer from a lack of new ideas. I remember visiting a major Japanese company in the late 1990s whose executive leadership team universally agreed that dual DVD recorder players would be their next hit product. I expressed my view that it was more likely to be a niche product, because I suspected that, as with VCRs, users would be more interested in the "play" button than the "record" button. They looked at me as if I were crazy. But the market proved me right, and the company suffered mightily.

This is not to say that a heterogeneous corporation's path to success will be smooth. A diverse population produces diverse ideas that, from time to time, can generate conflict. As a relatively young country, the United States is divided over highly charged social issues (for example, abortion, capital punishment, immigration, gun control), which are not top-of-mind concerns in countries with common religions, cultures, ethnicities, and deeper histories, or which have smaller immigrant populations.

Still, homogeneity is greatly overrated. In my 2011 book, *The Comeback*, I argued that the incredible diversity of our nation is what gives us unique strength. The mosaic of people in our immigrant nation collectively make us the most entrepreneurial and innovative country in the world. Attracting many highly skilled immigrants—the best and brightest—helps create companies and jobs. And it's not just about tech—diversity across all sectors is important. According to a Harvard Business School study,[1] like-minded venture capital partners have lower returns than teams of diverse partners: "[T]he success rate of acquisitions and IPOs was 11.5 percent lower, on average, for investments by partners with shared school backgrounds than for those by partners from different schools. The effect of shared ethnicity was even stronger, reducing an investment's comparative success rate by 26.4 percent to 32.2 percent."

In *Ninja Innovation*, I argued that one of the strengths of ninja team leaders is that they know their weaknesses: They deliberately seek colleagues who are different from them and can fill the gaps in their skills. Research bears this out: In her 2018 Internet Trends report,[2] Mary Meeker finds that more than half of the most valuable U.S. tech companies were founded by first- or second-generation immigrants—innovators like Jeff Bezos, Sergey Brin, and Jensen Huang—with extraordinary ideas and a passion to try something new.

We're seeing signs of forward progress in diversity across

STEM education and the tech industry. African-American employees represent 21 percent[3] of Amazon's workforce, according to a 2018 analysis by *Re/code*. Thirty-six percent of Lyft employees in leadership positions are women. And most big tech companies have implemented plans to boost diversity among their ranks.

In some areas, like gender diversity, we are seeing signs of parity. Girls Who Code, a group CTA supports and which promotes STEM by offering after-school clubs and summer coding classes, says it's on track[4] to having just as many women as men in entry-level computer science jobs by 2027. So we're heading in the right direction, but unfortunately, there aren't enough women in the tech world. We can't pin this problem on any one factor; like most complex trends, the number, visibility, and success of women in tech are influenced by a constellation of factors. It's clear we have relatively few women in visible senior technology positions. There are many possible reasons for this, too. Despite many strong female role models in public-facing positions, there are not enough—yet. And we see gender bias in education, sexism in the workplace, lack of investment in female entrepreneurs, and a culture that discourages girls from pursuing STEM education and women from entering tech fields.

So we need more Girls Who Code. We need more underrepresented populations and women choosing to study in STEM fields. And we need more diversity-driven hiring initiatives. The United States leads in so many industries—in content creation, in health care, in technology—because our culture of innovation and risk-taking is fueled by the experiments and experiences of our immigrant culture and history. Our heterogeneity is a competitive strength. Diversity in the workforce makes us better, stronger, and smarter.

Status vs. Skills

Across the river from CTA's offices sits George Washington University, known around here as GW. In the spring of 2018, the school named Marcia McNutt—president of the National Academy of Sciences (NAS)—as its 2018 commencement speaker. In announcing the decision, GW president Thomas LeBlanc said, "Marcia McNutt is not only one of our nation's foremost scientific leaders, but she also sets a powerful example as the first woman to lead one of the National Academies."[5]

A geophysicist by training, McNutt holds a Ph.D. in earth sciences and is the first woman to serve as NAS president. For four years, she was the director of the U.S. Geological Survey, during which time her team responded to major disasters including the Deepwater Horizon oil spill. McNutt led the team that helped cap the well and contain the spill.

The class of 2018 didn't respond to the news the way I would have expected. A few days after the announcement, the editorial board of the *Hatchet*, the university's student newspaper, published this:

> *The University has long sustained a pattern of high-profile speakers for the ceremony on the National Mall. Previous speakers have included Apple*

CEO Tim Cook in 2015, Sen. Cory Booker, D-N.J., in 2016 and Sen. Tammy Duckworth, D-Ill., last year. GW is a university full of students with a variety of interests who study many different disciplines, but it is still known for fields like international affairs, political science and journalism. McNutt is not a public figure and clearly breaks away from this trend. Most students on campus didn't even know her name before the announcement. . . .[6]

LeBlanc said in a radio interview it was mostly non-STEM students who complained about the pick—students he described as "privileged."[7] But to me, the problem runs much deeper. In America, we idolize athletes and movie stars, viewing the ability to close a deal or break a record as more important than the ability to code, build hardware, or map systems. Our celebrity culture has elevated a few nontraditional players, including Mark Zuckerberg, Jeff Bezos, and Bill Gates, to elite status, but these are exceptions. We have to change things to make tech cooler. The tech industry, Hollywood, and the media can do a better job telling stories about ninja women like Marcia McNutt, who too seldom receive credit for working wonders behind the scenes. The 2016 hit *Hidden Figures* tells the story of three brilliant African American women mathematicians working for NASA—Katherine Johnson, Dorothy Vaughan, and Mary Jackson—who helped John Glenn launch into space. We need to shine a light on more untold stories, introduce more STEM role models, and make the industries and institutions they represent more accessible to the next generation of ninja innovators.

Leading the Way

CTA has an unparalleled platform for this kind of education and inspiration. As the producer of CES, the biggest and most visible business event in the world, my team and I have a unique opportunity—and, I would argue, responsibility—to champion women and underrepresented groups throughout our programming. We have to be part of the solution.

According to a 2018 survey conducted by LivePerson, just 8 percent of Americans say they can name a female CEO of a technology company. And when pressed for a name, only 4 percent actually can come up with one.[8] Despite the ubiquity of tech companies, their tremendous impact on our economy, and their cache within our culture, we have a shortage of visible female role models.

This is not the case within CTA; we have an exceptional record of hiring and promoting women. Roughly two-thirds of our staff of almost two hundred employees are women. This ratio holds at every level, through senior vice president. Two of our top leaders are Glenda MacMullin, our COO and CFO, and Karen Chupka, our executive vice president, CES. Almost all of Karen's direct reports—the ones running the global CES events—are women.

The entire CES team is responsible for attracting the world's innovative companies to CES in January to launch their products and deliver thought-provoking visions of the future. We have done this successfully for more than fifty years.

But in 2018 our status as a diversity ninja was challenged. The debate centered on the perceived lack of diversity on the

CES 2018 keynote stage. We announced our 2018 keynote lineup based on a range of factors, including the time of final speaker confirmation. Ultimately we announced three men, up front, in succession—the CEOs from Ford, Huawei, and Intel. We neglected to share that we had almost three hundred women speakers—many of whom were CEOs. But that didn't matter either, because in late 2017, the industry began to hear from women reflecting on sexual harassment in the workplace. Then in October, the #MeToo movement went viral after several high-profile stories of sexual misconduct in Hollywood came to light.

At exactly the moment women rightly began demanding more accountability from powerful industries, we missed an opportunity to lead by example. This experience highlighted for us the need to not only be more inclusive within our industry, but to shun sexism by vocally defending and championing women in tech—at all levels. We have to take full advantage of our role as leaders in the tech industry to increase the visibility of women and underrepresented groups. This doesn't mean we will simply look to have equal representation of male and female speakers—but it does mean we will create opportunities that diversify our speaker pool to include traditionally underrepresented groups throughout the show.

We need more girls and women—and more boys and men—from all backgrounds to pursue careers in science, math, coding, engineering, and data analysis. We know these are the building blocks of artificial intelligence, robotics, self-driving cars, the Internet of Things, augmented and virtual reality, and other areas of rapid innovation. We know these industries are the future. We know we already face a talent shortage. We must not fail to find a way to engage all our talented youth and turn them into future ninjas.

Diversity in Tech

Our commitment to diversity is borne out by most measures in our hiring at CTA. In addition to our strong African American, Asian, and Hispanic employment numbers, we work hard to hire veterans and people with disabilities (though we can do better). We also support programs to boost employment for veterans and connect older adults and people with disabilities with technology. And the benefits of these investments play out across the CES show floor.

Eighty-two-year-old Carol Staninger was a first-time exhibitor at CES 2018. She created Save Our Loved Ones, a device that prevents young people, seniors, or pets left in a car from dying. She debuted her innovation in Eureka Park. Another CES success story: Xyla Foxlin is founder and CEO of Parihug—you may have seen her company featured on a Microsoft Surface commercial. Today she runs Beauty and the Bolt, an online maker movement teaching kids about STEM, and exhibits at CES to promote her program to future maker/engineer/creative ninjas. Within seven months after CES, her subscription base for Beauty and the Bolt grew five-fold. And sixteen-year-old Robert West, son of entrepreneur, educator, and CTA member Skip West, debuted FeedScore, a sentiment analysis tool for social media, at CES 2018. Robert was one of our youngest ninja innovators ever to exhibit at CES.

We are the primary funder of U.S. Tech Vets, a free service that connects more than one million job-seeking veterans with thousands of hiring companies through software that translates military skills to civilian jobs. We also support Black Girls Code, a group that promotes STEM education for young girls in underrepresented communities. I serve on the D.C.-area board of the United Service Organizations (USO). Our CTA Foundation supports groups using technology to help people with disabilities, and we have worked side by side with many disability groups to deliver empowering technologies.

We are both an advocate and a leader on lesbian, gay, bisexual, and transgender (LGBT) issues. Our goal is to hire and keep the best employees possible; their sexual orientation shouldn't impact that at all. Our board agrees and has been generous in allowing us to be vocal on these issues.

We are the first to say that the tech industry as a whole needs to make gains with traditionally underrepresented groups to improve our diversity record. While more than half (57 percent) of professional jobs are held by women in the United States, only about one-quarter (26 percent) of computing jobs are held by women.[9] And of that 26 percent, only 3 percent are held by African American women. Reports filed by Google, Facebook, and Twitter show that fewer than 2 percent of their combined workforce were African American.[10] And a report from the National Urban League found that in companies across the tech industry, African Americans comprise less than 5 percent of the workforce.[11]

And sadly, the inflow of women and people of color into STEM fields has actually declined in some areas in the last twenty-five years. A Pew study found that "while there has been significant progress for women in the life and physical sciences since 1990, the share of women has been roughly stable in other STEM occupational clusters and has actually gone down 7 percentage points in the area with the largest job growth over this period: computer occupations, a job cluster that includes computer scientists, systems analysts, software developers, information systems managers, and programmers." [12]

Hundreds of programs encourage students to go into tech at earlier and earlier ages. But no single program of which I am aware has been consistently successful in ramping up underrepresented populations in STEM fields. We need to double down on these investments and ensure they succeed. Earlier, I mentioned our strong support for Girls Who Code; we also work with EVERFI to sponsor a digital learning course called Future Innovators across more than three dozen public schools in Clark County, Nevada. I personally support the Ron Brown Foundation, a program that provides financial support and mentorship for top-performing students of color who are entering college. More than 99 percent of its awardees graduate from college.

One amazing example is the model set by my friend, the scientist and inventor Dean Kamen. In addition to inventing the Segway and better ways to desalinate salt water, Dean created a robot-building contest for students (more on Kamen's STEM work in Chapter 5). The contest began in 1992 with teams of students from 28 schools. By 2018, the contest included 90,000 students from 27 countries. And of these participants, 31 percent are female, 18 percent are African American or Hispanic, and 20 percent are part of a free or reduced-price lunch program. [13] Dean's contest also attracts notable judges, including Colin Angle, who created and runs iRobot, the world's most successful robot company. In fact, Colin met his wife—a former programmer and fellow judge—at the contest! With stories like this, I am starting to think if we can fully engage all students at a young age, we tech nerds can inherit the earth.

Reforming Our Immigration System

At CES 2017, we met Robbie Cabral, an immigrant to the United States with an innovative security solution. Robbie was born and raised in the Dominican Republic in what he describes as "a tough environment." Robbie founded his startup, BenjiLock, a fingerprint-enabled gym locker lock that can be used just about anywhere, when he was out of work and going to the gym to keep himself motivated. "BenjiLock is my startup. It turned me from a depressed, unemployed father to a driven, 24-7 machine," he wrote in the *Los Angeles Business Journal*.

Four years later, Robbie debuted his product in Eureka Park, where BenjiLock won an Innovation Award. After the show, he got involved with the work we do at CTA. And we watched proudly as he won funding on *Shark Tank*, backed by Kevin O'Leary.

First-generation immigrants like Robbie account for 30 percent of all new U.S. entrepreneurs, according to a Kauffman Foundation study. Restricting immigration, whether legal or illegal, would mean slower labor force growth and hence slower employment growth. And strategic immigration reforms that encourage foreign-born entrepreneurs and U.S.-educated immigrants to remain in the United States will help build businesses and create domestic jobs. High-skilled immigration has allowed the United States to attract the world's most talented software developers, engineers, statisticians, and mathematicians to help create and maintain some of the latest cutting-edge technology Americans love.

Slashing immigration not only throttles our economy, it betrays our values. We must embrace strategic immigration reform that boosts our industry without compromising our humanity.

The failures of the U.S. system are not lost on other countries. Canadian private-sector firms are enticing skilled immigrants and snapping up U.S. startups. France has developed a visa expressly for tech innovators. And Britain has increased its Exceptional Talent visas by 100 percent. The competition for top talent is stiff—and it will grow only more intense.

A Competitive Advantage

Some may argue that workforce diversity is not important. They see U.S. companies doing well and argue that it is because tech is a merit-based field—because these hypercompetitive companies select and hire only the best candidates, who in turn build the most prosperous businesses. I don't buy this argument.

I believe strongly that advocating diversity is not just the right thing to do—hiring and promoting people from different backgrounds and experiences gives organizations a competitive advantage. Just think about the life cycle of any business. *Harvard Business Review* describes the five stages of small business development like this: existence, survival, success, takeoff, and resource maturity. The nature, size, management, and growth potential of businesses will vary widely, but "they experience common problems arising at similar stages in their development." [14] A diverse team with different life and business experiences can help respond to specific challenges, anticipate future scenarios, and contribute to strategies that ensure the entity's survival and growth.

I wrote about this at length in *Ninja Innovation*. In the 1990s, eBay was a relatively small-scale internet auction site. Its founder, Pierre Omidyar, knew he had a great idea, but also understood that he wasn't the right person to take eBay public— so he brought in Meg Whitman. Although Whitman's background seemed to clash with eBay's ethos (she was a Harvard MBA and seasoned corporate executive), she turned out to be exactly what eBay needed. Under her leadership, the company went public in less than a year, launching the e-commerce age.

Everything starts with an idea. Then you need to take that idea to market. That requires money. You can self-fund. You can ask your family and friends for money. Increasingly, you can get off the ground by using crowdfunding platforms such as Kickstarter and Indiegogo (CTA successfully fought for a law allowing startups to raise equity capital via crowdfunding). But for most innovators, at some point you have to grow and must turn to outside investors.

Most people assume good *ideas* get funded. But the fact is that *people* get funded—and men control the investment funds. A study at Luleå University in Sweden found female startup founders received 25 percent of their ask from governmental venture capitalists, compared to 52 percent for startups founded by men.[15] At a 2018 conference in Washington, a panel of investors agreed that funding is made largely on the basis of chemistry—"clicking" with the founder. According to panelist Merom Klein, a principal at Courage Growth Partners, "It's a lot like with dating—and you kind of develop a methodology for finding the people, the right teams to fit you as an investor." [16] It is human nature to gravitate toward people with whom you feel most comfortable.

The same thing is true in hiring. We must fight our natural bias to select people like ourselves. In *Ninja Innovation*, I argued that successful innovation requires diversity. In my view, diversity is a core American strength, and one we hope others will emulate. We think diversity is so important to innovation that it was one of the twelve criteria we used to rank countries in our International Innovation Scorecard. We based our rankings on the United Nations migration data, as well as the ratio of male-to-female participation in the workforce. Unsurprisingly, most of the thirteen countries we honored as top-tier Innovation Champions in 2018 also earned the highest grades in measures of diversity.

Leading the Pack

All employers have to work hard to ensure diversity in the workforce and with regard to their investors. It's possible that homogeneous populations may have less discord, but I'd argue that they're also less innovative. When you combine diverse backgrounds and perspectives with inclusive practices and a team environment—where employees work across cultures, differences, even languages—then a company has a great shot at leading a pack instead of being just one of many followers.

I applaud former Intel CEO Brian Krzanich for leading the pack: At CES 2016 he announced that by 2020 he wanted a workforce that reflected the demographics of America. At CES 2018, he announced the company had met this goal. Most companies, however, are struggling to become future ninjas because the talent pool is not there for hire, and it appears to be getting even shallower.

What can other businesses learn from our experience? Ninja innovators already understand that hiring and promoting people from different backgrounds with different skills will bestow a competitive advantage on almost any organization. It's also worth noting that stronger companies tend to have more diverse boards. Corporations with female board members do better financially, according to a 2016 survey by the Peterson Institute for International Economics.[17] Norway, Iceland, Spain, and France require that 40 percent of board members be women.[18] And pressure is building from large, actively managed pension funds, including the California Public Employees' Retirement System, to pass diversity tests or be disqualified from fund investing. Any company lacking diversity at the board and executive level is threatening its reputation, share price, and ability to tap the largest talent pool at every level of employee.

One solution is to recruit diverse board members and executives. Publicly traded company boards should include not only CEOs, former CEOs, and trustworthy friends of founders or CEOs, but also those who can add expertise in key areas such as government, environment, technology, cybersecurity, partnering, and strategy. And they should include representatives from other countries and cultures. Diversity is our national strength—it should be a corporate strength and corporate culture, too. And it should be in play in every facet of human resources, starting with the hiring of interns. Junior employees need role models in the boardroom and the executive suite.

Amazon's leadership principles guide its efforts to innovate in diversity, inclusion, and equality. Salesforce is committed to employee diversity, driven by the mantra "Equality for All." Intel pledged $300 million in investments to mirror our national diversity. You don't have to be Amazon or Intel or Salesforce, but CEOs and boards must not only commit to diversity and opportunity—they must also loudly and visibly show it. Facebook chief operating officer Sheryl Sandberg's bestselling book *Lean In* documents the unique challenges women face with workplace discrimination and as mothers. And she lays out concrete suggestions for employers to leverage the strengths of *all* employees, instead of holding them back.

We can create workplaces that better reflect our country's diversity by stretching toward those who are leaning in. This means pulling them up through mentoring, and reaching out and targeting underrepresented groups for recruitment and executive career paths.

The United States is the undisputed leader in so many industries—content creation, health care, technology—because our culture of innovation and risk-taking is fueled by the different views and experiments of our immigrant culture and history. Our heterogeneity is a competitive strength. Diversity in the workforce makes us better as a nation.

I am proud of our record. I know we can do better. Innovation is too important to not seek, tap, and develop talent from every corner and community—it's what helps the U.S. economy grow and thrive. It's what will ensure we remain a nation of ninjas.

Resilience

Diversity may be the foundation of the economy and society of the ninja future—but we need to make sure we also fortify our organizations so that they can achieve their mission when confronted with external threats or adversity. In short, we need resilience.

Innovation has been the buzzword for the past decade. *Resilience* is the watchword of the future.

Not all technological innovations are new; sometimes it's worth looking to the past when building for the future, so as not to overlook hard-won lessons. This hit home for me in 2017. Moved by the suffering and courage of those impacted by the year's many disasters, our association donated $1 million to charity efforts that helped each affected area recover from its crisis. Four of these were natural disasters—the hurricanes in Florida, Texas, and Puerto Rico and the fires in Napa Valley; one was the result of human cruelty—the mass shooting in Las Vegas. People were hurting everywhere disaster had struck, but the suffering in Puerto Rico was especially high. We believed these Americans faced a particularly long and difficult recovery, so we directed half of our overall donations there.

But while organizationally our biggest impact was in Puerto Rico, the greatest impact for me personally came in Napa Valley. It was there that I learned the importance of resilience—or the ability to withstand and recover from hostile events.

In early October 2017, our governing board met at a beautiful new hotel in Napa Valley. The rooms had wonderful views and the electric blackout shades let us sleep deeply beyond the dawn. Each room was also equipped with a high-tech toilet that raised its cover as soon as you entered the bathroom.

The final night of our stay, wind gusts buffeted the valley and knocked out the area's electricity. In the wee hours, the hallway emergency lights sputtered on and off. Sirens followed. Few of us could sleep. At this point, the rooms were pitch black, and the heavy electric-powered blinds could not be opened. The room lights were useless, landline hotel telephones were dead, and our smartphones soon became unusable for anything other than their power-sucking flashlight function.

Tired guests gathered in common areas to commiserate. We learned that forest fires were spreading nearby; briefly there was talk of evacuating the hotel. But there also was word of long lines of bumper-to-bumper traffic and a concern the fire was approaching the main roads.

The hotel quickly set up a cold buffet breakfast outside and delivered candles to each room. We were urged to pack. This presented a special challenge for me as my suitcase was on the balcony, which could only be reached by first raising the electronically controlled blackout shades. We decided to bump up our meeting time and benefit from the team of experts who had flown in to brief our board on a critical issue: security procedures for CES.

In a sunlit room without electricity, phone connectivity, or coffee, we spent the next couple of hours exploring this important and substantive topic. Without distractions, the group was laser focused and soon concluded an important and productive meeting. We quickly left on a bus and wove our way around some massive, smoky fires that sadly cost dozens of lives and thousands of homes.

In retrospect, I'm immensely grateful for all that went wrong. I found the experience transformational in several ways. Not only did it serve as a kind of rehearsal ahead of CES 2018—when unprecedented rainfall led to power outages in parts of the Las Vegas Convention Center for about two hours—it also changed the way I thought about disaster preparedness.

Most of us assume we'll always have access to basics like water, electricity, and a phone signal. Yet our cities, towns, and homes are increasingly vulnerable due to real changes in our environment and our dependence on technology. (See Chapters 3 and 6 for more on environmental shifts.) We need to start thinking differently about how we can prepare for a rapidly changing world—and resilience will be the key. As extreme weather conditions grow more common, we need to take preparing and planning seriously. Add frequent power outages, periodic cyber-intrusions, looming nuclear threats, and rumbling trade wars to the mix, and we're looking at many major cultural, economic, and social shifts that require us all to be future ninjas.

In a 2018 interview in *Washingtonian* magazine, Washington, D.C.'s first-ever chief resilience officer, Kevin Bush, compared the idea of resilience to your body's immune system. "Cities are complicated systems of systems; there's road systems, there's health systems, there's housing systems. They all come together and interact in ways we don't always recognize." He added that his job is to think about "How is our immune system weak and how is it strong? How can we build up immunities to things that we can expect coming on down the line?"[19] Or, as CTA board member Dr. Carmichael Roberts, founder and managing partner at Boston-based Material Impact, a fund that invests in technologies that solve real-world problems, explained at CTA's 2018 CEO Summit event: "Resilient technologies are those that even in the face of adversity keep the world healthy, safe, warm, powered, fed, and secure."

My Dutch friend Martijn van der Linden, of NXP, agrees that resilience is critical, and he believes we should look to younger generations and startups—future ninjas—for the solutions. Older generations, he says, helped cause climate change, and as such focus primarily on reducing our environmental impact. Younger people, by contrast, are accustomed to abrupt changes in the environment and are providing practical solutions to confront and leverage these changes.

He highlighted two examples. The first was a group of Dutch students who, seeing the pollution caused by carbon-based fuels, developed a solar-powered car. The second was a company called LINA that transforms plants into 3-D-printed cars instead of using nonrenewable materials.

Other regions and sectors have also started to prioritize resilience. In the nonprofit sector, the Bill and Melinda Gates Foundation—the largest private foundation in the United States—expanded its focus beyond education and health care to include emergency response and energy sustainability. Thanks to generous contributions from the foundation, several regions, including the Middle East, have been able to invest in resilience initiatives. And the Gates Foundation asked Carmichael, a serial entrepreneur and material sciences expert, to lead its investments in companies that offer solutions to energy dependence and promote resilience.

Not everyone is on board with this; some say it's not enough to simply be resilient. Author Nassim Nicholas Taleb argues in *Antifragile* that resilience is not the opposite of fragility, as it implies. It's not about simply building protections against adverse events. He characterizes resilience as defensive and incomplete, as it does not account for the unique strengths and advantages that can only arise from adversity.

Taleb makes the analogy to the human immune system: The body builds immunities by fighting off disease. It can only grow stronger in those specific ways by withstanding specific infections or overcoming certain suboptimal circumstances. Writ large, he contends that the health of a system—from the human body to a national economy—*requires* the failure of individual cells or businesses. Individual cells die. Startups fail. Yet the marketplace—like the body—succeeds *because* of failure, not in spite of it. He says the opposite of fragility is actually antifragility and that resilience alone is not enough.

Taleb, who also wrote about improbable events that are difficult to plan for in *The Black Swan*, and became a successful Wall Street investor, makes some fascinating and interesting points. Mainly, defensive planning is not enough to ensure survival: You must be able to adjust quickly to changing situations. Taleb calls it "antifragile." I call it being a ninja.

These two ideas are mutually reinforcing—a both/and situation. Some companies may focus more on resilience, others on antifragility. As an industry, we need to do both: build bulwarks against bad situations *and* position ourselves to respond nimbly when things don't go as planned. As painful as they are, the natural disasters like the devastating fires in Napa offer valuable learning opportunities and reinforce the need for this kind of protection and planning.

Resilience is all about surviving in the face of challenging or unexpected conditions or forces. People, groups, businesses, geographic entities, and governments can all be—must all be—resilient. And they are all starting to realize it. In the last decade, Google searches for "resilience" have grown nearly 130 percent.[20] In light of this growing interest, we dedicated an entire exhibit area and conference program to resilience at CES 2019.

There are three key components of resilience: redundancy, independence, and investment.

Redundancy

Our reliance on technology makes us vulnerable if we depend on these vital technologies without some type of backup plan in place. During the Napa Valley fires, we lost light in our hotel rooms, but many in our group had tiny flashlights on hand. In some countries, including Japan, all hotel rooms are equipped with flashlights. I keep a few flashlights in my home but had never considered traveling with one. I do now.

The loss of electric light was serious because the blackout blinds could not be opened manually. This was not only frustrating, but could also be a major safety issue if there were a fire at my front door. Makers and buyers of products affecting ingress should consider real-life scenarios. In the case of the Napa Valley hotel, the electric blinds needed a manual override.

Being cut off from communication was unnerving. We were only able to get a radio signal by going to the parking lot and turning on our car radios. To arrange an earlier bus we had to drive to the bus dispatch office. Every group and facility should have a portable, solar, or hand-cranked radio, or a phone with a working FM radio option. Isolated facilities and homes should consider investing in a satellite phone. Backup chargers were valuable for those who used their phone's flashlight capabilities.

The level of redundancy should be tied to the harm from technology failure and the cost and inconvenience of redundancy. Redundancy doesn't have to be expensive. Carrying a battery charger and a tiny flashlight in a travel kit is cheap but potentially essential. Every airplane is required to have redundancy in all critical systems, even though it is expensive and may never be needed. We accept the redundancy because one failure out of 1,000 flights is not acceptable.

Indeed, sometimes the safety stakes are so high the answer is obvious. As we shift to self-driving vehicles, companies designing and building them are considering different technical strategies to ensure safety, such as car-to-car communication, smartphone-based spectrum and dead reckoning, GPS, and onboard computers. To me, the answer is obvious: We need redundancy to ensure safety.

In the HDTV debate of the 1990s, the five finalist inventors argued for their different systems, each having a different number of lines of resolution. I learned that it did not take much to create a chip that could receive all formats. So I proposed that every TV set be required to receive all formats, and let the set maker choose how to display that format. Manufacturers were fine with this solution, and it allowed us to shift gracefully and easily to a fantastic national HDTV system.

I was thankful to survive and learn from the Napa Valley power blackout and fires. But I am all too aware that others were not so lucky, and am committed to promoting redundancy as a vital factor in my future tech planning. By the way, the toilet in our hotel room had a manual flush option. Simple, low-cost redundancy is often the best and simplest solution.

Independence

Being resilient also means being independent.

This is not to diminish the power of the connected world enabled by technology. The internet and broadband connectivity give us unprecedented access to information and to one another. Connectivity of our utilities lets us buy and sell efficiently across multiple sources depending on supply and demand. The physical connectivity provided by airports, roads, and water means we can travel and trade easily.

But none of us is oblivious to the risks of connectivity. Internet connectivity also enables cyber intrusions and exposes people to unwanted solicitation and even identity theft. Utility connectivity introduces greater systemic vulnerability, including electric outages, water poisoning, and domestic terrorism. Physical connectivity allows vulnerability to crime, disease, and—again—terrorism.

Independence isn't a zero-sum game. Again, it isn't resilience *or* antifragility; it's another instance of "both/and." We can protect our institutions with a layered security approach, starting with perimeter or border security to deter cyberbots, terrorists, or other harmful entrants. If bad actors do get through, they can be isolated in smaller units or cells to minimize damage—and we should use every one of these failures to grow stronger and defend ourselves better going forward.

Independence also means not being reliant on other countries for goods. The "shop local" movement supports local economies, cuts down on the environmental cost of transporting food, and encourages community building, but it does not have to be an exclusive mandate.

Independence and resilience are tied to the concept of "grit." Research has shown young children who are willing to delay eating a single marshmallow or cookie if they know they'll get *two* treats later—those willing to stick it out and delay gratification—are more likely to succeed in life. Grit, or the willingness to stick with something without quitting, is present in some people but not others. The young soccer players who survived almost two weeks stranded in a dark cave in Thailand had grit. Would American kids have done as well?

Investment

Each of us can and should invest in making our homes and businesses both more independent and more resilient. As I write this, I hear my neighbor's electric generator running after a brief-but-intense windstorm that caused multiple power outages in the Detroit area where I live. Let's say the generator cost him

$4,000. That's a lot of money—but it pays dividends every time snow or wind knocks out the power and his family can carry on as if nothing has happened.

Many people store extra potable water and canned food, and back up their computers or even keep them off the grid. At CES 2018, Zero Mass Water took this idea to the next level, demonstrating technology that pulls water or humidity out of the air. Increasingly, governments are mandating that new homes be built to meet certain earthquake, flood, and wind damage criteria.

This is a global challenge. According to a 2016 World Bank report, "If cities fail to build their resilience to disasters, shocks, and ongoing stresses, climate change and natural disasters will cost cities worldwide $314 billion every year by 2030." [21] We can start with investments in infrastructure.

By 2050, the majority of the world will be living in cities. [22] Now is the time to lay the groundwork for smart building and infrastructure. This means building buildings with backup water and energy systems that harness the power of renewable energy sources. It means investing in standardized emergency bridges, like those used in Haiti following 2016's Hurricane Matthew, that can be quickly assembled with ready-made, interchangeable pieces. And it means developing resilient internet systems built on decentralized, distributed networks that can preserve our data in the wake of emergencies.

Smart cities are the urban landscapes of the ninja future. Powered by the ubiquitous connectivity of the Internet of Things, smart cities collect data on a variety of factors, from pollution to traffic, and employ that data to make cities safer and more sustainable. CES now has an area of the show floor dedicated to Smart Cities. A recent report cosponsored by CTA and the United Parcel Service (UPS), *The Evolution of Smart Cities and Connect Communities Study,* predicts that the market value of smart cities will jump from $14.85 billion in 2015 to $34.35 billion by 2020.[23] This represents a compound annual growth rate of 18 percent. Many cities have read the tea leaves and hired chief technology officers and innovation officers to implement smart-city technologies. Ninja innovators should engage now with leaders who have a vision and understanding of their local needs.

Make no mistake: These are serious investments. The hardware, sensor, and transmitter costs of implementing these systems are not insignificant, but they will, at least, decrease over time—and they will create new jobs. Technicians will be needed to install and maintain the systems. Data analysts are going to be needed to interpret the data. Architects, builders, construction trades, and others will be essential to designing, building, and changing towns to accommodate and apply the data. These will be good, well-paying jobs requiring a diverse array of skills.

New technologies and tools equipped with sensors and big data analytic capabilities will solve many of the fundamental concerns underlying the resilience movement. Technology is an incredible force for good, particularly for responding to natural or man-made disasters. Americans recognize and appreciate the value these tech tools present: According to a 2017 Pew study, Americans say technology will be the most important factor in improving their lives in the decades to come.[24]

Government, citizens, and the tech industry should work together to address personal cybersecurity challenges and national security to fortify our systems and communities so they can withstand disasters and keep running smoothly. If necessity is the mother of invention, resilience is the mother of innovation—and innovation requires flexibility and collaboration. Let the work begin!

CHAPTER 12

PRINCIPLES FOR FUTURE NINJAS

I STARTED WORKING AT A very young age—so I've had a lifetime to think about the attributes that ninja innovators possess. Over the years, everyone from students to startups to business leaders has asked me for career advice. Each person's background and aspirations are different, so whenever possible I try to customize my advice. For the purposes of this chapter, I've organized my thoughts on professional and personal development into eight principles for future ninjas.

Be Compassionate

When I was six or seven years old, my father would leave work as a teacher and head to the local factory to pick up piecework.

He'd bring home big, foam structures and we'd punch out hair curlers and put them together, working as a family to earn some extra money. Across the seasons, I was always shoveling snow, mowing lawns, delivering newspapers—in other words, working.

When I was about fifteen years old, my older brother was working for a temp agency. One day he couldn't take a job request that had come in, so I pretended I was him, said I was of legal age, and spent the day working in a lamp factory. It was a life-altering experience. When my dad picked me up after I'd spent a full day repeating the same action over and over, I told him, "Dad, I'm going to college."

The next summer, I nabbed my dream job, as a summer camp counselor and lifeguard at the 4-H sleepaway camp on the Long Island Sound where I had been a camper for many years. I loved working with the kids and I loved the environment and 4-H culture. One particularly hot evening, I impatiently sat through an all-staff meeting as I looked forward to hanging out with my first real girlfriend. I barely listened as the camp director talked about recent problems with alcohol use by counselors and announced a zero-tolerance policy.

A few days later, I had a day off, so my girlfriend and I spent it together away from camp. Along the way, we got a six-pack, and I managed to finish the first beer of my life. I carried the remaining few beers in hand as we walked back into the camp and crossed paths with the camp director. He confiscated the beers and said he would talk to me about it in the morning.

I was shocked the next day when he fired me. I thought having beer on my day off was my business. But bringing the beer onto camp property was exactly what he had said was verboten. I was devastated.

I called my father and asked him to pick me up. I remember my humiliation and tears on the ride home. But I remember something else much more vividly: My dad never chided or scolded me. He certainly could have; I felt I deserved it. But he saw my pain and knew I had learned a lesson. His great judgment and love for me meant that he could be silent—which, in that moment, was the very definition of compassion.

I think about that transformative experience often. It taught me that actions have consequences. If you violate a rule, be prepared to pay the price. Even today, whenever I consider consciously violating a rule—whether it's jaywalking or speeding—I assess whether the likely penalty or safety risk is worth the consequences.

But it also taught me the importance of compassion. When someone is down, that's when he or she most needs support. That's when parents, friends, colleagues, and bosses matter most. Applauding excellence and achievement is easy. Calling a friend or acquaintance who's been fired, even for cause, is more important. And firing someone with empathy is even harder and more important.

Being fired is a mortifying experience. Having lived through it, I insist, as CEO, on approving every employee termination. I leave it to the lawyers to assess the legal risk; my job is to make sure we have been fair to the person. When you're the boss, it's important to be empathetic. My dad didn't pile on. Remembering that formative experience, I can't help but empathize with employees being fired, and ask multiple questions before any termination. Was there one bad act or a series? Did they receive feedback and a chance to change? Was it performance or personality? Absent fraud or transgression, is there a different job in the organization the employee could succeed at? How do we tell them and what, if any, severance is offered? What help can we offer in finding another job more suited to their skills? How can we preserve their dignity?

Nine times out of ten, the best advice in such a situation is to err on the side of compassion—even if that means shortening the pain by escorting an employee out of the building the same day.

Be Collaborative

Nothing teaches us more about empathy than working on a team. For a team to function well, each member must always be working to better understand and relate to one another. And when you have strong teams, you can draw a straight line from collaboration to ninja innovation.

Once upon a time, employees could steadily move up in one division of a company and switch positions within that division. That's rarely the case anymore. The silo approach of individual excellence isn't enough in our connected world. You must expand your view to grow within a company. This is a particular strength of MBA programs—they teach you how to work with diverse teams. They hone active listening, which is the core of empathy. The more you listen to your customers, your colleagues, and your teammates, the better—that's where you will get the best ideas.

CEOs should lead by example. Great CEOs know they are not always right, not always the best source for new ideas, and could not have achieved success without teamwork. In *Ninja Innovation*, I made the case that Amazon's monstrous success is due in large part to Jeff Bezos' mantra of putting the customer first and working backward from there. That is more than a strategy—being aware of and sensitive to the needs of others is the definition of empathy.

Mike McGuire, CEO of professional services firm Grant Thornton, once told me that to drive innovation in his organization, he takes an "upside-down pyramid" approach. Instead of dictating new ideas from the executive suite to the full team, he's building a model that turns the pyramid upside down so that all the great ideas employees have across the firm can funnel down to the leadership team.

The company is implementing an innovation software platform that enables every employee to contribute ideas, such as how to improve business functions, interact better with clients, or deliver services more effectively. "This is what we mean by our 'people-first' growth strategy," McGuire told me. "We have thousands of people on our team who constantly think of new ways to create value for our clients." In this way, Grant Thornton, a nearly century-old company that serves clients globally, is moving beyond the status quo and into its new brand positioning—"Status Go"—to innovate and move quickly and nimbly as an organization.

Great CEOs like Bezos and McGuire are driving transformational change by listening to other people's ideas, adopting the best ones, and encouraging everyone in the company's orbit—including customers or external partners—to pitch ideas for the next ninja innovation.

Be Curious

You never know when inspiration will strike. In 2018, I spoke at a conference about blockchain held at the French embassy in Washington, D.C. The host was Don Upson, who served as Virginia's secretary of technology, the nation's first state cabinet-level technology secretary, and was the mastermind behind the legal framework governing the internet. Don and I go way back, so even though I am by no means an expert on blockchain, I was happy to participate and to learn from other speakers.

After I spoke, I listened to a presentation on the evolution of the science of voting and decision making. Much of it was developed by French mathematicians and philosophers. The speaker described how airplane pilots and copilots make decisions, of which there are basically only three to be made—keep going, return to their base, or shift course. He suggested that rather than making "yes/no" decisions to a checklist of facts before a decision, the pilot and copilot consider four choices: "yes, strong no, moderate no, weak no." With these four choices, and only two people, the pilots can make better decisions than the simple two inputs of "yes" or "no."

My hand shot up the moment he was finished: "First, this is fascinating, but what does it have to do with blockchain? Second, can my wife and I use this to make decisions?"

He responded patiently that his talk was aimed at how computers verify facts necessary for blockchain to work: The greater the number of independent computers with more choices, the higher degree of certainty of the facts, and the greater the likelihood that the predicate conditions will be considered satisfactory for the blockchain transaction to proceed. He then responded to my marriage question by saying this method would indeed allow me to make better decision making . . . if I had ten wives. (I guess this is blockchain humor.)

For the first time in years I wondered if I had asked a really stupid question. I rarely feel foolish asking questions; it's how I learn. And in my experience, if you have a nagging question, chances are many others in the audience are wondering the same thing. The more pressing questions: Who's going to raise their hand? Who's overly concerned about looking stupid? It is amazing what a large percentage of people have this fear.

Many of these thoughts went through my head as I realized that my question conveyed that I had totally missed the point of the speaker's presentation and exposed my ignorance to a room full of high-level executives. I steeled myself for looks of pity as I headed out of the room for the break. But before I reached the door, a business leader approached me and, to my relief, told me he also didn't understand the connection to blockchain and appreciated my question. This happened several more times throughout the day.

The lesson: Curiosity leads to better decision making. Everyone is afraid of looking stupid. But asking questions is a life skill that's worth practicing every day. It's key to great "small talk" at business events. If you're in a situation where you don't know anyone, it's difficult to walk up to a group and insert yourself. One way to do this is to walk up to anyone standing alone or not engaged with the group, introduce yourself, and ask, "What brings you here?" Ask about their connection to the group, what they do, and what they're looking to learn. When you are seated next to strangers at a business lunch or a dinner, take the opportunity to pick their brains and learn something about their areas of expertise or interest. While most people find commonality over sports and weather and avoid politics, I prefer to get reactions to the events of the day, ask what they think the stock market will do, what they invest in, or what their favorite device or app is. I also like to hear what technology they think will be popular or useful in their business or for entertainment.

When asking questions, think about how you structure them. If you want more than a "yes" or "no" answer, it's best to begin with "why," "what," "how," or "tell me." This is much more likely to evoke answers that go beyond relevant facts, including personal stories that offer insight into how people made the decisions that led them to where they are today. I learned this technique from philanthropist and Carlyle Group founder and host of Bloomberg's *Peer to Peer*, David Rubenstein. After leaving the Carter White House, he joined a law firm, where I worked closely with him on issues involving the legality of new technologies. At our weekly meetings, David would always have a lengthy to-do list on a yellow legal pad. He rarely gave his opinion without first asking a series of thoughtful questions.

David chairs the Economic Club of Washington, D.C., a prestigious group of area business leaders who gather frequently for a series of onstage interviews with well-known leaders in business and government. With his prodigious memory, wry sense of humor, and casual delivery of questions, David manages to elicit incredibly personal and interesting responses from his featured and famous interviewees. I was there in 2014 when David got Donald Trump to say publicly that he was likely running for president. (I was sitting next to CNN Washington Bureau Chief Sam Feist, who nearly jumped out of his seat as he told me that CNN would cover Trump "nonstop" even though he wasn't a "serious" candidate; Sam knew CNN ratings spiked whenever Trump spoke.)

David often asks his interviewees what they aspire to, what they will do next, and why or how they chose their given field. These interactions don't seem like interviews; you feel you're listening to a conversation between two equals, and that's what makes them so powerful and memorable. We are hardwired to explore the world by connecting with one another, not by looking down at our devices. Kids naturally ask a series of "why" questions as they try to figure out the world. Questioning, and active listening, should come just as naturally to adults. Live, meaningful conversations are how we come to empathize with and learn from each other.

Be Connected (But Not Too Connected)

Ninja businesses arise from and depend on relationships. The best ideas often spring from different people putting different concepts together. Asking questions is the most direct route to innovation. Relationships are harder to describe and define than they once were. But it should be clear that relationships are distinct from "contacts" or "connections."

We seem to need increasingly high levels of stimulus simply to stay engaged. We grab for our smartphones at any momentary lull in the action of life—even sitting at a stoplight—rather than welcome the quiet or take time for introspection. We avoid talking to strangers, email colleagues who sit five feet away, tweet in 280 characters, or text emojis to one another, rather than write in longer form or even speak directly to a person. Yet innovative technologies, no matter how marvelous, don't replace the need for human interaction or the benefits of solitude and self-reflection.

Let's think about what phones were originally designed to be: a way to connect us with one another. While a first-year law student, I went to work in the office of Representative Mickey Edwards of Oklahoma. I spent some time responding to constituent concerns and learned that the phone is your most valuable tool. Like everything else, lawmaking and lobbying hinges upon meeting people where they are and really listening to them. You might have an astounding technology or product that you consider life-changing. People aren't going to run out and buy it just because you say so. They need to have a reason to trust your advice.

This is why there are so many lobbyists in Washington—relationships with politicians often matter more than money. No matter their political persuasion or stripes, elected officials tend to be smart, passionate people who really care about the constituents they represent. They work hard to examine every side of an issue, build consensus, and solve problems, always starting from the same place: What does this mean for real people? How will it affect them and their families? And you can't answer those questions by scanning polling data or guessing based on your own experience. You have to truly connect with fellow human beings. Even small interactions can become meaningful relationships. With those in place, results follow.

Be Assertive

Since its earliest concept days in the 1980s, I was 100 percent certain consumers would embrace high-definition television (HDTV). To me, HDTV was to viewing what the CD was to listening. With the latter, some people resisted change, but most were glad to give up the hiss, crackle, and scratch of vinyl records for the near-clean, perfect sound of the CD. Similarly, HDTV offered five times the picture quality, phenomenal surround sound, and a wider, more realistic 16x9 picture than standard definition. I was so excited about HDTV that I joked I wanted my tombstone cut to the 16x9 aspect ratio.

On the other hand, I was every bit as convinced 3DTV would flop with consumers. I believed 3-D viewing was at best a bonus feature useful for certain types of movies and maybe some sports, but less-than-great for most programming. More, it required wearing heavy, battery-powered glasses that wouldn't necessarily work if you were lying down on the sofa. And because each TV manufacturer had its own system, none of them were interoperable.

In a December 2010 interview with the *Wall Street Journal* on 3DTV, I expressed my view that 3DTV was not a "product" but rather a "feature" that had been overhyped.[1] My good friend Bryan Burns, an executive at ESPN with whom I had worked to make HDTV succeed, thought my comments in the *Journal* would sabotage the success of 3DTV. He had brilliantly led ESPN to invest in HDTV and he saw a similar opportunity with 3DTV. While I understood his feelings, I disagreed with his optimism. I brought my case to our governing board, arguing that we should be cautious promoting this technology given its uncertain prospects. As an organization, our association's credibility was on the line. And even though I am a paid cheerleader for the industry, I need to believe in the products and services we're promoting. I even offered to resign my position if my lack of enthusiasm for 3DTV was a bridge too far.

But the board understood where I was coming from and got behind me. Given this vote of confidence in me rather than 3DTV, I moved on to more relevant and exciting projects. In January 2012, the president of Sony America, who was on our top board, invited me to the Sony Open golf tournament to offer my thoughts on 3DTV to the Sony global executive team and top retailers. He himself had had little luck dimming the optimism of his bosses in Japan and wondered if I could persuade them. I agreed to speak, and suggested that my wife speak, too. As an ophthalmologist, she saw some benefits to 3DTV, especially regarding eye exercise for those likely to become myopic or recovering from a stroke.

We did a good-cop/bad-cop routine: She outlined the benefits of 3DTV. I outlined several flaws in the user experience. Not surprisingly, the Sony executives liked her better! While the retailers in the room agreed with me, the Sony executives disagreed with my assessment and my assertion that their 3DTV couldn't be viewed lying down.

Shortly thereafter, the Sony president who had invited me to speak left the company. 3DTV was a marketplace failure (U.S. sales actually peaked in 2012).[2] Little content was produced. No one talks about 3DTV anymore. The entire Sony management team has turned over since then; the present management team has had many successful products after pivoting away from 3DTV.

The lesson here is to be assertive and stand up for what you believe in. The "experts" aren't always right. Trust your own instincts and judgment. Preserve your integrity. Sometimes a job is about following orders—but when you have built up equity in your reputation, you shouldn't risk it all on someone else's judgment. Assert your own.

Be Decisive

Failure and success both hinge on making decisions—small and big. Life decisions are tough. A decision is a commitment and commitments foreclose options. Limiting options can produce anxiety, especially if you view life as I do, one big buffet table full of choices—I want to sample almost everything! I am all too familiar with indecision. I never really knew what I wanted to be when I grew up, and to this day I often find myself leaving my options open.

When it came time for college, I was ready to live away from home. My high school grades were good, but nothing to brag about. But I always did well on standardized tests, and thanks to my PSAT score, I received an academic scholarship, provided I went to a public New York school. I had heard the State University at Binghamton was nice, so I took a train to Manhattan, slept on the floor in Grand Central Terminal, and caught the early morning bus to Binghamton. I enjoyed the campus tour, made a friend who offered to host me for the night, and decided I wanted to go there. That was the extent of my college search.

I had enough credits to graduate from high school early, so within a few weeks I was living away from home at age seventeen. Most courses were already full, so I took an eclectic sampling of disciplines and lots of intro classes. When I returned in the fall, something clicked. I still couldn't figure out what I wanted to do for my career, but I decided I needed good grades to keep my options open. So I lived in the library, rewarded my mastery of a subject with pinball games, and started earning high marks. I loaded up on courses and credits. I worked on the weekends, studied at night, *and* had a girlfriend. I was firing on all cylinders.

I had enough credits to graduate early but *still* didn't know what I wanted to do, so I took the business, law, and graduate qualifying tests all in one month and filled out more than a dozen law school, graduate school, and business school applications. A few accepted me and a few rejected me—most of them wait-listed me. But just a week before fall term started, I was accepted to Georgetown Law School. I figured law school would keep my options open, so I borrowed tuition from the bank and started three days later.

I enjoyed law school immensely—but knew I didn't really want to be a lawyer. I also enjoyed living on Capitol Hill during my first year, working on legislation updating how rules are made by government. Little did I know I was actually starting my career. My second year, I joined a small firm doing antitrust and competition work. They had a great culture, gave me real work, and soon merged into a much bigger firm. I became a summer associate, and when I graduated, they offered me a full-time associate position.

I was twenty-three and it was the first decision I truly labored over. I didn't like the big law firm atmosphere where every partner could and often did command your time, including your weekend time. One partner offered advice that stuck. He said, "Put in a couple of years and get the big firm experience. Then, you'll have plenty of options to do anything you want." So I did. And through this firm, as a law student, I started working for what is now the Consumer Technology Association, first as a client and eventually in-house. Funny how life works.

Everyone has a different story, and some of our decisions carry more weight than others. It's more about risk and reward. It's important to take risks, but the potential reward should be commensurate with the risk. The most important thing is to be decisive. The "five-year commitment" approach I talked about earlier goes a long way toward reducing the sense that every decision is irrevocable, unless it is a decision about whom to marry, whether to have children, or whether to commit a felony. Be decisive now—you can always change your mind later.

Be Bold

I've talked a lot about the value of failure. I'm not alone in believing that failure is best viewed as an opportunity to learn. In his leadership book *Failing Forward*, John C. Maxwell defines failure as "simply a price we pay to achieve success." [3] In *The Gift of Failure*, Jessica Lahey delves into the critical role of failure in children's development. "Failure is too often characterized as a negative: an F in math or a suspension from school," she says. "However, all sorts of disappointments, rejections, corrections, and criticisms are small failures, all opportunities in disguise, valuable gifts misidentified as tragedy."[4]

I couldn't agree more: If we want to raise a generation of ninja innovators, parents have an obligation to instill confidence in their kids, not to bulldoze every obstacle in their path. If you do a good job building confidence, then kids will be bold enough to take some risks and take their lumps instead of avoiding risk and potential failure. When you succeed, you learn some things—but not the most important things. You just think you're smart—but you're probably also lucky. You might have randomly made a good decision. But real success takes experimentation and a certain degree of failure.

This is a uniquely American attitude: In most other cultures, if you fail, you're out for good. That's not the case in the United States—and that's the reason we're worldwide leaders of innovation. We accept and embrace failure. We're willing to take risks and make bets. We accept that some strategies don't work. Some products don't launch. Some brilliant ideas will end in obscurity.

Future ninjas know that if you stay still, you'll be surpassed. If you're approaching life and business right, you will fail. But if you fail, you will also learn. You'll strive harder. You'll make better decisions. Innovation favors the bold!

Be Committed

Ninja innovators balance risk with reality. Not every startup will be the next Lyft or Postmates or Airbnb or Twitter. But they don't all need to be. Whenever I'm asked for career advice, I encourage people to match their aspirations to their abilities. The world needs an endless variety of marketable skills: Accountants and architects. Teachers and tailors. Electricians and editors. Coaches and coders. Scientists and social workers. Figure out what you're good at. Explore the career paths that will let you leverage your strengths. And then: commit.

Way back when my mother was selling encyclopedias, she told me, "You can't sell something if you're not passionate about it." As usual, she was right. I love the Consumer Technology Association and wouldn't want to work anywhere else—but it's not CTA itself that fuels my passion and inspires my commitment.

I'm committed to innovation and invigorated by the ways it will influence our future and redefine our definition of what problems are, from health care to transportation, energy to agriculture.

I'm committed to rising to the challenge of figuring out ways of using the tools we have to solve complex problems.

I'm committed to harnessing the brilliance in and around CTA to strive toward a ninja future.

CONCLUSION

The Ninja Future

WE ARE GENERALLY SAFER TODAY than at any time in history. We live more than twice as long as we did in 1900.[1] And we communicate and travel great distances in shorter periods of time. You can jet from New York to Mumbai in less time than it once took to ride a horse from New York to Philadelphia.[2]

Life is a one-way journey. As we grow up, the carefree anticipation of our youth is replaced by a more serious obligation to foster the next generation. Our duty as parents is to make our children's lives better and ensure they have more opportunities than we had. As I noted in *Investor's Business Daily* in 2017, our duty as an industry is to do the same for innovators: to usher in a generation of future ninjas and do everything possible to support their inspiring work.

That's easier said than done. Too often, change is resisted by naysayers intent on maintaining the status quo. We see it today: Self-driving vehicles will increase safety, improve the environment, and empower older adults and people with disabilities. Yet government officials in India blocked them because these vehicles will displace some jobs. In the United States, commercial truck drivers compelled members of Congress to exclude commercial vehicles from legislation that will advance self-driving vehicles, even though we face a massive truck driver shortage. And trial lawyers have resisted legislation to advance self-driving vehicles because fewer road accidents mean fewer lawsuits.

The fear that innovation will hasten job loss is not new, and it's not unjustified. History has proven that innovation is a mixed bag. Technological advancements have rocked the job market from the invention of the wheel to the rise of artificial intelligence. Some jobs have disappeared, and more may be eliminated—but these same ninjas driving innovation are also creating entirely new jobs. More, the impact of automation can be hard to predict. For example, most people assumed that automatic teller machines (ATMs) would displace bank tellers. In fact, by lowering the cost of opening new branches, ATMs increased the overall number of bank teller jobs. And now the market is shifting again thanks to mobile banking and AI.

Millions of people worldwide drive on ride-sharing platforms, benefiting from the flexibility these jobs offer. Hundreds of thousands of jobs are now open in the rapidly growing field of data analysis and artificial intelligence. Short-term rentals allow homeowners to pay off their mortgages and expand revenue for businesses located far away from hotels. Voice assistants create opportunities for programmers, developers, and hardware manufacturers. Drones require drone operators—a job category that did not exist a few years ago. Robots and self-driving vehicles need vendors, designers, manufacturers, and mechanics.

But innovation, technology, and industrialization do more than simply create jobs: They allow average people of every race, gender, ethnicity, and income level to live longer, healthier, more productive, and more comfortable lives. As I write this, disruptive innovations including augmented reality, biometrics, robotics, and blockchain are shifting from mere ideas to daily realities. Even in early stages, these technologies have already expanded our choices and improved our health and safety.

Lyft and Uber have expanded mobility options (and collision-avoidance technology has prevented countless accidents). Airbnb and HomeAway give travelers new, more affordable lodging choices. Artificial intelligence helps predict, diagnose, and treat medical conditions. Voice-activated assistants give us access to information anywhere, anytime, without having us view or even touch a screen. Drones deliver medicine and search for survivors of natural disasters. Robots clean up oil spills and dismantle explosives.

Our world is changing rapidly. It's understandable that some of us are wary. But our moral obligation is clear: We must be proactive in setting up the next generation for success. It's up to us to ensure that innovation can flourish. It's up to us to empower future ninjas to create the life-changing products and services of the future. That means we have to educate our children—our future workforce—differently. We have to offer apprentice programs to teach new skills. We have to focus on the issue of jobs and competition and what we will need to compete in the global marketplace.

If we embrace innovation boldly and with our eyes wide open, we can cure incurable diseases, solve impossible environmental challenges, and create unimaginable opportunity and prosperity. Today these are tantalizing possibilities. I have every confidence that innovators will turn them into realities in the ninja future.

ACKNOWLEDGMENTS

A BOOK IS RARELY A solo performance. This one was a beautiful ninja orchestra with a magnificent conductor and fabulous instrumentalists!

While I conceived and wrote most of my first two books, this one was different. Beginning in 2017, Rachel Horn, a CTA communications director, suggested repeatedly that I write another book. I often responded that I had several ideas that were good, but no ideas that were great. She broke through my reluctance, stating she had reviewed scores of commentaries I had written since my last book and saw a consistent big idea of a better future thanks to the innovation we knew was coming.

In early 2018, we released CTA's first International Innovation Scorecard—a ranking of more than thirty countries by how innovation-friendly they are. This was a pet project of mine, but it provoked valuable internal discussions on what it takes for a nation to be innovative. This is a question I often get from national political leaders as I travel the globe speaking about innovation. After a lot of hard work, CTA's 2018 International Innovation Scorecard succeeded beyond our expectations and is an important set of guideposts underlying much of this book.

Our CTA Scorecard team agreed on key parameters. We debated and eventually agreed on not only the criteria and their measurements, but also our fundamental commitment to transparency, honesty, and the ability to take input and keep improving the product over time. Headed by another great communications pro, Izzy Santa, the project benefited from the quantitative analysis of Jack Cutts, the communications sagacity of Tyler Suiters, the research skills of Angela Titone, the promotion prowess of Bronwyn Flores, and the policy expertise of Walter Alcorn—each of whom also helped develop and review content for this book—and the organization of Johanna O'Keefe.

With the Scorecard as a backdrop, Rachel and I agreed on a book aimed at government leaders and business executives, as well as those interested in understanding the many changes—and challenges—we know are coming. Rachel offered to craft an outline with the concepts from my commentaries and move the process forward. Once she delivered an outline and brief first draft, I was inspired to add to its depth and interest by adding the values expressed in the global scorecard along with real-life stories, advice, and experience.

HarperCollins, the publisher of my last book, was excited about the idea of sharing my updated perspective on how ninja innovators will embrace our digital future. I appreciate the enthusiasm of HarperCollins, and in particular Nick Amphlett, for the topic, as well as their support for this project and belief in my voice and value.

The editor of my last two books was not available, so Rachel recruited and worked closely with a fabulous book editor, Shannon Last. Although Shannon, Rachel, and I never sat down all together in person, through the innovation of Google Docs we organized the structure and turned several different sections into (hopefully) interesting and cohesive prose.

Along the way, we received substantive input from many other members of the CTA team, including Curtis Kincaid (manuscript review); Katherine Rutkowski and Eriq Ocampo (general research); Caitlin Cline (citations); Sage Chandler, Doug Johnson, Julie Kearney, Jamie Boone, Michael Hayes, Katie Reilly, Nathan Trail, and Maya Sharma (all on various policy content); Jennifer Taylor and Jacqueline Black (workforce content); Loren Wray (HR content); Dave Wilson and Mike Bergman (technology expertise); Steve Koenig, Ben Arnold, and Lesley Rohrbaugh (industry trends content); and John T. Kelley, Allison Fried, and Sasha Spellman (CES-related content).

I could not have completed the book without the daily support from several people on the CTA executive team:

Chief Operating Officer and Chief Financial Officer Glenda MacMullin heads the team who beautifully manages so many aspects of CTA, sparing me time and concern.

Executive Vice President of CES Karen Chupka and her team ensure CES and other CTA events gather and inspire innovators and innovation.

Senior Vice Presidents Michael Petricone (government and regulatory affairs) and Tiffany Moore (political and industry affairs) and their teams not only push for pro-innovation policies and a workforce trained for the future, but are always advocating for and raising the interests of the groups who can and should gain from innovation: small businesses, entrepreneurs, creators, traditionally underrepresented groups, and the less fortunate.

Senior Vice President Brian Markwalter (research and standards) sets an example for his skilled and dedicated team, one that's committed to delivering high-quality market insights and making consumers' technology experiences easier and more efficient.

I am also grateful to Senior Vice President Jean Foster (marketing and communications) and her lieutenants Tyler Suiters, Michael Brown, and Sean Perkins, who eagerly took on this project, even though it was outside their expertise. I must also acknowledge their work built on that of our former marketing head Susan Littleton, who touched so many of us before her untimely passing in 2018.

I want to thank John J. Kelly, Kara Maser, and Gaby Chavez for getting through legal issues. I also want to thank my scheduler Tyler Stenberg for not only making this book a priority in my schedule, but also transcribing many of my hard-copy edits to our shared online document. Tyler, Kailey Adametz (who runs my office), and Jacqueline Black (who until recently ran my office) are true ninjas who always break down brick walls to make things happen.

I am so proud that these and our other CTA employees are so effective, dedicated, relentless, and creative in pursuing our cause of innovation. They inspire me with their resourcefulness, passion, and belief that technology and innovation can provide a better world. It is our sacred mission to ensure the events, government policies, and information and technology environment is right to help us realize our best future.

This book could not have proceeded without the blessing and support of the CTA Executive Board: Chairman David Hagan, Vice Chairmen Mike Dunn and Steve Tiffen, Industry Executive Advisor Pat Lavelle, past chairman Daniel Pidgeon, and board members Mike Fasulo, Randy Fry, Bridget Karlin, Jim Mault, Laura Orvidas, Eliott Peck, John Penney, Joe Stinziano, and Fred Towns. Also, a big dose of gratitude goes to ex officio board member John Shalam, whose grace, dignity, generosity, and wisdom to CTA and me have made him my mentor and father figure. This is one ninja board which focuses on the big picture, is willing to take a stand, and is always principled and passionate about the cause of innovation.

Additionally, I appreciate the work of the Pinkston Group. David Fouse—a longtime partner of CTA—Lauren Carl, Nancy Ritter, and Julia Smith helped frame my thoughts and bring this book to life. Their strategic approach in helping develop and promote my public voice served as the basis for many parts of this book.

The work CTA does for innovation is supported by so many worthy groups. The Center for Democracy and Technology ensures privacy and innovation can coexist. The Media Institute protects our freedom of speech. Third Way and No Labels are bipartisan groups proposing innovative solutions to real problems. Other trade groups and think tanks, including BSA | The Software Alliance, CompTIA, the Computer & Communications Industry Association, CTIA, Information Technology Industry Council, Internet Association, Northern Virginia Technology Council, R Street Institute, Software & Information Industry Association, TechNet, and the Technology CEO Council, work hard with government to ensure innovation can flourish. And events including CEDIA, Collision, InfoComm, Mobile World Congress, NAB Show, South by Southwest, and Unbound facilitate entrepreneurs and innovation.

Although I have tried to stay out of politics in this book, CTA honors those special political leaders from both sides of the aisle who have championed the cause of innovation—we call them "Digital Patriots." We also rate and recognize the top states for innovation, which our U.S. Innovation Scorecard recognizes as Innovation Champions. Special thanks to Valerie Hoffenberg and Pascal Cagni for their diplomacy and help understanding the exceptionalism of France.

My additional thanks go to Debbie Taylor Moore, Don Upson, Darrell Issa, and David Leibowitz for encouraging me to produce yet one more book.

Innovation is never about one person, it is about teams of ninjas working together to move the cause forward. I am so thankful for the conductor, Rachel, and all those listed above who helped this book and our cause move forward.

Of course, I could not have done any of this without the support and love of my wife, Dr. Susan Malinowski. She encourages my writing and inspired some sections, such as the five-year personal plan horizon. She is a special ninja—her creativity and innovation as a retina surgeon will save hundreds of thousands of people from a lifetime of blindness. She inspires, humbles, and keeps me grounded!

And I deeply thank her parents, Drs. Edward and Jolanta Malinowski, who so generously help Susan and me raise our children, making them better humans and allowing us to pursue exceptional careers.

My older two sons, Steve and Doug, always make me proud—thank you. My younger boys, Mark and Max, didn't love the time I spent on this book. I hope they forgive me in the future.

NOTES

PREFACE

1. Noah Robischon, "Why Amazon Is the World's Most Innovative Company of 2017," *Fast Company*, February 13, 2017, https://www.fast company.com/3067455/why-amazon-is-the-worlds-most-innovative -company-of-2017.

CHAPTER 1: THE EDGE OF TOMORROW

1. "The Development of Agriculture," Genographic Project, accessed 2018, https://genographic.nationalgeographic.com/development-of-agri culture/.
2. Meagan Gambino, "A Salute to the Wheel," Smithsonian.com, June 17, 2009, https://www.smithsonianmag.com/science-nature/a-salute-to-the -wheel-31805121/.
3. Denise Schmandt-Besserat, "The Evolution of Writing," last modified January 25, 2014, https://sites.utexas.edu/dsb/tokens/the-evolution-of -writing/.
4. Elizabeth Palermo, "Who Invented the Printing Press?," Live Science, February 25, 2014, https://www.livescience.com/43639-who-invented-the -printing-press.html.
5. "Model T," *Encyclopædia Britannica*, accessed 2018, https://www.britan nica.com/technology/Model-T.
6. David Lumb, "One Billion Hours of YouTube Are Watched Every Day," *Engadget*, February 27, 2017, www.engadget.com/2017/02/27/youtube -one-billion-hours-watched-daily/.
7. Tess Townsend, "Eric Schmidt Said ATMs Led to More Jobs for Bank Tellers. It's Not That Simple," *Recode*, May 8, 2017, https://www.recode

.net/2017/5/8/15584268/eric-schmidt-alphabet-automation-atm-bank
-teller.

8. Alicja Grzadkowska, "When Will Machines Take Over Insurance Jobs?,"
Insurance Business America, April 2, 2018, https://www.insurancebusi
nessmag.com/us/news/technology/when-will-machines-take-over-insur
ance-jobs-96400.aspx.

9. U.S. Department of Defense, DoD News Briefing—Secretary Rumsfeld
and Gen. Myers. Washington: Federal News Service Inc., February 12,
2002, http://archive.defense.gov/Transcripts/Transcript.aspx?Transcript
ID=2636.

10. Randy Alfred, "March 25, 1954: RCA TVs Get the Color for Money,"
Wired, March 25, 2008, https://www.wired.com/2008/03/dayintech-0325/.

11. Geoffrey Morrison, "TV Resolution Confusion: 1080p, 2K, UHD, 4K,
8K, and What They All Mean," *CNET*, January 25, 2016, https://www
.cnet.com/news/tv-resolution-confusion-1080p-2k-uhd-4k-and-what
-they-all-mean/.

CHAPTER 2: CHANGES IN CULTURE AND COMMERCE

1. Monica Anderson and Jingjing Jiang, "Teens, Social Media & Technology 2018," Pew Research Center: Internet, Science & Tech, May 31,
2018, http://www.pewInternet.org/2018/05/31/teens-social-media-tech
nology-2018/.

2. "Lethal Weapon (1987) Trivia," IMDb, accessed August 13, 2018, https://
www.imdb.com/title/tt0093409/trivia.

3. Movieclips, "Patriot Games (3/9) Movie CLIP - Road Rage (1992) HD,"
YouTube, October 9, 2011, https://www.youtube.com/watch?v=AKOtvc
IssZk.

4. Maggie Fox, "World Health Organization Adds Gaming Disorder to
Disease Classifications," NBC News, June 19, 2018, https://www.nbc
news.com/health/health-news/who-adds-gaming-disorder-disease-clas
sifications-n884291.

5. Jean Twenge, "Have Smartphones Destroyed a Generation?," *Atlantic*,
March 19, 2018, https://www.theatlantic.com/magazine/archive/2017
/09/has-the-smartphone-destroyed-a-generation/534198/.

6. Ibid.

7. Ibid.

8. "Population Projections for the United States from 2015 to 2060 (in Millions)," digital image, Statista, 2018, https://www.statista.com/statistics/183481/united-states-population-projection/.

9. Barbranda Lumpkins Walls, "Effect of Poverty on Older Adults Revealed in Aging Conference," AARP, March 24, 2016, https://www.aarp.org/politics-society/advocacy/info-2016/effect-of-poverty-on-older-adults.html.

10. Gregory J. Norman, Kristann Orton, Amy Wade, Andrea M. Morris, and Jill C. Slaboda, "Operation and Challenges of Home-Based Medical Practices in the US: Findings From Six Aggregated Case Studies," BMC Health Services 18, no. 1 (January 27, 2018): doi:10.1186/s12913-018-2855-x.

11. Lynnette Khalfani-Cox, "Can You Afford to Age in Place?," AARP, accessed July 17, 2018, https://www.aarp.org/money/budgeting-saving/info-2017/costs-of-aging-in-place.html.

12. Renee Stepler, "Smaller Share of Women Ages 65 and Older Are Living Alone," Pew Research Center Social & Demographic Trends Project, February 18, 2016, http://www.pewsocialtrends.org/2016/02/18/smaller-share-of-women-ages-65-and-older-are-living-alone/.

13. Grayson Brulte, "This Is What an A.I.-powered Future Looks Like," VentureBeat, October 7, 2016, https://venturebeat.com/2016/10/07/this-is-what-an-a-i-powered-future-looks-like/.

14. United Nations Department of Economic and Social Affairs, World Population Prospects: The 2017 Revision, Key Findings and Advance Tables, 2017, https://esa.un.org/unpd/wpp/Publications/Files/WPP2017_Key Findings.pdf.

15. Consumer Technology Association, "Active Aging Tech Can Help 85 Million Americans, Says New CTA Report," news release, March 23, 2016, Consumer Technology Association, https://www.cta.tech/News/Press-Releases/2016/March/Active-Aging-Tech-Can-Help-85-Million-Americans,-S.aspx.

16. Larry Elliott, "Economics: Whatever Happened to Keynes' 15-Hour Working Week?," Guardian, August 31, 2008, https://www.theguardian.com/business/2008/sep/01/economics.

17. Derek Thompson, "The Myth That Americans Are Busier than Ever," Atlantic, May 21, 2014, https://www.theatlantic.com/business/archive/2014/05/the-myth-that-americans-are-busier-than-ever/371350/.

18. "World Population Projected to Reach 9.8 Billion in 2050, and 11.2 Billion in 2100," United Nations, June 21, 2017, https://www.un.org/development /desa/en/news/population/world-population-prospects-2017.html.

19. Rana Sen, William D. Eggers, Mahesh Kelkar, Deloitte, *Building the Smart City*, 2018, https://www2.deloitte.com/content/dam/Deloitte/us /Documents/public-sector/us-fed-building-the-smart-city.pdf.

20. Lauren Thomas, "Under-the-radar Store Closures Are Leaving Big Gaps and Putting More Malls at Risk," CNBC, January 12, 2018, https://www .cnbc.com/2018/01/12/hundreds-of-retailers-arent-renewing-leases-put ting-malls-at-risk.html.

21. Josh Sanburn, "Why the Death of Malls Is About More than Shopping," *Time*, July 20, 2017, http://time.com/4865957/death-and-life-shopping -mall/.

22. Steve LeVine, "Axios Future," *Axios*, May 2018, https://www.axios.com /newsletters/axios-future-ca246c67-295d-411e-8802-e4f11e11512.html ?chunk=2#story2.

23. Sanburn, "Why Death of Malls."

24. Marc Bain, "Even Macy's Is Surprised at How Well Macy's Is Doing," *Quartz*, May 16, 2018, accessed June 26, 2018, https://qz.com/1279473 /macys-first-quarter-earnings-even-macys-was-surprised-at-its-great-start -to-2018/.

25. Lauren Hirsch, "Macy's Launches Pop-up Marketplaces in Its Stores," CNBC, February 6, 2018, https://www.cnbc.com/2018/02/05/macys -launches-pop-up-marketplaces-in-its-stores.html.

26. Nandita Bose, "Best Buy CEO Says Turnaround Done, Room to Compete with Amazon," Reuters, March 9, 2018, https://www.reuters.com /article/us-best-buy-ceo/best-buy-ceo-says-turnaround-done-room-to -compete-with-amazon-idUSKCN1GL2Y8.

27. Vicki Howard, "The Rise and Fall of Sears," Smithsonian.com, July 25, 2017, https://www.smithsonianmag.com/history/rise-and-fall-sears-1809 64181/.

28. Hayley Peterson, "Sears Is Closing 150 Stores," *Business Insider*, January 4, 2017, http://www.businessinsider.com/list-of-sears-and-kmart -stores-closing-2017-1.

29. Sears Holdings Corporation, Form 10-Q for the Period Ending May 5, 2018 and April 29, 2017 (filed May 31, 2018), from Securities and Ex-

change Commission website, https://www.sec.gov/Archives/edgar/data
/1310067/000131006718000014/shldq12018.htm, accessed September 10,
2018.

30. Michael Ingram, "With Amazon Deal, Sears Is Coming Full-Circle,"
Tire Review, May 14, 2018, http://www.tirereview.com/with-amazon
-deal-sears-is-coming-full-circle/.

31. Consumer Technology Association, "Emerging Tech to Edge Holiday
Tech Spending to Reach Record Setting Levels, Says CTA," news release, October 12, 2017, Consumer Technology Association, https://
www.cta.tech/News/Press-Releases/2017/October/Emerging-Tech-to
-Edge-Holiday-Tech-Spending-to-Rea.aspx.

32. Nathaniel Meyersohn, "Dollar General Is Opening 900 New Stores Next
Year," *CNNMoney*, December 7, 2017, http://money.cnn.com/2017/12
/07/news/companies/dollar-general-store-openings/index.html?iid=EL.

33. Alan Wolf, "Radio Shack: A Brief History of Time," *Twice*, February 16, 2015, https://www.twice.com/retailing/radioshack-brief-history
-time-56040.

34. Chris Woodyard, "RadioShack, Closing 1,000 Stores, Leaves Only
These 70," *USA Today*, June 1, 2017, https://www.usatoday.com/story
/money/business/2017/05/31/radioshack-closes-1000-stores-week-these
-70-left/102372912/.

35. Carl Swanson, "The Store (It Would Seem) Is Not Dead (at Least for
Now)," *The Cut*, May 16, 2018, https://www.thecut.com/2018/05/retail
-success-in-the-age-of-amazon.html.

36. *Economic Impact Report: United States 2017*, report, Google, 2017.

37. Facebook, "Refresh Your Space with Facebook Marketplace," news release, March 20, 2018, MultiVu, http://www.multivu.com/players/En
glish/81601510-facebook-marketplace-spring-cleaning.

38. Source: Facebook.

39. Guadalupe Gonzalez, "Facebook Is Investing $1 Billion in Small-
Business Initiatives This Year. Why the 'Likes' Aren't Pouring In," *Inc.*,
March 30, 2018, https://www.inc.com/guadalupe-gonzalez/facebook
-mark-zuckerberg-jobs-tool-review-small-business-1-billion-investment
.html.

40. Olivia Pulsinelli, "Facebook Community Boost Program for Businesses
and Job Seekers Announces Houston Dates," *Houston Business Journal*,

January 18, 2018, https://www.bizjournals.com/houston/news/2018/01/18/facebook-community-boost-program-for-businesses.html.

41. "Retail Sales Workers: Summary," U.S. Bureau of Labor Statistics, April 13, 2018, https://www.bls.gov/ooh/sales/retail-sales-workers.htm.

CHAPTER 3: NINJA FUTURE ECONOMY

1. Tom Verde, "Aging Parents with Lots of Stuff, and Children Who Don't Want It," *New York Times*, August 18, 2017, https://www.nytimes.com/2017/08/18/your-money/aging-parents-with-lots-of-stuff-and-children-who-dont-want-it.html.

2. Sarah Boumphrey and Caroline Bremnerm, "How Should Business Respond to the Rising Demand for Experiential Consumption?," *Euromonitor International*, October 30, 2017, https://blog.euromonitor.com/2017/10/experiences-overtaking-consumers-buying.html.

3. Sam Chambers, "Zara Greets London Shoppers with Robots, iPads and Connected Mirrors," Bloomberg, May 18, 2018, https://www.bloomberg.com/news/articles/2018-05-17/zara-greets-shoppers-with-robots-ipads-and-connected-mirrors.

4. "Starpower to Open New 15,000 Square Foot Luxury Living Showroom in Southlake, Texas"; "William Lyon Homes Announces Agreement to Acquire RSI Communities, a Southern California and Texas Based Homebuilder," Business Wire, August 4, 2016, https://www.businesswire.com/news/home/20160804005058/en/Starpower-Open-New-15000-Square-Foot-Luxury.

5. Airbnb, *Airbnb UK Insights Report*, September 11, 2017, https://www.airbnbcitizen.com/wp-content/uploads/sites/48/2017/09/Airbnb-UK-Insights-Report_Final_Digital_v3.pdf.

6. "Airbnb Policy Tool Chest," Airbnb Citizen, Airbnb, 2016, https://www.airbnbcitizen.com/airbnb-policy-tool-chest/.

7. Airbnb, *Airbnb UK Insights Report*.

8. Ali Mogharabi, "What Will Uber Shares Be Worth?," Morningstar, July 30, 2018, http://www.morningstar.co.uk/uk/news/169192/what-will-uber-shares-be-worth.aspx.

9. "The Perilous Politics of Parking," *Economist*, April 6, 2017, https://www.economist.com/leaders/2017/04/06/the-perilous-politics-of-parking.

10. Biz Carson, "Lyft Doubled Rides in 2017 as Its Rival Uber Stumbled,"

Forbes, January 16, 2018, https://www.forbes.com/sites/bizcarson/2018
/01/16/lyft-doubled-rides-in-2017/.

11. Johana Bhuiyan, "Uber Powered Four Billion Rides in 2017. It Wants
to Do More—and Cheaper—in 2018," Recode, January 5, 2018, https://
www.recode.net/2018/1/5/16854714/uber-four-billion-rides-coo-barney
-harford-2018-cut-costs-customer-service.

12. Recode, "Mary Meeker's 2018 Internet Trends."

13. Ljubica Nedelkoska and Glenda Quintini, "Automation, Skills Use and
Training," OECD Social, Employment and Migration Working Papers,
no. 202 (2018): 7, https://doi.org/10.1787/2e2f4eea-en.

14. Anand Rao and Gerard Verweij, "Size the Price," PwC, 2017, https://
www.pwc.com/gx/en/issues/analytics/assets/pwc-ai-analysis-sizing-the
-prize-report.pdf.

15. "Graduate Enrollment and Degrees," Council of Graduate Schools,
accessed August 10, 2018, https://cgsnet.org/graduate-enrollment-and
-degrees.

16. France, *Elysee*, 2018, http://www.elysee.fr/declarations/article/tran
scription-du-discours-du-president-de-la-republique-emmanuel-macron
-devant-le-congres-des-etats-unis-d-amerique/.

17. Elena Holodny, "Extreme Weather Events Are on the Rise," *Business Insider*, March 23, 2016, http://www.businessinsider.com/extreme-weather
-events-increasing-2016-3.

CHAPTER 4: NINJA INNOVATION TODAY

1. *State of the USPTO*, PDF, Dallas, Texas: USPTO Texas Regional Office,
April 19, 2018.

2. United States, USPTO, "Patenting Trends Calendar Year 1997," 1997,
https://www.uspto.gov/web/offices/ac/ido/oeip/taf/pat_tr97.htm.

3. J. W. Knutti and H. V. Allen, "Trends in MEMS Commercialization," in
Enabling Technologies for MEMS and Nanodevices (Weinheim: Wiley
-VCH, 2004), 35.

4. James Carbone, "Sensor Market to Grow Despite Price Declines," *Electronics Sourcing*, March 28, 2018, http://www.electronics-sourcing.com
/2018/03/28/sensor-market-to-grow-despite-price-declines/.

5. "YouTube for Press," YouTube, accessed August 11, 2018, https://www
.youtube.com/yt/about/press/.

6. Stephen Shankland, "How 5G Will Push a Supercharged Network to Your Phone, Home, Car," *CNET*, March 2, 2015, https://www.cnet.com /news/how-5g-will-push-a-supercharged-network-to-your-phone-home -and-car/.

7. Ibid.

8. Cisco, *Cisco Visual Networking Index: Global Mobile Data, Traffic Forecast Update, 2016–2021*, 2017, https://www.cisco.com/c/en/us/solutions /collateral/service-provider/visual-networking-index-vni/mobile-white -paper-c11-520862.pdf.

9. Accenture, *Smart Cities*, 2017, https://api.ctia.org/docs/default-source /default-document-library/how-5g-can-help-municipalities-become-vi brant-smart-cities-accenture.pdf.

10. Kumba Sennaar, "How America's Top 4 Insurance Companies Are Using Machine Learning," *TechEmergence*, July 19, 2018, https://www .techemergence.com/machine-learning-at-insurance-companies/.

11. Kaveh Waddell, "Algorithms Can Help Stomp Out Fake News," *Atlantic*, December 7, 2016, https://www.theatlantic.com/technology/archive /2016/12/how-computers-will-help-fact-check-the-internet/509870/.

12. Kirsten Stewart, "10 Algorithms That Are Changing Health Care," Algorithms for Innovation, accessed October 10, 2015, http://uofuhealth .utah.edu/innovation/blog/2015/10/10AlgorithmsChangingHealthCare .php.

13. Joy Buolamwini and Timnit Gebru, "Gender Shades: Intersectional Accuracy Disparities in Commercial Gender Classification," MIT Media Lab, February 4, 2018.

14. Dom Galeon and Christianna Reedy, "Ray Kurzweil Claims Singularity Will Happen by 2045," Ray Kurzweil in the Press, March 14, 2017, http://www.kurzweilai.net/futurism-ray-kurzweil-claims-singularity-will -happen-by-2045.

15. Nick Bostrom, "How Long Before Superintelligence?," *International Journal of Future Studies* 2 (1998).

16. "Experts Predict When Machines Will Be Better than You at Your Job," *MIT Technology Review*, May 31, 2017, https://www.technologyreview .com/s/607970/experts-predict-when-artificial-intelligence-will-exceed -human-performance/.

17. Matt McFarland, "The Eyes Expose Our Lies. Now AI Is Noticing,"

CNN, October 4, 2017, https://money.cnn.com/2017/10/04/technology /business/eyedetect-lies-polygraph/index.html.

18. Antonio Villas-Boas, "The Company Behind the Galaxy S8's Iris Recognition Says It's Superior to the FBI's Fingerprint Tech," *Business Insider,* April 13, 2017, http://www.businessinsider.com/samsung-galaxy-s8-iris -scanner-fbi-fingerprint-tech-princeton-identity-2017-4.

19. Dave Mosher, "Ears Could Make Better Unique IDs than Fingerprints," *WIRED,* November 12, 2010, https://www.wired.com/2010/11/ears-bio metric-identification/.

20. Nadeem Unuth, "What IP Means and How It Works," Lifewire, May 13, 2018, https://www.lifewire.com/internet-protocol-explained-3426713.

21. Marco Iansiti and Karim R. Lakhani, "The Truth About Blockchain," *Harvard Business Review,* March 6, 2018, https://hbr.org/2017/01/the -truth-about-blockchain.

22. Graham Rapier, "From Yelp Reviews to Mango Shipments: IBM's CEO on How Blockchain Will Change the World," *Business Insider,* June 21, 2017, https://www.businessinsider.com/ibm-ceo-ginni-rometty-block chain-transactions-internet-communications-2017-6.

23. Russ Juskalian, "Inside the Jordan Refugee Camp That Runs on Blockchain," *MIT Technology Review,* April 12, 2018, https://www.technol ogyreview.com/s/610806/inside-the-jordan-refugee-camp-that-runs-on -blockchain/.

24. Consumer Technology Association 2014. "From Cowboys to Movie Stars: CEA Inducts 12 Industry Leaders into the 2014 CE Hall of Fame," https://cta.tech/News/Press-Releases/2014/November/From-Cowboys -to-Movie-Stars-CEA-Inducts-12-Industr.aspx.

25. Bill Visnic, "Nvidia's Newest AV Processor: 30 Trillion Operations per Second on 30 Watts," SAE International, January 11, 2018, https://www .sae.org/news/2018/01/nvidias-newest-av-processor-30-trillion-operations -per-second-on-30-watts.

26. Randy Alfred, "Aug. 12, 1981: IBM Gets Personal With 5150 PC," *WIRED,* August 12, 2011, https://www.wired.com/2011/08/0812ibm -5150-personal-computer-pc/.

27. Ashraf Eassa, "1 Way Apple Inc. Played It Safe with the A11 Bionic Chip," *The Motley Fool,* September 15, 2017, https://www.fool.com/investing /2017/09/15/1-way-apple-inc-played-it-safe-with-the-a11-bionic.aspx.

28. Katie Litchfield, "In the wrong hands, quantum computers have the potential to break modern encryption methods we thought it would take the lifetime of the universe to break," LinkedIn, 2018, https://www .linkedin.com/feed/update/urn:li:activity:6409723372774789120/.

29. Bernard Marr, "6 Practical Examples of How Quantum Computing Will Change Our World," *Forbes*, July 10, 2017, https://www.forbes.com /sites/bernardmarr/2017/07/10/6-practical-examples-of-how-quantum -computing-will-change-our-world/#7f292d680c18.

CHAPTER 5: NINJA INNOVATION TOMORROW

1. Jennifer Latson, "Why the 1977 Blackout Was One of New York's Dark-est Hours," *Time*, July 13, 2015, http://time.com/3949986/1977-blackout -new-york-history/.

2. "Personal Weather Station: Overview," Weather Underground, accessed July 20, 2018, https://www.wunderground.com/weatherstation/overview .asp.

3. James Vincent, "Walmart Is Using Shelf-Scanning Robots to Audit Its Stores," *Verge*, October 27, 2017, https://www.theverge.com/2017/10/27 /16556864/walmart-introduces-shelf-scanning-robots.

4. Jennifer M. Ortman, Victoria A. Velkoff, and Howard Hogan, *An Aging Nation: The Older Population in the United States*, U.S. Census Bureau, May 2014, https://www.census.gov/prod/2014pubs/p25-1140.pdf.

5. Yasmeen Abutaleb, "U.S. Healthcare Spending to Climb 5.3 Percent in 2018: Agency," Reuters, February 14, 2018, https://www.reuters.com/ar ticle/us-usa-healthcare-spending/u-s-healthcare-spending-to-climb-5-3 -percent-in-2018-agency-idUSKCN1FY2ZD.

6. Centers for Medicare & Medicaid Services, "National Health Expen-ditures 2016 Highlights," news release, accessed July 19, 2018, https:// www.cms.gov/Research-Statistics-Data-and-Systems/Statistics-Trends -and-Reports/NationalHealthExpendData/downloads/highlights.pdf.

7. "Cancer Stat Facts: Cancer of Any Site," Surveillance, Epidemiology, and End Results Program, accessed July 20, 2018, https://seer.cancer.gov /statfacts/html/all.html.

8. Haidong Wang, Christopher Murray, and Alan Lopez, "Global, Re-gional, and National Life Expectancy, All-Cause Mortality," *Lancet* 388, no. 10053 (October 2016).

9. Aju Mathew, "Global Survey of Clinical Oncology Workforce," *Journal of Global Oncology*, February 8, 2018, http://ascopubs.org/doi/full/10.1200/JGO.17.00188.

10. Sy Mukherjee, "This New AI Can Detect a Deadly Cancer Early with 86% Accuracy," *Fortune*, October 30, 2017, http://fortune.com/2017/10/30/ai-early-cancer-detection/.

11. Taylor Kubota, "Deep Learning Algorithm Does as Well as Dermatologists in Identifying Skin Cancer," *Stanford University News*, January 25, 2017, https://news.stanford.edu/2017/01/25/artificial-intelligence-used-identify-skin-cancer/.

12. Satya Ramaswamy, "How Companies Are Already Using AI," *Harvard Business Review*, April 14, 2017, https://hbr.org/2017/04/how-companies-are-already-using-ai.

13. National Highway Traffic Safety Administration, U.S. Department of Transportation, *Critical Reasons for Crashes Investigated in the National Motor Vehicle Crash Causation Survey*, February 2015, https://crashstats.nhtsa.dot.gov/Api/Public/ViewPublication/812115.

14. Invest in Canada, *Canada—A Leader in Artificial Intelligence*, accessed July 25, 2018, http://www.international.gc.ca/investors-investisseurs/assets/pdfs/download/Niche_Sector-AI.pdf.

15. Mark Zuckerberg, "I'm excited to announce that we've agreed to acquire Oculus VR, the leader in virtual reality technology," Facebook, March 25, 2014, https://www.facebook.com/zuck/posts/10101319050523971.

16. Entertainment Software Association, *2018 Sales, Demographic, and Usage Data: Essential Facts about the Video Game and Computer Industry*, April 2018, http://www.theesa.com/wp-content/uploads/2018/05/EF2018_FINAL.pdf.

17. "Virtual Reality Offers Real Pain Relief," Cedars-Sinai Blog, May 3, 2017, https://blog.cedars-sinai.edu/virtual-reality-offers-real-pain-relief/.

18. Ailsa Sherrington, "Broadband Speeds Are Slowing the Adoption of VR," The Next Web, April 24, 2018, https://thenextweb.com/events/2018/04/24/broadband-slowing-adoption-vr/.

19. Mattias Fridström, "The Bandwidth Problem: 5 Issues the VR Industry Must Resolve," *VentureBeat*, May 6, 2017, https://venturebeat.com/2017/05/06/the-bandwidth-problem-5-issues-the-vr-industry-must-resolve/.

20. Mathew Ingram, "Medical Students Are Using Augmented Reality to

Study Patients in 3D," *Fortune*, May 3, 2017, http://fortune.com/2017/05 /03/medical-augmented-reality/.

21. Gerald Lynch, "AR Warfare: How the Military Is Using Augmented Reality," *TechRadar*, September 16, 2017, https://www.techradar.com/news /death-becomes-ar-how-the-military-is-using-augmented-reality.

22. Jonathan Vanian, "Here's What UPS Finds Interesting About Drones," *Fortune*, October 4, 2016, http://fortune.com/2016/10/03/ups-drones-de livery-testing/.

23. Andrew J. Hawkins,"Volocopter Envisions 'Air Taxi' Stations That Can Handle 10,000 Passengers a Day," *Verge*, April 17, 2018, https://www .theverge.com/2018/4/17/17243214/volocopter-flying-car-landing-station -infrastructure.

24. Joshuah Stolaroff, Constantine Samaras, Emma O'Neill, Alia Lubers, Alexandra Mitchell, and Daniel Ceperley, "Energy Use and Life Cycle Greenhouse Gas Emissions of Drones for Commercial Package Delivery," *Nature Communications*, February 13, 2018, https://www.nature .com/articles/s41467-017-02411-5#article-info.

25. Keith Schoonmaker, "UPS' Extensive Shipping Network Produces Industry-leading Margins and ROICs," Morningstar, April 26, 2018, http://analysisreport.morningstar.com/stock/research/c-report?&t =XNYS:UPS&region=usa&culture=zh-CN&productcode=QS&cur =&urlCookie=8056723522&e.

26. Darryl Jenkins and Bijan Vasigh, New Economic Report, AUVSI, 2013, http://www.auvsi.org/our-impact/economic-report.

27. "Global Market for Commercial Applications of Drone Technology Valued at over $127bn," PWC blog, May 9, 2016, http://pwc.blogs.com /press_room/2016/05/global-market-for-commercial-applications-of -drone-technology-valued-at-over-127bn.html.

28. Jenkins and Vasigh, *New Economic Report.*

29. Geekwire, "Amazon CEO Jeff Bezos Shares His Vision for Package Delivery with Prime Air Drones," YouTube, October 23, 2016, https://www .youtube.com/watch?v=6WYrPSYqEXE.

30. "1957-1959 Imperial," HowStuffWorks, October 8, 2007, https://auto .howstuffworks.com/1957-1959-imperial9.htm.

31. Dean Gibson, "Cruise Control and Adaptive Cruise Control: The Complete Guide," *Auto Express*, January 9, 2017, https://www.autoexpress.co

.uk/car-tech/98225/cruise-control-and-adaptive-cruise-control-the-complete-guide.

32. Gary Shapiro, "3 Reasons to Get Excited About Self-Driving Cars," *U.S. News & World Report*, September 20, 2017, https://www.usnews.com/opinion/op-ed/articles/2017-09-20/3-reasons-to-get-excited-about-self-driving-cars.

33. Consumer Technology Association, "Revved Up and Ready: Most Consumers Are Excited About Driverless Cars and Their Many Benefits, Says CTA Study," news release, October 7, 2016, https://www.cta.tech/News/Press-Releases/2016/October/Revved-Up-and-Ready-Most-Consumers-are-Excited-A.aspx.

34. "General Statistics," IIHS, accessed July 17, 2018, http://www.iihs.org/iihs/topics/t/general-statistics/topicoverview.

35. "Road Traffic Injuries," World Health Organization, last modified February 19, 2018, http://www.who.int/news-room/fact-sheets/detail/road-traffic-injuries.

36. "Drunk Driving," NHTSA, last modified April 23, 2018, https://www.nhtsa.gov/risky-driving/drunk-driving.

37. *Critical Reason for Crashes*, National Highway Traffic Safety Administration.

38. Oliver Suess and Jan-Henrik Foerster, "Self-Driving Cars to Cut U.S. Insurance Premiums 40%, Aon Says," Bloomberg, September 11, 2016, https://www.bloomberg.com/news/articles/2016-09-11/self-driving-cars-to-cut-u-s-insurance-premiums-40-aon-says.

39. Henry Claypool, Amitai Bin-Nun, and Jeffrey Gerlach, *Ruderman White Paper—Self-Driving Cars: The Impact on People with Disabilities*, January 2017, https://issuu.com/rudermanfoundation/docs/self_driving_cars_-_the_impact_on_p.

40. Waymo, *Say Hello to Waymo*, https://waymo.com/static/documents/introduction.pdf.

41. Mary Chapman, "Self-Driving Cars Could Be Boon for Aged, After Initial Hurdles," *New York Times*, March 23, 2017, https://www.nytimes.com/2017/03/23/automobiles/wheels/self-driving-cars-elderly.html?_r=1.

42. Claypool, Bin-Nun, and Gerlach, *Ruderman White Paper*.

43. "Excited About Driverless Cars," Consumer Technology Association.

44. https://www.wired.com/story/tesla-autopilot-self-driving-crash-california/.

45. "Air Traffic by the Numbers," Federal Aviation Administration, November 14, 2017, https://www.faa.gov/air_traffic/by_the_numbers/.

46. Simon Calder, "Airline Safety: 2017 Was Safest Year in History for Passengers Around World, Research Shows," *Independent*, January 1, 2018, https://www.independent.co.uk/travel/news-and-advice/air-safety-2017-best-year-safest-airline-passengers-worldwide-to70-civil-aviation-review-a8130796.html.

47. Alexis Egeland, "60 Years Ago, 2 Planes Collided Over the Grand Canyon and It Changed the World," *The Arizona Republic*, June 30, 2016, https://www.azcentral.com/story/news/local/arizona-history/2016/06/30/60-years-ago-2-planes-collided-over-grand-canyon/86529858/.

48. Airbus, *A Statistical Analysis of Commercial Aviation Accidents 1958–2017*, 2018, https://www.airbus.com/content/dam/corporate-topics/publications/safety-first/Airbus-Commercial-Aviation-Accidents-1958-2017.pdf.

49. Rob Verger, "Why No One Has Died in a Commercial Passenger Jet Crash in More than a Year," *Popular Science*, January 3, 2018, https://www.popsci.com/why-air-travel-became-so-incredibly-safe.

50. SOURCE: (35,092 total # of traffic deaths x .94)/365.

51. Alex Hutchinson, "How a Fitbit May Make You a Bit Fit," *New York Times*, March 19, 2016, https://www.nytimes.com/2016/03/20/opinion/sunday/how-a-fitbit-may-make-you-a-bit-fit.html.

52. "Facts & Figures," International Diabetes Federation, last modified 2017, https://www.idf.org/aboutdiabetes/what-is-diabetes/facts-figures.html.

53. Gary Arlen, "Robots All Around," *i3*, January 7, 2016, https://www.cta.tech/News/i3/Articles/2016/January-February/Robots-All-Around.aspx.

54. International Federation of Robotics, "31 Million Robots Helping in Households Worldwide by 2019," news release, December 20, 2016, IFR, https://ifr.org/ifr-press-releases/news/31-million-robots-helping-in-households-worldwide-by-2019.

55. Consumer Technology Association, "A Completely Simulated Organism: David Hanson's Sophia," news release, March 26, 2018, https://www.cta.tech/News/i3/Articles/2018/March-April/A-Completely-Simulated-Organism-David-Hansons-So.aspx.

56. "At A Glance," FIRST, accessed September 11, 2018, https://www.firstinspires.org/about/at-a-glance.

57. "Dean Kamen Explains Why he Started the First Robotics Competition," *WIRED*, August 7, 2009, https://www.wired.com/2009/08/dean-kamen-explains-why-he-started-the-first-robotics-competition/.

58. Nat Eliason, "Lessons from Sapiens by Yuval Noah Harari," accessed July 23, 2018, https://www.nateliason.com/lessons/sapiens-yuval-noah-harari/.

59. Peter Rudegeair and Akane Otani, "Bitcoin Mania: Even Grandma Wants In on the Action," *Wall Street Journal*, November 29, 2017, https://www.wsj.com/articles/bitcoin-mania-even-grandma-wants-in-on-the-action-1511996653.

60. Daniel Shane, "Bitcoin Mania: What the Big Names of Finance Are Saying," *CNNMoney*, January 2, 2018, http://money.cnn.com/2018/01/02/investing/bitcoin-finance-top-quotes/index.html.

61. "Historical Rates for the GBP/USD Currency Conversion on 30 June 2018," Pound Sterling Live, accessed August 10, 2018, https://www.poundsterlinglive.com/best-exchange-rates/british-pound-to-us-dollar-exchange-rate-on-2018-06-30.

CHAPTER 6: NINJA RISKS, NINJA REWARDS

1. Ian Sherr, "Microsoft's Nadella Says Privacy Is a Human Right, and It Needs to Be Protected," *CNET*, May 7, 2018, https://www.cnet.com/news/microsofts-nadella-says-privacy-is-a-human-right-and-it-needs-to-be-protected-build-2018/.

2. Consumer Technology Association, *Data Privacy: Consumer Attitudes & Behaviors*, May 31, 2018, https://www.cta.tech/Research-Standards/Reports-Studies/Studies/2018/Data-Privacy-Consumer-Attitudes-Behaviors.aspx.

3. Aliya Ram, "Google Receives 2.4m Requests to Delete Search Results," *Irish Times*, February 27, 2018, https://www.irishtimes.com/business/technology/google-receives-2-4m-requests-to-delete-search-results-1.3407979.

4. Consumer Technology Association, *2018 International Innovation Scorecard*, 2018, https://www.cta.tech/cta/media/policyImages/policyPDFs/IntlScorecard/Intl-Innovation-Scorecard-FULL.pdf?utm_source=Website&utm_campaign=IntlScorecard.

5. Alexandra Ma, "China Has Started Ranking Citizens with a Creepy

'Social Credit' System [...]," *Business Insider*, April 8, 2018, http://
www.businessinsider.com/china-social-credit-system-punishments-and
-rewards-explained-2018-4.

6. Zack Whittaker, "FBI Sought iPhone Unlock Order Before Exhausting
Tech Options," *ZDNet*, March 27, 2018, https://www.zdnet.com/article
/fbi-had-no-way-to-access-locked-iphone-after-san-bernardino-shooting/.

7. Andrew Soergel, "In America's Rural-Urban Divide, Age, Earnings
and Education Are Prominent," *U.S. News & World Report*, December 8, 2016, https://www.usnews.com/news/articles/2016-12-08/in-amer
icas-rural-urban-divide-age-earnings-and-education-are-prominent.

8. "2010 Census Urban Area Facts," U.S. Census Bureau, 2013, https://
www.census.gov/geo/reference/ua/uafacts.html.

9. Brian Thiede, Lillie Greiman, Stephan Weiler, Steven Beda, and Tessa
Conroy, "6 Charts That Illustrate the Divide Between Rural and Urban
America," PBS, March 17, 2017, https://www.pbs.org/newshour/nation
/six-charts-illustrate-divide-rural-urban-america.

10. "Measuring America: Our Changing Landscape," U.S. Census Bureau,
December 8, 2016, https://www.census.gov/library/visualizations/2016
/comm/acs-rural-urban.html.

11. "Rural Hosts in the US Earn $494 Million in the Past Year," *Airbnb Cit-
izen*, June 27, 2017, https://www.airbnbcitizen.com/rural-hosts-in-the-us
-earn-494-million-in-the-past-year/.

12. Brad Silver, Michal Mazur, Adam Wisniewski, and Agnieszka Babicz,
Welcome to the Era of Drone-Powered Solutions, PWC, 2017, https://
www.pwc.com/gx/en/communications/pdf/communications-review
-july-2017.pdf.

13. Courtney Columbus, "Could Drones Help Save People in Cardiac Arrest?," NPR, June 13, 2017, https://www.npr.org/sections/health-shots/2017
/06/13/532639836/could-drones-help-save-people-in-cardiac-arrest.

14. "Online Job Ads Decreased 51,000 in May," Conference Board,
May 30, 2018, https://www.conference-board.org/press/pressdetail.cfm
?pressid=7442.

15. Bachelor's Degrees Conferred by Postsecondary Institutions, by Field
of Study: Selected Years, 1970-71 through 2015-16 (Washington, D.C.:
National Center for Education Statistics, August 2017), table 322.10,
https://nces.ed.gov/programs/digest/d17/tables/dt17_322.10.asp.

16. Master's Degrees Conferred by Postsecondary Institutions, by Field of Study: Selected Years, 1970-71 through 2015-16 (Washington, D.C.: National Center for Education Statistics, August 2017), table 323.10, https://nces.ed.gov/programs/digest/d17/tables/dt17_323.10.asp.

17. Industry Analysis and Technology Division, Federal Communications Commission, *Internet Access Services: Status as of December 31, 2016,* February 2018, https://transition.fcc.gov/Daily_Releases/Daily_Business/2018/db0207/DOC-349074A1.pdf.

18. Kelly Cole, "Modern Rules Are Needed to Build Our Wireless Future," CTIA, June 28, 2018, https://www.ctia.org/news/modern-rules-are-needed-to-build-our-wireless-future.

19. Center for Climate and Energy Solutions, *China's Contribution to the Paris Climate Agreement,* July 2015, https://www.c2es.org/site/assets/uploads/2015/07/chinas-contribution-paris-climate-agreement.pdf.

20. "Explore the Data," State of Global Air, accessed June 28, 2018, http://www.stateofglobalair.org/data/.

21. John Vidal, "Air Pollution Rising at an 'Alarming Rate' in World's Cities," *Guardian,* May 11, 2016, https://www.theguardian.com/environment/2016/may/12/air-pollution-rising-at-an-alarming-rate-in-worlds-cities.

22. OECD, *The Economic Consequences of Outdoor Air Pollution,* June 2016, http://www.oecd.org/greengrowth/the-economic-consequences-of-outdoor-air-pollution-9789264257474-en.htm.

23. United Nations, *World Urbanization Prospects: 2014 Revision,* 2014, https://esa.un.org/unpd/wup/publications/files/wup2014-highlights.pdf.

24. *The World Factbook,* s.v. "People and Society: World," accessed August 13, 2018, https://www.cia.gov/library/publications/the-world-factbook/geos/xx.html.

25. Stephane Hallegatte, Colin Green, Robert J. Nicholls, and Jan Corfee-Morlot, "Future Flood Losses in Major Coastal Cities," *Nature Climate Change* 3, no. 9 (August 2013): 804, https://doi.org/10.1038/nclimate1979.

26. Hannah Fingerhut, "Race, Immigration, Same-Sex Marriage, Abortion, Global Warming, Gun Policy, Marijuana Legalization," Pew Research Center for the People and the Press, March 1, 2018, http://www.people-press.org/2018/03/01/4-race-immigration-same-sex-marriage-abortion-global-warming-gun-policy-marijuana-legalization/.

27. "Green Generation: Millennials Say Sustainability Is a Shopping Priority," Nielsen, November 11, 2015, http://www.nielsen.com/us/en/insights/news/2015/green-generation-millennials-say-sustainability-is-a-shopping-priority.html.

CHAPTER 7: NINJA REGULATION

1. This sentence and the paragraph above originally appeared here: Gary Shapiro, "How the EU's War on U.S. Innovation Stifles European Creativity," *Investor's Business Daily*, September 12, 2016, https://www.investors.com/politics/commentary/how-the-eus-war-on-u-s-innovation-stifles-european-creativity/.

2. Renae Merle, "Apple Owes $14.5 Billion in Back Taxes, European Authorities Say," *Washington Post*, August 30, 2016, https://www.washingtonpost.com/business/economy/apple-owes-145-billion-in-back-taxes-european-authorities/2016/08/30/e7f6ed80-6ea2-11e6-9705-23e51a2f424d_story.html?utm_term=.12c4bba80b0e.

3. Chris Merriman, "Google and Facebook Rack Up £6.7bn in GDPR Lawsuits on Day One," *Inquirer*, May 29, 2018, www.theinquirer.net/inquirer/news/3033111/google-and-facebook-rack-up-gbp67bn-in-gdpr-lawsuits-on-day-one.

4. Gary Shapiro, "Don't Trust Antitrust Tactics: Why America Must Push for Parity in Europe," *Morning Consult*, May 19, 2017, https://morningconsult.com/opinions/dont-trust-antitrust-tactics-america-must-push-parity-europe/.

5. Pamela McClintock, "MPAA Touts Netflix, Streamers for Driving Growth in Movie Spending," *Hollywood Reporter*, April 4, 2018, https://www.hollywoodreporter.com/news/mpaa-touts-netflix-streamers-driving-growth-movie-spending-1099560.

6. Tumblr Staff, "Yesterday We Did a Historic Thing," Tumblr, November 17, 2011, https://staff.tumblr.com/post/12930076128/a-historic-thing.

7. Jenna Wortham, "A Political Coming of Age for the Tech Industry," *New York Times*, January 17, 2012, https://www.nytimes.com/2012/01/18/technology/web-wide-protest-over-two-antipiracy-bills.html?scp=11.

8. Sean Buckley, "Sandvine: Pirated Live TV Could Cost Service Providers $4B in Revenue in 2017," *FierceCable*, November 1, 2017, https://www

.fiercecable.com/online-video/sandvine-pirate-tv-could-cost-service
-providers-4b-revenue-2017.

9. Joshua P. Friedlander, *News and Notes on 2017 RIAA Revenue Statistics,
Recording Industry Association of America*, 2017, https://www.riaa.com
/wp-content/uploads/2018/03/RIAA-Year-End-2017-News-and-Notes
.pdf.

10. Keith Caulfield, "U.S. Vinyl Album Sales Hit Nielsen Music-Era Record
High in 2017," *Billboard*, January 3, 2018, https://www.billboard.com/ar
ticles/columns/chart-beat/8085951/us-vinyl-album-sales-nielsen-music
-record-high-2017.

11. "Twitter Usage Statistics," Google Search Statistics—Internet Live Stats,
accessed July 5, 2018, http://www.internetlivestats.com/twitter-statistics/.

12. Lyft, *2017 Economic Impact Report*, 2017, https://take.lyft.com/eco
nomic-impact/2017/Lyft-Drives-Economy-pre.pdf.

13. "New Survey: Drivers Choose Uber for Its Flexibility and Convenience,"
Uber, December 7, 2015, https://www.uber.com/newsroom/driver-part
ner-survey/.

14. Airbnb, "Airbnb: Generating $6.5 Billion for Restaurants Around the
World," news release, September 20, 2017, https://press.atairbnb.com/wp
-content/uploads/sites/4/2017/09/Restaurant-Spending-Report-2017.pdf.

15. Gatwiri Muthara, "Older Airbnb Hosts Are Making Serious Money,"
AARP, April 25, 2018, https://www.aarp.org/money/budgeting-saving
/info-2018/airbnb-hosts-making-money.html.

16. "The World's Most Admired Companies for 2018," *Fortune*, 2018, http://
fortune.com/worlds-most-admired-companies/list.

CHAPTER 8: NINJA NATIONS

1. Claire Sergent, "Emmanuel Macron's Party Wins Majority in French
Parliamentary Elections," *Independent*, June 18, 2017, https://www.inde
pendent.co.uk/news/world/europe/france-parliament-elections-results
-national-assembly-emmanuel-macron-win-en-marche-party-marine-le
-a7796496.html.

2. "France Given Boost as Economy Grows Faster than Expected," *Local*,
February 28, 2018, https://www.thelocal.fr/20180228/france-given-boost
-as-economy-grows-faster-than-expected.

3. Bruce Sterling, "Emmanuel Macron Talking to WIRED About Artificial Intelligence," *WIRED*, March 31, 2018, https://www.wired.com/beyond -the-beyond/2018/03/emmanuel-macron-talking-wired-artificial-intelli gence/.

4. "French President Emmanuel Macron Addresses U.S. Congress," France in the United States, April 25, 2018, https://franceintheus.org /spip.php?article8612.

5. Clem Chambers, "Who Needs Stock Exchanges?," Mondo Visione, July 14, 2006, http://www.mondovisione.com/exchanges/handbook-arti cles/who-needs-stock-exchanges/.

6. "Henry Hudson and His Crew Sailed into the River That Would Bear His Name," America's Library, accessed July 10, 2018, http://www.amer icaslibrary.gov/jb/colonial/jb_colonial_hudson_1.html.

7. European Commission, *Europeans and Their Languages Report*, June 2012, http://ec.europa.eu/commfrontoffice/publicopinion/archives/ebs /ebs_386_en.pdf.

8. "#75 Royal Dutch Shell," *Forbes*, 2018, https://www.forbes.com/compa nies/royal-dutch-shell/.

9. "Most Innovative Companies: Royal Dutch Shell," *Fast Company*, 2016, https://www.fastcompany.com/company/royal-dutch-shell.

10. "Banks, Bulbs, Beer and Oil: The 10 Largest Dutch Companies," Dutch News.nl., September 8, 2017, https://www.dutchnews.nl/features/2017 /09/banks-bulbs-beer-and-oil-the-10-largest-dutch-companies/.

11. "What's Cooking in the Blockchain Kitchen?," ING, January 26, 2017, https://www.ing.com/Newsroom/All-news/Whats-cooking-in-the-block chain-kitchen.htm.

12. "Global 2000: The World's Largest Public Companies," edited by Halah Touryalai and Kristin Stoller, *Forbes*, 2018, https://www.forbes.com /companies/philips/.

13. Consumer Technology Association, Innovation Leader: Netherlands, 2018, https://www.cta.tech/cta/media/policyImages/policyPDFs/Intl Scorecard/2018-Intl-Innovation-Scorecard-Web-Netherlands.pdf.

14. Abigail Hess, "The 10 Most Educated Countries in the World," CNBC, February 7, 2018, https://www.cnbc.com/2018/02/07/the-10-most-edu cated-countries-in-the-world.html.

15. Gerrit De Vynck, "A Big Chunk of Israel's Tech Scene Is Actually Based in New York," Bloomberg, March 28, 2018, https://www.bloomberg.com/news/articles/2018-03-28/a-big-chunk-of-israel-s-tech-scene-is-actually-based-in-new-york.

16. Michael Wines, "Majority of Chinese Now Live in Cities," *New York Times*, January 17, 2012, https://www.nytimes.com/2012/01/18/world/asia/majority-of-chinese-now-live-in-cities.html.

17. Ross Garnaut, Ligang Song, and Cai Fang, eds., *China's 40 Years of Reform and Development: 1978–2018* (Canberra, AU: Australian National University Press, 2018), 17, http://press-files.anu.edu.au/downloads/press/n4267/pdf/ch01.pdf.

18. Demographia, Demographia World Urban Areas, April 2018, http://www.demographia.com/db-worldua.pdf.

19. Willige, "The World's Top Economy."

20. Robin Yates, "China's Age of Invention," interview by NOVA, PBS, February 2, 2000, http://www.pbs.org/wgbh/nova/ancient/song-dynasty.html.

21. Isabella Steger, "China's Two-Child Policy Has Already Stopped Working," *Quartz*, January 19, 2018, https://qz.com/1183692/after-ending-chinas-one-child-policy-in-2015-its-two-child-policy-has-already-stopped-working-as-births-decline/.

22. Lauri Myllyvirta and Li Danqing, "China Halts More than 150 Coal-fired Power Plants," Unearthed, November 10, 2017, https://unearthed.greenpeace.org/2017/10/11/china-halts-150-coal-fired-power-plants/.

23. Robert Rohde and Richard Muller, "Air Pollution in China: Mapping of Concentrations and Sources," *PLoS One* 10, no. 8 (August 20, 2015), https://doi.org/10.1371/journal.pone.0135749.

24. Dan Harris, "China's 12th Five Year Plan: A Preliminary Look, Part II," China Law Blog, March 6, 2011, https://www.chinalawblog.com/2011/03/chinas_12th_five_year_plan_a_preliminary_look_part_ii.html.

25. "High-Technology Exports (% of Manufactured Exports)," World Bank Group, accessed July 28, 2018, https://data.worldbank.org/indicator/TX.VAL.TECH.MF.ZS?locations=CN.

26. Scott Kennedy, "Made in China 2025," CSIS, June 1, 2015, https://www.csis.org/analysis/made-china-2025.

27. Niall McCarthy, "The Countries with the Most STEM Graduates," *Forbes*, February 2, 2017, https://www.forbes.com/sites/niallmccarthy/2017/02/02/the-countries-with-the-most-stem-graduates-infographic/.

28. Brian Wang, "Future Tech Dominance—China Outnumber USA STEM Grads 8 to 1 and by 2030 15 to 1," Next Big Future, August 2, 2017, https://www.nextbigfuture.com/2017/08/future-tech-dominance-china-outnumber-usa-stem-grads-8-to-1-and-by-2030-15-to-1.html.

29. *The Power of International Education, Open Doors Fact Sheet: China*, 2017, https://p.widencdn.net/ymtzur/Open-Doors-2017-Country-Sheets-China.

CHAPTER 9: AMERICAN NINJAS

1. "Tech Workers: They're Just like Us—Can't Find Affordable Housing," Open Listings Blog, February 13, 2018, https://www.openlistings.com/blog/can-engineers-afford-homes-near-work-in-sf-la/.

2. Greg Hack, "Kansas City's No. 7 in Ranking for Women-Owned Businesses," *Kansas City Star*, February 22, 2016, https://www.kansascity.com/news/business/article61731997.html.

3. Benjamin Freed, "70 Percent of the World's Web Traffic Flows Through Loudoun County," *Washingtonian*, September 20, 2016, https://www.washingtonian.com/2016/09/14/70-percent-worlds-web-traffic-flows-loudoun-county/.

4. "Analysis of Post-Recession Job Trends Suggests Existence of 'Two Pennsylvanias,'" Penn State University, June 11, 2018, https://news.psu.edu/story/524675/2018/06/11/research/analysis-post-recession-job-trends-suggests-existence-two.

5. Salve Juris, "Fully Automatic? Boston Restaurant Takes Just 180 Secs to Prepare a Meal," *Kicker Daily News*, May 19, 2018, https://kickerdaily.com/posts/2018/05/fully-automatic-boston-restaurant-takes-just-180-secs-to-prepare-a-meal/.

6. iRobot, "iRobot Reports Record Fourth-Quarter and Full-Year Revenue," news release, iRobot, February 7, 2018, http://media.irobot.com/2018-02-07-iRobot-Reports-Record-Fourth-Quarter-and-Full-Year-Revenue.

7. "Amazon Expands Tech Hub in Boston, Massachusetts," Area Development, May 2, 2018, http://www.areadevelopment.com/newsItems/5-2-2018/amazon-tech-hub-boston-massachusetts.shtml.

8. Arren Kimbel-Sannit, "22 Dallas–Fort Worth Companies Make the 2018 Fortune 500 List," *Dallas News*, May 21, 2018, https://www.dallas news.com/business/economy/2018/05/21/22-dallas-fort-worth-compa nies-make-2018-fortune-500-list.

9. "Texas," 2018 US Innovation Scorecard, Consumer Technology Association, 2018, https://usinnovationscorecard.com/map/overall/texas.

10. Danielle Abril, "Dallas Business Leaders at Rise of the Rest: The Future is in Entrepreneurs," *D*, May 7, 2018, https://www.dmagazine.com/busi ness-economy/2018/05/dallas-business-leaders-spotlight-entrepreneurs -during-rise-of-the-rest/.

11. Peter Wilkins, "How Chicago's Startup Exits Stack Up against 4 Other Major Cities," *VentureBeat*, May 12, 2018, https://venturebeat.com/2018 /05/12/how-chicagos-startup-exits-stack-up-against-4-other-major-cities /.

12. "Illinois," 2018 US Innovation Scorecard, Consumer Technology Association, 2018, https://usinnovationscorecard.com/map/overall/illinois.

13. Daniel Howes, "Take Note, Self-driving Car Skeptics: Detroit Could Field the First Truly Autonomous Cars," Michigan Radio, January 13, 2018, http://michiganradio.org/post/take-note-self-driving-car-skeptics -detroit-could-field-first-truly-autonomous-cars.

14. Matt Burns, "Detroit's Startup Scene Is Exploding and Here Are the Numbers to Prove It," *TechCrunch*, July 10, 2017, https://techcrunch .com/2017/07/10/detroits-startup-scene-is-exploding/.

CHAPTER 10: CORPORATE NINJAS

1. Steve Trousdale, "GM Invests $500 Million in Lyft, Sets Out Self-driving Car Partnership," Reuters, January 5, 2016, https://www.reuters.com/ar ticle/us-gm-lyft-investment/gm-invests-500-million-in-lyft-sets-out-self -driving-car-partnership-idUSKBN0UI1A820160105.

2. Alan Murray, "Fortune 500 CEOs See A.I. as a Big Challenge," *Fortune*, June 8, 2017, http://fortune.com/2017/06/08/fortune-500-ceos-survey-ai/.

3. Hallmark, "Mother's Day Gift Ideas from Hallmark to Show You Care Enough," news release, April 20, 2018, https://corporate.hallmark.com /news-article/mothers-day-gift-ideas-hallmark-show-care-enough/.

4. Intel Capital, *Backgrounder*, May 2018, http://www.intelcapital.com/as set/docs/Intel-Capital-Backgrounder.pdf.

5. Brian Merchant, "The Secret Origin Story of the iPhone," *Verge*, June 13, 2017, https://www.theverge.com/2017/6/13/15782200/one-device-secret-history-iphone-brian-merchant-book-excerpt.

6. Tim Ryan, David Sapin, Anand Rao, and Cristina Ampil, *US Business Leadership in the World in 2018*, 2018, https://www.pwc.com/us/en/library/ceo-agenda/pdf/21st-annual-global-ceo-survey-us-supplement.pdf.

7. Jorge Paulo Lemann, Jim McCaughan, Jim Sloan, and Julie Sweet, "Strategy and Leadership in an Age of Disruption," Milken Institute video, 1:00:15, posted 2018, http://www.milkeninstitute.org/videos/view/strategy-and-leadership-in-an-age-of-disruption.

8. Victor Luckerson, "Here's Proof That Instagram Was One of the Smartest Acquisitions Ever," *Time*, April 19, 2016, http://time.com/4299297/instagram-facebook-revenue/.

9. Josh Constine, "Instagram Hits 1 Billion Monthly Users, Up from 800M in September," *TechCrunch*, June 20, 2018, https://techcrunch.com/2018/06/20/instagram-1-billion-users/.

10. Scott Kirsner, "Hire Today, Gone Tomorrow?," *Fast Company*, July 31, 1998, https://www.fastcompany.com/34457/hire-today-gone-tomorrow.

11. "Cyberstates 2018," Computing Technology Industry Association, March 2018, www.cyberstates.org/pdf/CompTIA_Cyberstates_2018.pdf.

CHAPTER 11: DIVERSITY AND RESILIENCE

1. Paul Gompers and Silpa Kovvali, "The Other Diversity Dividend," *Harvard Business Review*, July–August 2018, https://hbr.org/2018/07/the-other-diversity-dividend.

2. Recode, "Mary Meeker's 2018 Internet Trends Report," YouTube, May 30, 2018, https://www.youtube.com/watch?v=HdjcdZqODoE.

3. Rani Molla, "How Facebook Compares to Other Tech Companies in Diversity," Recode, April 11, 2018, https://www.recode.net/2018/4/11/17225574/facebook-tech-diversity-women.

4. "Girls Who Code Reaches 90K, on Track to Achieve Gender Parity," Girls Who Code, April 9, 2018, https://girlswhocode.com/2018/04/09/2017-annual-report/.

5. "National Academy of Sciences President Marcia McNutt Will Deliver GW Commencement Address," *GW Today*, March 5, 2018, https://gw

today.gwu.edu/national-academy-sciences-president-marcia-mcnutt-will -deliver-gw-commencement-address.

6. "Choosing Marcia McNutt for Commencement Speaker Was a Mistake," GW *Hatchet,* March 8, 2018, https://www.gwhatchet.com/2018 /03/08/choosing-marcia-mcnutt-for-commencement-speaker-was-a-mis take/.

7. "LeBlanc on Hot Mic: 'Doesn't Anybody Have Any Shame' About Graduation Speaker Criticism," GW *Hatchet,* April 5, 2018, https://www .gwhatchet.com/2018/04/05/leblanc-on-hot-mic-doesnt-anybody-have -any-shame-about-graduation-speaker-criticism/.

8. Alistair Charlton, "Just 8.5% of Americans Said They Could Name a Female Tech Leader—Then a Quarter Said Siri and Alexa," Gearbrain, March 22, 2018, https://www.gearbrain.com/just-8-5-of-americans-said -they-could-name-a-female-tech-leader-then-a-quarter-said-siri-and -alexa-2551222905.html.

9. National Center for Women & Information Technology, *Women and Information Technology by the Numbers,* 2017, https://www.ncwit.org/sites /default/files/resources/btn_04042018_web.pdf.

10. Jesse J. Holland, "Tech Companies Not Hiring Blacks Despite Ownership Rates," *Washington Times,* May 3, 2018, https://www.washington times.com/news/2018/may/3/tech-companies-not-hiring-blacks-despite -ownership/.

11. "Powering the Digital Revolution," State of Black America, National Urban League, 2018, http://soba.iamempowered.com/sites/soba.iamem powered.com/themes/soba/flexpaper/SOBA2018-ExSum/.

12. Cary Funk and Kim Parker, "Women and Men in STEM Often at Odds Over Workplace Equity," Pew Research Center, January 9, 2018, http:// www.pewsocialtrends.org/2018/01/09/diversity-in-the-stem-workforce -varies-widely-across-jobs/.

13. Tala Salem, "FIRST Robotics Championship Boosts Diversity," *U.S. News & World Report,* May 9, 2018, https://www.usnews.com/news /stem-solutions/articles/2018-05-09/first-robotics-championship-makes -strides-in-diversity.

14. Neil C. Churchill and Virginia L. Lewis, "The Five Stages of Small Business Growth," *Harvard Business Review,* November 18, 2015, https:// hbr.org/1983/05/the-five-stages-of-small-business-growth.

15. Dan Primack, "Study Shows Gender Bias in Venture Capital," *Axios*, May 19, 2017, https://www.axios.com/study-shows-gender-bias-in-venture-capital-1513302441-4dbc0ce7-54d8-468e-ae07-7f4b43bd2ee8.html.

16. Morgan Eichensehr, "Local Angels on Investing: It's like Falling in Love," *Baltimore Business Journal*, April 24, 2018, https://www.bizjournals.com/baltimore/news/2018/04/24/local-angels-on-investing-its-like-falling-in-love.html.

17. Marcus Noland, Tyler Moran, and Barbara Kotschwar, *Is Gender Diversity Profitable? Evidence from a Global Survey*, Peterson Institute for International Economics, February 2016, https://piie.com/publications/working-papers/gender-diversity-profitable-evidence-global-survey.

18. Oliver Staley, "You Know Those Quotas for Female Board Members in Europe? They're Working," *Quartz*, May 3, 2016, https://qz.com/674276/you-know-those-quotas-for-female-board-members-in-europe-theyre-working/.

19. Luke Mullins, "How DC's First Chief Resilience Officer Is Planning for Disaster," *Washingtonian*, July 23, 2018, https://www.washingtonian.com/2018/07/23/how-dc-first-chief-resilience-officer-is-planning-for-disaster/.

20. "Resilience," Google Trends, Google, accessed October 1, 2018, https://trends.google.com/trends/explore?date=2008-09-01%202018-10-01&geo=US&q=resilience.

21. "How Can We Finance the Resilient Cities of the Future?," World Bank, October 12, 2016, http://www.worldbank.org/en/news/feature/2016/10/11/how-can-we-finance-the-resilient-cities-of-the-future.

22. Mark Wilson, "By 2050, 70% of the World's Population Will Be Urban. Is That a Good Thing?," *Fast Company*, March 12, 2012, https://www.fastcompany.com/1669244/by-2050-70-of-the-worlds-population-will-be-urban-is-that-a-good-thing.

23. Consumer Technology Association, *The Evolution of Smart Cities and Connected Communities*, January 30, 2017, https://www.cta.tech/Research-Standards/Reports-Studies/Studies/2017/The-Evolution-of-Smart-Cities-and-Connected-Commun.aspx.

24. Mark Strauss, "Four-in-Ten Americans Credit Technology with Improving Life Most in the Past 50 Years," Pew Research Center, October 12, 2017, http://www.pewresearch.org/fact-tank/2017/10/12/four-in

-ten-americans-credit-technology-with-improving-life-most-in-the-past
-50-years/.

CHAPTER 12: PRINCIPLES FOR FUTURE NINJAS

1. Don Clark, "Trade Show Chief Touts Many Gadgets, but Not 3D TV," *Wall Street Journal*, December 16, 2010, https://blogs.wsj.com/digits /2010/12/16/trade-show-chief-touts-many-gadgets-but-not-3d-tv/.
2. Source: CTA Market Research.
3. John C. Maxwell, *Failing Forward: Turning Mistakes Into Stepping Stones for Success* (Nashville: Thomas Nelson, 2007).
4. Jessica Lahey, *The Gift of Failure* (New York City: Harper, 2016).

CONCLUSION: THE NINJA FUTURE

1. Source: World Health Organization: 31 in 1900; 72 in 2016.
2. Gary Shapiro, "The Jobs of Today Are Created by Change," *Investor's Business Daily*, November 17, 2017, https://www.investors.com/politics /commentary/the-jobs-of-today-are-created-by-change/.

INDEX

INDEX

INDEX

INDEX